T0277827

Coping with Christmas

Coping with
Christmas

FANNY
& JOHNNIE
CRADOCK

HarperCollins Publishers

Coping with Christmas

FANNY & JOHNNIE CRADOCK

HarperCollins*Publishers*

HarperCollinsPublishers
1 London Bridge Street
London SE1 9GF
www.harpercollins.co.uk

HarperCollins*Publishers*
1st Floor, Watermarque Building, Ringsend Road
Dublin 4, Ireland

First published by Fontana Books 1968
This edition published by HarperCollins*Publishers* 2022

10 9 8 7 6 5 4 3 2 1

A catalogue record of this book is available from the British Library

ISBN 978-0-00-853227-7

Printed and bound in the UK using 100% renewable electricity at CPI Group (UK) Ltd

This book is produced from independently certified FSC™ paper
to ensure responsible forest management.

For more information visit: www.harpercollins.co.uk/green

WHEN USING KITCHEN APPLIANCES PLEASE ALWAYS FOLLOW
THE MANUFACTURER'S INSTRUCTIONS

*To Alison, who has worked so hard
with us in editing this book*

CONTENTS

CONTENTS

FOREWORD

By Felicity Cloake

When even the obituaries describe someone as the 'preposterous character . . . you loved to loathe',[1] their status as a pantomime villain seems set for all eternity – and Fanny Cradock, with her 'mad glittering eyes, the face of a supercilious horse, the maquillage of a French clown and demeanour of a woman in constant search of an argument'[2] fits the bill perfectly. Her fate was sealed when, in 1976, she demolished a Devon housewife's cooking on national television. 'Not since 1940 can the people of England have risen in such unified wrath,' the *Daily Telegraph* reported – and just like that, the 20-year career of the 'original celebrity chef' collapsed like one of her famous souffles . . . though not one made by Fanny herself, obviously.

Yet almost half a century later, even those of us who never saw her on screen the first time round know the legend of Fanny Cradock. She's gone, but she's more alive than ever online: *Fanny Cradock Cooks for Christmas*, a series made the year America pulled out of Vietnam, popped up on the BBC's iPlayer service in 2017, where it remains a festive fixture to this

---

1. Paul Levy, 'Obituary: Fanny Cradock', *Independent* (29 December 1994).
2. 'Fanny Cradock: First Lady of Food', *Independent* (19 February 2009).

day – a fact that led the *Telegraph* to declare, 'Forget Nigella . . . Fanny Cradock is the true queen of Christmas cooking'.[3]

There's no danger of Nigella forgetting Fanny at Christmastime either; she credits 'the great' woman for teaching her that vodka is 'the best spirit for flambéing the pud on the big day', while Jamie Oliver recently revealed that Fanny appears on his dream dinner-party guest list – along with Shakespeare and Bob Marley. And although the idea of them all sitting down to his Gnarly Cauliflower Curry has *me* reaching for the vodka, he's not the only one to want to resurrect her: Gordon Ramsay squeezed a whole television show out of his quest to find 'the next Fanny Cradock' – and I suspect it wasn't just because he loved her recipes.

Such is the unforgettable effect of her elaborately coiffed and aggressively hands-on television persona that this very analogue star has been honoured with that most twenty-first-century of digital tributes – a GIF, which allows internet users worldwide to convey their rage with an image of Fanny furiously stabbing a goose with a fork – type in 'think of someone you've never really liked' and there she is, resplendent in pink polyester! In the 30 years since her death, Fanny Cradock has gone from TV cook to national icon.

All this would have delighted Fanny herself, of course. After all, this is a woman who made her name cooking in a ballgown and diamonds at the Royal Albert Hall in 'a demonstration of international cookery' in front of a huge live audience – a shameless self-promoter with a keen eye for a headline. Her biographer, Kevin Geddes, suggests that Fanny might actually have been pleased at the notoriety that followed the 'Gwen Troake incident', as it came to be called – especially the press

---

3. Ben Lawrence, 'Forget Nigella: why Fanny Cradock is the true queen of Christmas cooking', *Telegraph* (12 December 2017).

outrage, which led to the programme being repeated the following year, garnering further publicity for its antihero, although the 67-year-old was never to front a television series again. The British public may love to hate a mean woman, but they don't want to eat her food . . . and Fanny was quietly replaced on the BBC by the distinctly gentler figure of Delia Smith.

All this drama was just a mischievous glimmer in her generously mascara-fringed eye a decade earlier when *Coping with Christmas* was published, however; a time when she was at the height of her fame, starring in two television series a year and popping out books as easily as her sidekick and husband Johnnie dispatched champagne corks. For those familiar with YouTube Fanny, a heavily made-up elderly woman madly pumping stuffing into turkeys in wildly inappropriate clothing, Writer Fanny's humour, common sense and sheer readability comes as something of a surprise. She's entertaining, self-deprecating and knowledgeable; someone to learn from, rather than laugh at. So who was the real Fanny Cradock?

The more I discover, the more she reminds me, quite unexpectedly, of Isabella Beeton, another keen-eyed business-woman who saw financial opportunity in the world of food and refashioned herself to exploit it – because although Fanny was the author of over 20 novels, she may well have been her own greatest work of fiction. Though this is not the place to dwell upon her two bigamous marriages, or the fact that she lied about her birthplace in her memoirs or claimed to be a descendant of the last wife of Henry VIII . . . it is, I think, relevant to state that, among other fabrications, she appears to have cooked up her expertise as a chef.

Indeed, she claimed variously to have learnt her culinary skills as a child from her grandmother, whom she described as a great society hostess in colonial India, or from hotel kitchens on the French Riviera while her rackety father was busy in the casinos – yet only decided to share her expertise at the age of 40, after stints washing up, working in shops, writing novels, dressmaking and selling vacuum cleaners door to door. As Geddes notes in *Keep Calm and Fanny On!*, this last job taught her 'a valuable lesson in persistence' and the importance of knocking on as many doors as possible in the hope one would yield results.

In a career that could most politely be described as 'portfolio' (as late as the 1970s she and Johnnie tried to relaunch themselves as faith healers), cookery turned out to be one of the most successful random door-knocks of all. Though she later hotly denied any affiliation with what she dismissed as 'women's libbers', in the mid-1940s Fanny nevertheless became involved with a women's group campaigning for improvements in the food ration (an association that also handily enabled her, newly returned to London from the country where she'd been busy churning out fiction potboilers, to get her name in the newspapers). Ever the entrepreneur, she realised the potential in marketing herself as an authority on such 'women's issues' to the press and, using the connections she'd made through United Women, finally found her niche as a writer for hire.

Initially covering everything from fashion to skincare for various newspapers – a familiar state of affairs to many a freelance journalist happy to rebrand as a specialist on whatever subject is currently in vogue – chance propelled her, in the early Fifties, into travel writing and restaurant reviewing, and from there into cookbooks, which she hoped would be more lucrative than fiction had proved to be. Ironically, for someone who dismissed Mrs Beeton as a 'fake' for passing off other people's recipes as her own, her former assistant, Wendy Colvin, told Geddes that Fanny collected old recipe books and had no qualms about tweaking their contents for her own use. (To be fair, this is not uncommon, though I note that, despite boldly proclaiming her willingness to 'fall over backwards in our all-out efforts to render unto Caesar by crediting whomsoever is the creator of a recipe which we quote', Fanny is only really willing to credit recipes to the dead, who presumably are unlikely to object.)

Yet whether self-taught from books or, as she boasted, by observation, she was clearly proficient in the kitchen. Not all of her recipes may be to everyone's taste – I must confess I quail at the notion of stuffing my Christmas turkey with pig's kidneys – but there's no doubt she could cook; even her contemporary Marguerite Patten, who freely confessed she did not like Cradock as a person, having had dealings with her at the Festival of Britain, was clear that she 'would defend her ability to the end of my days'.

Colvin also recalled that, as well as poring over old cookbooks, Fanny would practise techniques for hours, particularly before performing them on television: 'If there was something she could not do well, she would not do it. She never faked anything.' It paid off; the late Clarissa Dickson Wright was of the opinion that 'you can tell by watching who can cook and who can't . . . and you know that this is something she does on a regular basis, it's not just for television'. Delia Smith, her successor on the BBC, admits, 'I think I did learn things from Fanny Cradock,' while Prue Leith is adamant that 'she really did know what she was doing'.

One only has to open the following pages at random to discover that, beyond the frankly mad decorative ideas and infamous choux pastry swans, there's real wisdom here too. Her turkey roasting times, for example – 15 minutes per 450g, plus 30 minutes – are almost exactly the same as my own, in contrast to the usual advice to bake the poor bird into dusty submission, and I've rarely seen more straightforward guidance for portioning out the results. (N.B. The episode of *Fanny Cradock Cooks for Christmas* on BBC iPlayer and YouTube where she neatly demonstrates this skill, while haranguing men for their ineptitude in the carving department, is well worth a few minutes of your time.)

Without any formal culinary training, it seems Fanny became a culinary expert through sheer force of will and necessity – but the same restless energy that saw her leap from romance to children's fiction to sci-fi in the 1940s made her unable to confine herself to mere practical instruction in her cookbooks a decade later. Thus the casual reader, flicking through this collection in the hope of finding, perhaps, a recipe for prawn cocktail (a great Fanny favourite), might be startled, as I was, to happen upon a menu for Christmas dinner during the Siege of Paris, including camel 'roasted in the English fashion', or to learn that, according to Fanny, who claimed experience in this matter as in so many others, roast swan has a 'sickly sweet, predominantly fishy flavour . . . repellent to most modern palates'.

It cannot be denied that these constant diversions make her enormous fun to read; I was surprised to discover just how witty she could be, from the very first page where she concedes that, for all the earnest advice to come, 'the average wife and mum . . . would end up dead or ravers if she attempted to act upon all the suggestions we put forward in this book!' And she's right; just reading the 12-month plan for one day of celebration is exhausting – making cakes and puddings in January, bunking off work in June to collect rose petals in the full morning sun for pot-pourri and lugging back bits of driftwood and other 'winter decoration treasures' from your summer holidays . . . at which point your other half might reasonably start wondering if you'd like to go away for Christmas instead.

For a woman who worked hard to earn a living from the age of 20, when she found herself a single mother of two, she was oddly fond of creating pointless extra work for other women – because, let's face it, as Fanny makes clear, this is a book aimed at the 'cook/hostess/wife/mum' . . . the man's role here seems confined to drilling holes in the yule-log candle holder. Indeed, the very title, *Coping with Christmas*, is so ludicrously inappropriate one can almost see Fanny delivering it with a theatrical wink.

Yet, absurd as she may sometimes seem in her mania for what she archly termed 'the Cradock eccentric' – wrapping tables in tin foil or chasing the holy grail of a perfectly round Christmas pudding – she has a curious self-awareness that never seems to take itself too seriously. (She's also, at times, a lovely stylist of prose, if not ingredients. A Christmas Tale Which Happens to be True on p.28, for example, though as ridiculously rich as Gwen Troake's coffee cream pudding, is more than a little reminiscent of one of the greatest of her contemporaries, M. F. K. Fisher.)

If Fanny was acting a part, she expected no less from her culinary creations. One of the reasons her recipes feel so alien, even unappetising, to us today is her obsession – perhaps born out of insecurity about her lack of formal qualifications – with Making an Impression, in contrast to the modern preference for good ingredients, simply prepared. 'Above all,' she wrote elsewhere, 'professional chefs appreciate the value of Garnish and Presentation because, crafty and experienced as they are, they realise that half the daily battle in pleasing customers is won when the simplest and most economical foodstuffs have such visual glamour that the customer is charmed and tempted even before knife, spoon or fork has touched a portion'.

In this she was very much a product of her time. These days, the fashion is for things to look 'unstyled' – an artistically dripping spoon here, a few crumbs scattered just so there, but in the 1960s, a table was dressed to impress, a style Susan Bright describes in her history of food photography as 'epic'. Constance Spry, the 'Martha Stewart of her day', who, unlike Fanny, rarely comes in for mockery, devotes eight pages of her 1956 *Cookery Book* to 'the garnish and presentation of food', including such handy information as that Camembert ought to be served on a cabbage leaf and, more disturbingly, that fried bananas are the ideal accompaniment to fish.

As usual, however, Fanny couldn't resist taking things slightly too far, and this book represents the apotheosis of her terrible art, because, as she explains, 'at Christmas-time the garnish or decoration can be much more elaborate than at any other time in the year and indeed needs to be when it has to hold its own in a room garlanded and swagged, beribboned and sparkling with candlelight and glitter balls'. Hence the green brandy butter, the potatoes sculpted into pears, the stuffed eggs and cabbages and potatoes . . . and, most mysteriously of all to our eyes, the cold turkey arranged in the shape of a headless turbot. If something can be filled, covered in aspic or deep-fried, it usually is . . . Fanny just can't help herself.

In fact, one gets the sense from these pages that, in her eyes, the hostess's role is as much set designer and theatre director as caterer. From the hors d'oeuvres – 'the lifting of the curtains, the overture to a gastronomic opera' – onwards, the festive feast is a carefully orchestrated performance, packed full of extravagant dramatic flourish. Just as Fanny decries the 'startling lack of originality in so many Christmas decorations', she has no interest in promoting the same old food on the Christmas table, and, whether or not we're secretly quite fond of the season's greatest hits, it's still fascinating to go along with her for the ride.

After all, even allowing for Fanny's eccentricities, the 1960s were a very different world, when even family occasions had a certain, now rather exotic, formality to them. One was apparently expected to plan one's entire day around the proclamation from the palace, so if having Christmas 'luncheon' (a word that recently reduced my teenage niece to tears of mirth, so sure was she that I'd made it up) Fanny advises the reader to be sure to 'force the issue so that eating and drinking can be leisurely and still over with a few minutes to spare before the Queen speaks'. Whether the average British household back then actually had a separate dining room they could keep locked to protect their scarlet satin tablecloth carefully set with white pom-pom trees on a looking-glass lake – perfect for that four-course Christmas dinner with matched wines – or whether Fanny just liked to think they did is another matter.

Yet though these days we favour a more relaxed celebration (one shudders to think what the Cradocks would have made of families tucking into chocolate selection boxes on the sofa in matching Christmas pyjamas), this book still has much to offer the modern reader, and not just in the way of laughs. As well as the usual suspects – the roast meats and no fewer than nine takes on the plum pudding – there are some genuinely novel suggestions here: Brussels sprouts fritters, deep-fried turkey sandwiches, 'white' Christmas cake and a cream of pistachio soup 'very little known in England', which intrigues me half a century later. Fanny may be a festive figure of fun, but she's one who knows her onions; in my experience, her recipes work.

That said, she makes no allowances for individual tastes (unless they're her own), cheerfully describing well-done beef as 'ruined', and no apology for leaving bread sauce out of a book on Christmas because 'we think it so horrible and such a ruination to all upon which it imposes itself that we will not be associated with it'. Much as I love bread sauce, I have to admire her chutzpah in refusing to compromise on such a minor point. I also love the shameless sprinkle of swagger with which she seasons her prose: who could fail to thrill at the hint that a brandy butter recipe has been obtained by roundabout means from the royal family, or to be impressed by a casual reference to footmen standing guard over the candlelit Christmas tree (even if, one muses mean-spiritedly, such a servant would surely have been somewhat out of place in Fanny's suburban childhood home).

And though, despite her talk of Christmas being 'slave labour for the women' – a sentence she surely must have laughed at while typing – Fanny was avowedly not a feminist, it's also hard not to feel a certain sympathy for someone so irrepressibly themselves that they were, very clearly, branded a Difficult Woman by male commissioning editors, and who suffered professionally in consequence. For all her laughable airs and graces, she knew what it was to struggle to make ends meet, at one time leaving her infant son home alone while she walked four hours across London to wash up in a canteen, and the energetic work ethic that sees her recommending doing the Christmas shopping in the January sales is born out of necessity.

Not only is she obsessively thrifty (who else would hoard old tights for months to make decorative swags?), but also fierce in her determination to get the best value for money – I love her instructions for dealing with dodgy butchers: 'storm back with an offending tough slice [of meat] and demand explanation and compensation. Make him taste it . . . a nice practical conversion of the "eating his own words" phrase!'

Despite comparisons like 'the prototypical [Gordon] Ramsay'[4], even today we still find it hard to warm to such characteristics in a woman, preferring instead to dismiss Fanny as an aberrant 'dragon lady', as Esther Rantzen once memorably

---

4. 'Fanny Cradock: First Lady of Food', *Independent* (19 February 2009).

dubbed her,[5] rather than a strong woman prepared to work hard to get what she wanted, and who wasn't embarrassed to admit it. As she told the *Radio Times* in 1970, having started off in riches, known rags and achieved riches again, her prolific output (and, presumably, ballsy attitude) were all so she and Johnnie could 'have a ball' together, with 'a Rolls in the garage plus an MG [and] this divine house and garden . . .'

Yet the merry talk of children's parties and big family gatherings at these various grand homes disguises a lonelier truth about their life together. Like the twentysomething journalist Isabella Beeton pretending decades of experience in household management, Fanny plays the part of a great festive hostess, but with both she and Johnnie largely estranged from their families, it seems more than likely that this was another figment of her ever-fertile imagination. Indeed, she privately regarded Christmas lunch as 'the most monstrous intake of the world's most indigestible food' – telling the *Evening News* in 1963 that 'John and I barely touch anything. Instead, when it's all over, we creep upstairs to the pot of caviare we have waiting by our bed.' It's a rather tragic picture, but for all the popular image of Johnnie as a hen-pecked husband, I suspect the pair were happiest on their own.

Perhaps, then, the real Fanny, a woman who had cannily reinvented herself as a domestic goddess to pay the bills but who by all accounts was a rather slovenly housekeeper whose cutlery was usually crusted with dog food, can be found in her hilarious selection of Slap Happy 'Crisis' Substitutes for Serious Cookery at the end of the book, which one can easily imagine her resorting to after a hard day at the typewriter

---

5. Kevin Geddes, *Keep Calm and Fanny On!: The Many Careers of Fanny Cradock* (Fantom Publishing, 2019).

conjuring up mad ideas for Britain's housewives to busy themselves with:

(8) *Open a tin of salted pecan nuts* and tip into a small bowl.

(9) *Open a packet of pretzels* and tip into a small bowl.

(10) *Open a jar of cocktail onions* and tip into a small bowl.

(11) *Open a packet or tin of Twiglets* and tip into a small bowl.

Darling Johnnie, of course, would be ready, as he always was, with a cold glass of Montrachet '59 to wash it down with. And then they'd creep upstairs to bed – just the two of them, and not a piece of chicken wire or a royal-icing penguin in sight.

FELICITY CLOAKE
2022

PREPARING YOU FOR THE FRAY

Many years ago we brought down upon our heads a wrath of critics because we said when writing about Christmas preparations, 'Ideally, these begin in July with Preserved Raspberries for our Christmas Buffets.' On the face of it, daft of course! And currently even more so, because today almost every woman *is short of time for her standard daily chores*. Yet we are still muttering unrepentantly, 'The raspberry jazz is worth it!'

How dare we? . . . *Because we too are always short of time*, and because bitter experience has forced us to accept that in the matter of bulk entertaining life is much easier when advance lists are made and day-by-day or month-by-month forward chores are itemised and date-lined. Then when D-Day for the occasion finds us bleary-eyed and full of dread, we are fantastically heartened *if* we can console ourselves with the knowledge that we are already more than halfway there.

Let us not delude ourselves. If some preparations are not made in advance, Christmas can be sheer hell for the average wife and mum, especially if she is in for a Plague of Relations, as well as everything else! *But the same woman would end up dead or ravers if she attempted to act upon all the suggestions we put forward in this book!*

What we have set out to do primarily is to write a Fanny and Johnnie Cradock defence weapon in depth because every year, from September onwards, we have far more pleas for help from our 'followers' than Christmas cards from our friends. The framework of these letters is constant, and only the specific items vary, for each and every one confesses ruefully that the writer has 'unaccountably mislaid' some tried and approved recipe, or the instructions and diagram for some kind of garnish or decoration that she urgently wishes to repeat this year! Therefore each autumn when we should be writing something new, we are sent scurrying through old MSS and cutting-books for the missing gen, and when this is for a complete Christmas Plan of some kind or another, the subsequent typing turns our study into something very like an overcrowded aviary of demented woodpeckers.

So here it all is – our assembly of Christmas ideas, suggestions, plans and decorations, pruned and collated from material that has been published, broadcast or cooked by us on stage and television during the past 20 years, in the hopes that (a) it will meet at least some of your requirements, and that (b) it is solid enough not to mislay itself unaccountably and shove both you and us smartly back again into Square One.

Very sincerely,
FANNY and JOHNNIE CRADOCK

THROUGH THE YEAR
CHRISTMAS CALENDAR

'Your English housewife must be of chaste thought, stout courage, patient, diligent, witty and pleasant, constant in friendship, full of good neighbourhood, wise in discourse, but not too frequent therein, sharp and quick of speech, but not bitter or talkative, secrete in her affairs, comfortable in her consailes, and skilful in all the working knowledges that belong to her vocation.'

The Inward and Outward Virtues Which
Ought to be in a Complete Woman, 1615

Unless we are to be enemies from now onwards and you are to form the very justifiable impression that we are both stark raving mad, please read the following paragraph before you tackle our through-the-year Christmas calendar!

We *know* that none of us would make, dry, store, freeze, gather, scrounge or preserve every item that we are suggesting. We also know that however hard we try, we shall leave out something that somebody wants, so we have merely tried to put in a large enough assembly of suggestions for it to be possible for you to choose *the ones you want*. Therefore we will now confess that there has never yet been a family Christmas during which one or other of us has not exclaimed irritably, 'After all that we never froze the parsley cubes . . . made the Oxford sauce . . . got our chocolate leaves done in November.'

With these essential points clearly established between us, here is our calendar of items that can be advance-prepared for Christmas as well as general family consumption throughout the year.

OUR CALENDAR

January

Make Christmas Puddings (pp.216-17) for next Christmas. Steam for 10 hours and remove all coverings while puddings are still hot. When cold, brush tops with cooking brandy from a saucer. Cover with fresh butter papers, tie up firmly in clean cloths and hang in a *dry* place.

Make Christmas Cakes (pp.248-9) for next Christmas. Invert *in* cake tins onto cooling racks. When cold remove tins, turn right side uppermost and scissor away raised paper edges until level with cake top. Brush tops all over with brandy from a small saucer. Leave remaining papers in position. Wrap tightly in double thickness of kitchen foil and store in a dry place.

Twelfth Night! Down with all decorations! As soon as possible store or burn. Record all Christmas card names and addresses in new Christmas card list. Send any unwanted cards to children's wards of hospitals.

Open a Christmas Cook's File – then you can sling in through the oncoming months ideas, recipes and cuttings for reference when compiling Christmas plans again. When writing bread and butter letters for presents, start next year's Christmas present list.

While January sales are on and if you can afford it, keep a smart look-out for 'bargains', which can be tucked away for next year's Christmas presents or hoarded for decorations and garnish – study the relevant chapters to stimulate, we hope, your thinking. Hoard old nylon stockings for making Swags (p.69).

February to May

Give existing lists an occasional glance to remind yourself of whatever it is that has not been done yet, either because you have forgotten it or simply because you have not had a moment to get around to it. We think everyone has some laggard delinquents!

Make Dried-apricot Jam and/or Purée (p.264).

Gardeners, spare a corner of your garden in May for a few seed potatoes. When planted, cover area with black polythene, peg down securely and thus eliminate all earthing up. Delicate new potatoes will form on soil. Lift when small, store between layers of sawdust in biscuit tins and seal lids with adhesive tape. Then dig a hole, bury them, mark the place and lift them for eating on Christmas Day.

June

Make Muscat Jelly (pp.268-9) – gardeners will use their gooseberry thinnings.

Make Pickled Walnuts (pp.269-70) while these are still hard, unripe, very green and before centre kernels have had time to develop.

Start pot-pourri. The following instructions were given to us
by the late Constance Spry:

- First dry rose petals collected in the morning sun and
  after the dew has cleared. Put them in a jar with salt, a
  good handful of petals to a smaller one of rock salt. Mix
  together 1oz ground cinnamon, 1oz allspice, 1oz cloves,
  1oz nutmeg, 1oz powdered storax and 4oz powdered
  orris root. Then mix, separately, ½oz essence of lemon,
  ½oz oil of geranium, ½oz spirit of lavender, ½oz oil of
  bergamot and the finely chopped rind of three lemons.
  Mix together the powders, the liquids and some of the
  salted petals in the bottom of your chosen jar. This forms
  the nucleus of your pot-pourri. When the rose petals
  have soaked up some of the liquids, stir them thoroughly
  and add the rest of your salted rose petals. Pack them
  down firmly so that all become well impregnated with
  the oils. You may now add, without salting, more fresh
  rose petals, fresh violets and indeed any sweet-scented
  flowers that you fancy.

- The following leaves also make an excellent addition:
  sweet bay cut up into shreds, sweet verbena, bergamot,
  mint, sweet balm, geranium leaves all dried and crumbled and dried petals of marigolds. Lavender flowers,
  rosemary 'spikes' and thyme are also good additions. If
  mixture should be too moist, add powdered orris root;
  if too dry, add some rock salt. From the time of mixing
  the first rose petals with the oils until the final leaves are
  added, the jar should be kept tightly covered. Pot-pourri
  remains fragrant for a long time if it is not allowed to
  dry out so you may add from time to time brandy, lemon
  juice and freshly salted petals.

Bottle gooseberry purée for made-in-a-moment Gooseberry Fool. We use the George Fowler Lee steriliser method; otherwise follow the oven or top-of-the-stove method as given in all British schools of cookery and by all branches of the WI. Bottling of fruit in sugar syrup (p.274) is of course infinitely better than water-bottling, but *not* in terms of its appearance in the jar as the weight of the sugar syrup tends to force itself up and the fruit down. This is perfectly all right when the fruit is turned out and served but not suitable for display.

Gardeners, make out your list of pre-cooled bulbs that will flower at Christmas time – place your orders well in advance for August/September planting.

Start bunching and drying herbs for winter and Christmas use.

Start gathering mint and parsley for turning into deep-frozen cubes and continue throughout summer until stocks are satisfactory. Passionate cooks will develop this cube theme with other chosen herbs.

Pick the heads from well-washed parsley (use the stalks in the stock-pot) or pull the leaves from mint stems and nip off the tiny heads. Mill (very quick) or chop (far more laborious). Pack into the compartments of ice-cube freezing trays. Moisten with sufficient water to come to the brim. Freeze. If requiring trays again, remove cubes when frozen, wrap individually in scraps of kitchen foil, pack into polythene bags and put in the freezer to draw on as required.

July

Gardeners, begin to gather dried seed heads like iris. Bunch, tie, hang heads downwards in shed and use for Christmas decorations. From now onwards take some globe artichoke heads just before absolutely fully flowered, bunch and hang downwards.

Freeze raspberries, small strawberries (large ones taste like cotton wool), blackcurrants, blackberries, stoned cherries and stoned, quartered, unskinned apricots. Ideally, of course, these should be freshly gathered and frozen at once; in practice do the best you can in your particular circumstances.

Spread the fruit not more than ½in deep on large trays, weighing each amount carefully before so doing. The easiest way if you have sturdy scales is to weigh the tray, spread the fruit upon it, re-weigh and deduct the weight of the tray. Calculate the amount of soft brown (pieces) sugar that you will need in the ratio of 6oz sugar to every pound of fruit. Scatter the sugar carefully and evenly over the fruit on the tray and, using a scoop to avoid over-bruising the sugared fruits, half fill into polythene bags. Twist the necks, secure with plastic closures and pack into the freezer immediately. In our experience this method has always yielded fruits which taste almost exactly like fresh fruit, which is a good deal more than we have ever been able to say about bought frozen fruit. *Warning*: In old conservators it is advisable to cover sides, base and layers with newspapers; otherwise, and over a long period of storage, polythene tends to stick fiercely to freezer!

Start making soft fruit jams – when making strawberry jam, ladle some of the syrup (if you agree there is usually a surplus in your case as well as ours) into separate jars to use like Melba sauce throughout the year and at Christmas parties.

Make Crystallised Fruits (p.262), Preserved Raspberries (p.272), Maraschino Cherries (p.268) and Candied Cherries (p.262) from now onwards.

Bottle soft fruit purées (p.262) for sorbets and various puddings.

Make Redcurrant Jelly (pp.272-3).

Start Fruit Salad Pot (p.211).

Keep pot-pourri mixture going.

Make another raid on July sales.

Start freezing peas. Shell and, if finicky like us, pick out the tinies and the giants and then wash, plunge into boiling water for 1 minute, drain, plunge into cold water for 1 minute, drain and store exactly as described on p.8 for frozen fruits.

Overhaul Christmas cakes and puddings, treat them to another brandy-brushing and re-wrap as explained.

August

Check your address book and start recording on Christmas card list missing or changed addresses.

Start freezing French beans. Wash thoroughly in cold water, top and tail, plunge into boiling water for 3 minutes, drain, plunge into cold water for 1 minute, drain and store exactly as described on p.8 for frozen fruits.

Make Prunes in Port Wine (p.272).

Add fruits as available to Fruit Salad Pot (p.211).

Keep pot-pourri mixture going.

Store suitable dried items for decorations, remembering that dried flowers retain colour far better if wrapped in black tissue paper before hanging.

Gardeners, harvest garlic crop and pick unblemished raspberry leaves for gammon, tie together in small bunches, hang in cool place to dry, and thereafter rehang in dust-protecting polythene bags pierced with small holes to allow slight ventilation of contents.

Glance back at your existing files and see if there is any more to add.

Sort out your bulb containers and order special fibre for when the forcing bulbs arrive.

On country forays or holidays keep a smart look-out for bits of tree bark, driftwood and other winter decoration treasures.

Take Christmas present lists away with you on holiday.

September

Start freezing sliced runner beans (same as French beans, p.9) and polythene bagsful of small, firm tomatoes (stalk, wash, dry carefully and accept that they will give you excellent tomato pulp but will not be suitable for using either whole or halved and grilled).

Now is the time to start cleaning off and putting into jars the herbs which are already dry.

Dig up and pot a few clumps of chives and bring into kitchen for winter and Christmas use if no heated glasshouse is available.

Gardeners, slip squares of polythene underneath vegetable marrows marked down for winter storage, give them a shot in the arm with Liquinure to help them blow up like airships. Freeze corn on the cob.

Do final revision of Christmas card list. Either make your own cards or add to future shopping lists under one of two headings: Order in Bulk or Buy Gradually. If numbers are painful it is a good thing to buy a few stamps each week; then the blow is lessened around the 10th–15th December.

Do an overhaul of accumulated Christmas presents and tackle the missing ones on a list attached to whatever you take shopping.

Lay in fine string and a trussing needle for drying field mushrooms if your area makes this possible.

Make Mincemeat (p.219).

October

As soon as weather is cool enough, cure hams.

In areas where wild chestnuts occur, obtain necessary permission and glean these for home-made *Marrons glacés* (pp.270-72).

Gather walnuts before squirrels get them.

Pot up Oxford Sauce (pp.184-5).

Make Grandma's Indian Chutney (p.266) and finish your own favourite chutneys.

Turn windfalls into Apple Purée.

Gardeners, dig up salsify and plant in greenhouse under inverted flowerpots to blanch; gather last of cornheads, bunch and dry some for Christmas decorations. Bring in marrows; clean, dry and seal around both stalk and opposite ends with sealing wax, hang in nets. Harvest ornamental gourds; clean, dry completely and brush with colourless varnish.

If you can collect hazelnuts, treat as for walnuts.

Collect fir cones for Christmas decorations.

Check datelines at Post Office for overseas surface Christmas mail.

November

> *'Christmas is coming, the geese are getting fat,*
> *Please to put a penny in the old man's hat:*
> *If you haven't got a penny, a ha'penny will do,*
> *If you haven't got a ha'penny, God bless you!'*
>
> Beggar's Rhyme, anon.

Now get cracking in the evening with those Christmas decorations that can be made in advance. The late, great Constance Spry used to say every year, 'Now life starts to be all glitter dust.' Remember to save some of the simple, can-be-left-to-the-last-minute ones to keep the children out of mischief when they get back from school *and the heat is really on for YOU.*

Get all Christmas cards ready for posting and finish buying stamps before Post Office queues develop.

Complete buying of all decoration items.

Make Royal Icing Penguins (pp.286-7) and Plaques (p.286) and store in airtight tin.

Make Christmas stockings (pp.75–6).

Cover cake boards. Cut these to required size (round or square) in ply or hard-board and cover with shiny silver, gold or patterned Christmas wrapping papers. Once made, they can be used with different coverings over and over again.

Draw up Christmas menus in detail.

Make *Bagna Cauda* (p.100).

Overhaul all Christmas emergency stores.

Make lists of main perishable and non-perishable goods.

Make Worcestershire Sauce (p.275).

Make Chocolate Swan components (pp.279-80), Chocolate Leaves (pp.278-9) for Christmas garnish and Almond Paste Holly Leaves (pp.276-7).

Check your fairy lights are working.

Make ham frills by cutting a strip 8in wide and 18in long in red, white or green tissue paper. Fold over lengthwise. Make 1in-deep cuts closely together along the whole folded side (not the two edges). Open out and reverse the fold completely, thus making a rounded frilled panel. Wind this around the bone of the cold, cooked ham and secure with a paper clip (underneath) or with a dab of UHU. Do not use a pin! Cutlet frills are made in precisely the same way, with 2½in-wide and 9in-long strips.

Make cutlet frill decorations by winding a 4½in-long cutlet frill *slantwise* around a wooden cocktail stick so that it spirals down to within 1in of the tip. Secure end with UHU. These can be used in clusters or singly to decorate both sweet and savoury dishes. They are especially pretty if made with matching strips of red and green, or green and white, folded together, cut together and used as instructed. Larger ones on wooden skewers can be equally easily made in advance.

Make cake frills by cutting two 6in-wide frills of required length in one or two mixed coloured tissue paper strips and stick the two pairs of cut sides over each other with UHU. Then stick a narrow or gold or silver strip of bought cake paper down the centre and wrap around the cake.

December

Now do an overall check on everything we have suggested and insert anything that either you or we have overlooked, including the section on pp.317-20 entitled For Freezer and/or Refrigerator.

Check and cope with laundry, cleaning and pressing before deadline approaches.

Make final hair appointment.

Book overseas telephone calls and if 'that wretched tooth is starting to nag again', deal with it *now* and do not run the risk of letting it ruin your Christmas.

Remember to post Christmas cards and parcels on appropriate days!

Last but not least, rehearse your entire Christmas table and then pack everything away so that you can whip it all out and slap it into place at speed.

1st–14th
Study your Christmas food lists and make any of the following items which you will need:

Basic Butter Cream (refrigerator), Garlic Butter (refrigerator), Mayonnaise (refrigerator), Salted Almonds (store shelf), Peppermint Creams (store shelf), French dressing (store shelf), Fondants (store shelf), Almond Paste (store shelf in double polythene bags), Shortbread (in tin), Brandy Butter (refrigerator), Coconut Ice (tin), Stuffed Dates (tin), Lemon and Orange Creams (tin).

Pack pot-pourri into decorative bowls, cover lightly with wet cellophane and stick edges to bowl sides with UHU. When cellophane is dry and taut, tie up with ribbons.

Give chosen table napkins Christmas treatment.

Now turn to Battle Stations and may Heaven bless us all!

14th onwards

> *'Heap on more wood! – the wind is chill;*
> *But let it whistle as it will,*
> *We'll keep our Christmas merry still.'*
>   Walter Scott

There is no doubt that the hands that rock the cradle, scrub, clean, cook and decorate, have the labours of Sisyphus to contend with at Christmas. Having prepared your menus, listed and knitted in every single advance-made item, which you now have at your disposal, snatch one more quiet moment somehow. Work out everything else that remains to be done, divide your chores into separate days and so count down on your labours until you have turned the key on the dining-room door – Christmas table ready and glittering behind it – and can take yourself to bed knowing that in the morning you can, with just one cooker and with the help of the plan (Diagram 1), which Joan Jefferson Farjeon has drawn for us, just reach for your pots and pans, set them in position and thus have a comparatively easy day ahead.

Christmas Day

As you will see, the plan is geared to a four-burner, two-shelf oven cooker. On the left front burner is the kettle for

Diagram 1. Plan of Cooker

replenishing hot water in the bottom tier of the steamer, leaving the second tier available for you to fill to suit your pattern. The lid of this tier is inverted so that the small, lidded pan can sit on top holding your natural sauce or cleared juice from the roasted bird. On the back-right burner you have a double pan for either vanilla sauce or mulled wine and another one on the front-right burner for soup with a third sitting beside on the working unit, filled with the pre-made coffee, which in this type of container can be reheated over water and a thread of heat without any fear that it will boil. Grouped around this pan are (a) coffee pot, (b) soup bowls, (c) either pan or punch bowl or substitute for mulled wine or sauceboat for variation on other chosen sweet sauce. On the left-hand unit is the sauceboat for the sauce or gravy and the mince pie made, lightly baked, and still in its oven-proof container, waits to be slipped in when the bird is removed and at Gas Mark 1.

Now turn to the oven. The bird sits on the upper shelf, the sausage and bacon rolls or chipolatas on the second shelf alongside stuffing in a terrine or stuffing birds or independently roasted potatoes, leaving the floor of the oven clear for two pre-cooked casseroles of vegetables under foil to be slipped in for reheating at the appropriate time. Before you serve your first course, if cold, or when you serve a reheated soup, take out the bird and all its trimmings, reduce the heat to Gas Mark 1, tent the presentation dishes tightly in kitchen foil and start the meal knowing that you will only have to carry the dishes to table, slip in the mince pie and pour the natural (or any other chosen) sauce from a little pan into the waiting sauceboat.

If you are short of double pans, stand wine, soup, coffee, etc., in their pans on small pieces of wood in larger pans containing hot water; then cover the lot with pieces of kitchen foil.

Just remember to keep topping up the kettle with more water so that you have a little to spare for rinsing out sauceboats, punch bowl and soup bowls as an extra insurance that everything in these containers will stay piping hot. Be sure you have tea towels or oven gloves nearby, together with your serving dishes carefully tucked away into your warming drawer. Although this may not be independently heated, if you put your chosen dishes and plates for hot food in immediately you light your oven on Christmas Day, they will be fine and warm for you when you need them.

CHRISTMAS DINNERS

Escoffier wrote in the preface to his masterpiece – *A Guide to Modern Cookery* – 'Very few people know what an arduous task the composing of a perfect menu represents.' He was, of course, writing from the pinnacle of his profession, plumb in the middle of the Age of Elegance, when it was still a little daring for gentlewomen to venture into public restaurants, and when it would have been unthinkable for a dinner to consist of less than eight courses.

It is manifestly more of a problem to maintain a gastronomic balance in a meal sequence of eight courses than with the standard three courses served by the average cook/hostess today. Even so, we have our problems, because we are dealing primarily with Christmas Dinner, which traditionally should have a roasted bird and its accompaniments, a Christmas Pudding, some mince pies, Stilton cheese with celery and an assortment of desserts; yet even we can clearly remember a time when oysters were followed by clear soup, superseded by turbot in lobster sauce, and then the given traditional meal tacked on thereafter. This does as much as possible to obey the simplest of basic menu rules until it reaches the Christmas Pudding and what follows: for the oysters stimulate the tastebuds and cleanse the palate, then the clear brown soup changes the tempo ready for the white of the turbot and the brown of the roasted bird thereafter. After which, of course, the whole thing goes haywire, for you are required to pack in the rich black pudding, the equally rich mince pies, and the dessert items, an exercise which ends up with the diner feeling very much like an unfortunate Strasbourg goose.

All we can therefore do is give you some samples which honour tradition with the ultimate 'heavies' and try to lighten the load at the onset. We shall confine ourselves to three courses and dessert. Therefore, to save endless repetition, the large, labour-saving mince pies and the dessert will be given in the first example and left out thereafter. These menu examples of ours also strive to play a few permissible variations on the One Fixed Theme.

No. 1

BILL OF FARE	MENU
Melon Boats	Barquettes de Melon
Roast Turkey	Dinde Rôtie
Burgundy Sauce	Sauce Bourguignonne
Brussels Sprouts with Chestnuts	Choux de Bruxelles aux Marrons
Roast Potatoes	Pommes Rôties
Escoffier's Plum Pudding	Pouding des Rois Mages
Brandy Butter	Crème au Beurre au Cognac
Mince Pie	Mince Pie
Dessert	Dessert

No. 2 (rich and indigestible)

BILL OF FARE	MENU
Bortsch	Bortsch
Roast Goose with Chestnuts	Oie Rôtie aux Marrons
Red Cabbage	Chou rouge
Stuffed Jacket Roast Potatoes	Pommes Macaire
Escoffier's Plum Pudding	Pouding des Rois Mages
Brandy Butter	Crème au Beurre au Cognac

No. 3

BILL OF FARE	MENU
Potted Shrimps	Pâté de Crevettes
Stuffed Roast Turkey	Rôtie de Dinde Farcie
Monte Carlo Onions	Oignons Monte Carlo
Fried Potato Balls	Pommes Amandines
Escoffier's Plum Pudding	Pouding des Rois Mages
Brandy Butter	Crème au Beurre au Cognac

No. 4

BILL OF FARE	MENU
Brussels Sprouts and Chestnut Soup	Purée de Noël
Roast Turkey	Rôtie de Dinde
Creole Ham	Jambon à la Créole
Potato Croquettes	Pommes Rissolées
Chicory in Cheese Sauce	Endives Mornay
Christmas Pudding Ring	Pouding des Rois Mages en couronne
Rum Butter	Crème au Beurre au Rhum

No. 5

BILL OF FARE	MENU
Leek and Potato Soup	Vichyssoise
Pekin Duck	Caneton de Pekin
Ham in Puff Pastry	Jambon Feuilleté
Brussels Sprouts with Chestnuts	Choux de Bruxelles aux Marrons
Cumberland Sauce	Sauce Cumberland
Christmas Parcels	Petits Pacquets de Noël en Surprise
Champagne Sauce	Sauce Champagne

No. 6

BILL OF FARE	MENU
Hot Baked Grapefruit	Pamplemousses Chaudes
Foil-roasted Turkey	Dinde en Papillote
Gammon in Pastry Crust	Pièce de Bacon en Croûte
Potato Cake	Gâteau Lyonnais
Mme Jeanne's Cabbage	Choux Mme Jeanne
Christmas Pudding Roll	Pouding des Rois Mages en rouleau
Grand Marnier Butter	Crème au Beurre au Grand Marnier

No. 7 (for the bored sophisticate)

BILL OF FARE	MENU
Snails in Puff Pastry	Escargots Feuilleté
Pheasant with Foie Gras	Faisan Souvaroff
Potato Cakes	Crêpes Parmentier
Green Salad	Salade Verte
French Dressing with Grapes	Vinaigrette aux Raisins
Nesselrode Pudding	Pouding Nesselrode

No. 8

BILL OF FARE	MENU
Individual Mussel Moulds	Rémoulade de Moules
Boiled Turkey	Dinde Pochée
Onion Sauce	Sauce à l'Oignon
Creamed Carrots	Carottes à la crème
Swiss Potatoes	Roesti
Frozen Christmas Pudding	Pouding de Noël glacé
Punch Sauce	Sauce Ponche

No. 9

BILL OF FARE	MENU
Whitebait	Blanchailles Frites
Sucking Pig	Cochon au lait
Sou-Fassum	Sou-Fassum
Provence Sauce	Sauce Provençale
Christmas Fritters	Beignets de Noël
Champagne Sauce	Sauce Champagne

No. 10

BILL OF FARE	MENU
Avocados with French Dressing	Avocats Vinaigrette
Roast Leg of Pork	Gigot de Porc
Apple Sauce	Compôte de Pommes
Forcemeat Ducks	Petits Canards en farce
Artichokes in Cheese Sauce	Artichauts Mornay
Plum Pudding	Pouding de Noël
Brandy Butter	Crème au Beurre au Cognac

No. 11

BILL OF FARE	MENU
Avocados with Madeira	Avocats au Madère
Roast Capon with Mushroom Stuffing	Chapon farci aux Champignons
Brussels Sprouts with Chestnuts	Choux de Bruxelles aux Marrons
Dauphine Potatoes	Pommes Dauphine
French Plum Pudding	Pouding de Noël Français
Vanilla Sauce	Sauce Vanille

No. 12

BILL OF FARE	MENU
Prawn or Shrimp Cocktail	Cocktail d'Ecrevisses ou de Crevettes
South American Turkey	Dinde Sud-Americaine
Sweet Potatoes	Patates Douces
Cranberry Sauce	Sauce d'Airelles
Corn Fritters	Beignets de Maïs
French Plum Pudding	Pouding de Noël Français
Vanilla Sauce	Sauce Vanille

CHRISTMAS MENU – 1906

Frivolités
Caviar frais – Blinis de Sarrasin
Oursins de la Méditerranée
Natives au Raifort
Les Délices de St Antoine
Tortue Verte
Velouté de Poulet aux nids d'hirondelle
Sterlet du Volga à la Moscovite
Barquette de Laitance à la Vénitienne
Chapon fin aux Perles du Périgord
Cardon épineux à la Toulousaine
Selle de Venaison aux Cerises
Crème de marrons
Jeune agneau piqué de sauge à la Provençale
Sylphiaes de Roitelets
Gelée de Pommes d'Amour aux Ecrevisses
Fine Champagne 1820
Mandarines givrées
Caillies sous la cendre aux raisins
Bécassines rosées au feu de sarments
Salade Isabelle
Asperges de France
Foie gras poché au Vin de Moselle
Buche de Noël en Surprise
Plum Pudding – Mince Pie
Mignardises aux violettes
Etoile du Berger
Fruits de Serre chaude
Café Turc
Grandes Liqueurs

G. Escoffier

SIEGE OF PARIS CHRISTMAS DINNER
25 décembre 1870

Hors d'oeuvre
Beurre – Radis – Tête d'âne farcie – Sardines

Potages
Purée de haricots rouges aux croutons
Consommé d'éléphant

Entrées
Goujons frits – Le chameau rôti à l'Anglaise
Le civet de kangourou
Côtes d'ours rôties, sauce poivrade

Rots
Cuissot de loup, sauce chevreuil
Le chat flanqué de rats
Salade de cresson
La terrine d'antilope aux truffes
Crêpes à la bordelaise
Petits pois au beurre

Entremets
Gâteau de riz aux confitures

Dessert
Fromage de Gruyère

Vins: Premier Service	*Vins: Deuxième Service*
Xères	Mouton Rothschild 1846
Latour Blanche 1861	Romanée Conti 1858
Ch. Palmer 1864	Bollinger frappé
	Grand Porto 1827

Café et liqueurs
Café Voisin, G. Braquenas, 261, rue Saint-Honoré

Key (French/English): *âne* – donkey
chameau – camel
ours – bear
loup – wolf

A CHRISTMAS TALE WHICH HAPPENS TO BE TRUE
Pour amuser les autres

Once upon a time there were two sophisticated lovers, neither of whom was any longer in the first flush of youth. Because like invariably attracts like, they had two very close friends whose tastes were exactly similar, as were their situations. The four decided to dine together on Christmas night in an elegant but small London flat. The host and hostess settled their two guests in deep chairs before a log fire where, at small tables drawn before the chairs, they served Christmas Dinner to a muted background of Chopin, Liszt, Debussy and finally Ravel . . . just the *Bolero*.

They ate in ease and comfort:

Les papillotes de Caviar
Consommé en tasse
Les Cailles Périgourdine
Les petites Pommes Anna d'Escoffier
Ponche à la Romaine
Crème Ecossaise
Le Pouding de Noël
Sauce Sabayon au Madère
Moka

Explanation

They ate the little puff pastry envelopes filled with Russian caviare in their fingers and drank the soup from porcelain cups. They used fingers again for the boned *foie gras* and black truffle stuffed quail, and used a fork for the individual *Pommes Anna*; naturally finger bowls were provided. The iced champagne punch was served in crystal coupes with small spoons; the cheese cream spread on fingers of toast and the individual Christmas Puddings were also presented with forks.

They drank champagne beforehand in coupes, as none would have dreamed of using those old-fashioned, wide, shallow champagne glasses. They drank *Chambertin en magnum* from almost transparently thin Burgundy tulips and with the quail and the cheese cream; Madeira Terrantez 1795 in port glasses with the pudding, and paired the coffee with 1848 Armagnac from the cellars of the Sammalens brothers in Gascony – this, of course, in cold *balons*, which they warmed in their hands.

All of which constituted a compromise between distinction and tradition, and remarkably adult, romantic inclinations.

LIGHT LUNCHEONS AND SUPPERS FOR CHRISTMAS DAY

'Twas the night before Christmas, when all through
  the house,
Not a creature was stirring, not even a mouse;
The stockings were hung by the chimney with care,
In hopes that St. Nicholas soon would be there.'

Clement C. Moore

These little menu suggestions are based upon the assumption that you do the Christmas table on Christmas Eve, *after* the children have been thrust to bed and *after* the stockings and pillowcases have been filled – the last chore, in fact, before turning the key on the dining room door and either going up to bed or going out to midnight service. This procedure puts the dining room in baulk until Christmas-night dinner is over; unless you are such a paragon that you are prepared to clear the whole wretched mess up after Christmas luncheon, and re-do the same table for supper. The only other alternative is to clean and clear down, leave all the decorations and sup in the same festive setting. Otherwise, you will have to present light luncheon or light supper as we do ourselves *informally* in the kitchen or hallway when large enough, or the living room. All you really need do is cover a suitable table with a white or coloured cloth or table mats and have one easily movable Christmas centrepiece or backing piece to maintain Christmas flavour. Then stack at strategic points the cutlery, silver, glasses and such plates as do not require heating and add such beverages as do not require chilling, mulling or bringing up to boiling point. Red wines will, of course, *chambré* quite happily on the table.

If you are choosing luncheon, force the issue so that eating and drinking can be leisurely and still over with a few minutes to spare before the Queen speaks. While you are about all this, do not overlook some suitable containers for present wrappings if stripping the tree thereafter. If our memory serves us right, you will also need to apply a vacuum cleaner to the carpet, or spend the rest of the day like Caius Marius among the ruins of Carthage.

A PLEA ABOUT STILTON

If you are going to spend a considerable sum of money on a Stilton cheese, may we beg of you to treat it kindly and in such a manner that the very last inch is almost as edible as the first. There is no gloomier sight than the scooped-out cavity of a once-prime Stilton cheese; dried, powdered flakes of cheese moulting from its remaining walls and the whole thing painfully suggestive of decay and decomposition. We beg of you to cut your Stilton properly! There is a saying in Leicestershire, the birthplace of Stilton – which is both comprehensive and self-explanatory: 'Cut high, cut low, cut middle,' which, as you can now see for yourselves, means you cut wedges from the wall side all the way round and right across to the centre, maintaining the level as the cheese gets shorter and shorter and leaves no standing walls to crumble, so please banish your cheese scoops.

Luncheons

Potted Shrimps, Toast and Butter
Stilton Cheese, Celery and
    Biscuits
Fruit Salad Pot

Pork Pâté in a Pastry Case
Celeriac and Beetroot Salad
Assorted Cheese Board, Celery
    and Hot Bread
Mince Pie

Avocados with Shrimp or Prawn
    Cocktail Filling
Coulibiac
Green Salad
Stilton Cheese, Celery and
    Biscuits

Suppers

Hot or Cold Vichyssoise
Tuna Rice Bowl
Italian Trifle

Hot Baked Grapefruit
Smoked Trout or Buckling
Frozen Christmas
    Pudding

Cold Green Omelette
Mercedes Salad
Rum Sorbet

CHILDREN'S CHRISTMAS PARTIES' MENUS

Insofar as the young are concerned today, all but the very smallest react with extreme disfavour to pretty little pink cakes and nice wobbling jellies. They don't want to know! They like food which can be eaten in the hand, and they like *savouries*. Even the smallest go mad for fruit 'cocktails' – just fruit juice or fruit syrup shaken up with stiffly whipped egg white immediately before serving and poured into those beastly cocktail glasses.

Small fry prefer crisps and salted nuts to 'sweeties', though a few old diehards of about six can still be persuaded to toy with toffee apples. Their bias in eating and drinking is in complete accord with their bias about clothes; they prefer jeans to party clothes and therefore the food that goes with jeans.

No one could ever accuse us of having an orthodox approach to anything but gastronomy, so it is just possible that our suggestions for the entertainment of small and medium fry may bring down some parents with a touch of the screaming ab-dabs – nevertheless . . .

We scored our greatest success with the five-to-ten age group when we invited 40 of them to a winter party in a country house and wheedled their parents into allowing them to come in their go-into-the-farmyard-and-play clothes. Having lashed a fireguard 100 per cent securely into protective position across a huge log fire, we let the party in. One by one they were issued with a bundle, shovelled into the very big sitting room, and invited to dress up. We chose as many assorted sundries as one attic would yield, including one bundle with an admiral's hat, an ostrich feather boa and a pair of Wellington boots. We left them alone for five minutes, then marched in and announced tea. When they were awash with food and drink (non-alcoholic, of course) we tied them up in huge bath towels and let them do Apple Bobbing, while the attendant adults held up plaits and curls. When they had all been dried off we gave them a ballet to watch. This consisted of Johnnie, who is over 6 foot, and two other men of equal size, dressed in tutus with flowers in their teeth. Honestly we do not believe that they would have minded if they had not been given presents to take home. The result was a riotous success, the cost was minimal and nobody wanted to go home.

Such tactics will not work with totty teenagers. From them we learn that there are 'in' foods and 'out' foods, and that 'those awful fruit cups with drowned bits in' just go down the sink as soon as adult backs are turned. They all boast that they can fry (16 and over, of course) and adore kitchen parties 'because it is so nice when it gets a bit whiffy with frying and sloppings can easily be mopped up'. A stripped-down kitchen unit makes an ideal parking place for the record player 'with plenty of room to spread the records about' and there must be plenty of chunky candles about, firmly stuck into solid containers. Once they have done their frying, they are happiest in a dim, funereal light with plastic beakers: 'No broken glass to sweep up.' Remember 'bags of coffee, and don't scrimp the sugar'. We have also been taught to lay down tons of orange juice, no matter whether tinned or fresh, and, for the 18s and over, some 'nice cold wine, which does not taste like vinegar'. In our choice *we* err on the sweet side and do a bit of watering down for the younger ones. If the kitchen is by any happy chance in the basement, shove cushions up the stairway and then let them loose to get on with it alone.

MENUS

With the assistance of the relevant age group, the following list of ideal foods for small children has been compiled:

Peanuts; crisps; Twiglets; miniature sausage rolls; chipolatas on sticks; stuffed bridge rolls (savoury fillings only); tiny triangular egg and cress sandwiches (crusts off, please); hard-boiled egg swans; gingerbread men; toffee apples; jelly babies; chocolate cigarettes; fruit juice and egg white cocktails.

THE CAKE: A Chocolate Log Cake.

THE CENTREPIECE: A Gingerbread House.

For assorted teenagers choose from this list:

Dip-and-dunk assembly: Tuna Rice Bowl; Mum's Bangers; cold Beefsteak and Kidney Pie; Mrs Marshall's Fried

Sandwiches (ready to fry); French Potato Salad; a basket of raw vegetables; Mayonnaise and Vinaigrette; large Mince Pies; Blackcurrant Sorbets; a cheese board (labelled) with digestive biscuits and Dorset Knobs, celery and radishes; garlic bread; the Fruit Salad Pot.

Warning: If you are allowing your teenagers to fry in hot oil, will you please be sure to follow the simple precautions that really should be regarded as essential for everyone. Whatever pan is used, *never fill it more than one-third with oil*. If the pan has a long handle, either turn the handle inwards to the cooker or, better still, thread a wire through a hole at the tip of the handle and secure it to the back of the cooker. Then there is no fear that (a) seething oil can bubble over, (b) the pan can be knocked off, or (c) the pan can be tipped over.

IN PARENTHESIS AND AFTER SCRATCHING THROUGH OUR NOTEBOOKS

We find we have made a record of odd 'successes' with small children in the past. Only the squares of red cellophane remained when the children went home the year we gave each child a bag of popcorn in cellophane tied up with ribbons. They had somehow managed to stuff it all in during the afternoon, but the green cellophane bags of marshmallows were politely and disinterestedly taken away uneaten.

The year we cut elephants and rabbits and ducks in coloured blotting paper for place mats they all vanished with our guests, except two which were stuck to the table and sopping wet with spilt fruit juice cocktail. Last year one six-year-old brought his own disc of 'Puppet on a String' and requested that we should play it. All the funny little things began squirming about like their elder brothers and sisters and the party became a highly successful writhing session. The occasion when we left a half-finished jigsaw puzzle of our own on the corner table four very shy ones spent the entire afternoon completing it, and confided in us when they left that they would like to have jigsaws at all the parties they went to. We now use them as a bait for introvert types.

We were also astonished to find a queue of infants lining up to have the tiny posies we made for the girls and the carnations we put out for the boys safety-pinned onto them by us. This was the occasion when the 'thank you for having mes' included some additional 'thank you for our flowers'. We also have a note that says, 'Crackers are dicey – the squeakers are sometimes scared of the bangs.' Better to make cotton-wool snowballs with tiny presents in the middle and a bit of non-scratchy artificial holly stuck on top of each, together with a reminder for the future: 'What about soap pipes and bubble-blowing next time? It wouldn't cost much to sling a polythene poncho over each child!'

A nursery Christmas cake, which produced squeals of pleasure, was set on a board at least 4in wider all round than the base of the cake. When icing an adult rich fruit cake with royal icing, we stole a bit to pipe large rosettes ½in in from cakeboard edge, about 1½in apart. When the rosettes firmed sufficiently (about 15 minutes), we pushed small scarlet candles into them without their flopping over. When these were lit and carried into the darkened room, the cake looked as if it were encircled by flames (harmless ones).

Under our teenage records we find Pork Spare Ribs (p.166) the biggest success yet. They were very surprised we did not provide cigarettes. Should we next time? A lot of them asked for Coca-Cola, which we think is dreadful. We have also been informed recently by our most 'with-it' teenager that the most 'in' kind of teenage party is 'a pyjama party with all the lights out'. No comment.

We are not sure we ought to tell you, because we are uncertain as to whether we were right, when we hired an old bell and fruit gum machine – which took pennies only – and ran a roulette table with dummy coins and small financial returns to the winners at the end of the sessions. We must confess their comment was: 'Absolutely fab!'

THE CHRISTMAS BUFFET

This is one of our favourite forms of entertainment. Like all parties, we plan ours like battles, and in this house they go on for so long that the host and hostess have time not only to look after all their guests, but to talk to them as well! A buffet is also very much easier than any formal dinner, because unless the cook hostess goes mad in the head and decides to make something like a *Gâteau Réligieux* (which has to be made on the day of the party) it is pretty easy to advance-plan so that there is only garnish and set-up to do on the day.

A buffet table always looks much more effective and is more easily manageable if space for bodies can be allowed between the back of the buffet and the wall of the room. This eliminates having to hover between guests and puts you in a position from which you can explain without getting in the way when someone asks, 'What is this delicious-looking thing?' or 'Is there any mustard in that sauce? I'm allergic to it.'

Remember, too, that you can always arrange your display to far greater effect if you have a bit of height at the back. We have two sets of *Encyclopaedia Britannica* – one bogged down in the early nineteenth century and one contemporary. These are always brought into service to align along the back of the buffet table from end to end. Covered with drapes and with a decorative centre piece, they support the puddings and get them out of the way until the front-of-table-length-and-breadth of savoury items have been polished off. When the necessary

amount of table cloths is not available we fall back on sheets . . .
plain white ones for Christmas – one lot to wrap up the books
tidily (except for the back, which does not show!), and one lot
to cover the buffet table-top, front and sides – that come right
down to within a fraction of the floor. Once these are in position you can tear away with pre-made Swags (p.69) in either
scarlet or emerald-green tissue paper, or you can just use trails
of evergreens to dress the front and sides with sprays of wired
laurel and unblemished small lemons or oranges, whole garlic
heads or polished rosy apples arranged in crescents between
the dishes. To make these decorations (see Diagram 2), take
two small sprigs of uneven lengths of laurel, overlap the stems
centrally and secure with fine wire. Drive a piece of stem wire
through the base of a garlic head, apple, lemon or orange. Take
the two protruding ends of florists' stem wire and bend them
securely over the centre of the prepared laurel spray. These
sprays can be made several days in advance if set out carefully
on ordinary meat baking tins just base-covered with cold
water.

Use parsley, sage or rosemary in small tufts or sprigs to make
small, wired strands for decorating long rectangular, oval or
square flat dishes. Just wind the herbs together with fine
florists' wire exactly as described for Tissue Paper Swags
(pp.84-5); only one difference – when making several days
before the party, and after wiring, coil them into bowls
containing water. They will then keep well and are simply lifted
out, shaken free of water and patted in a dry cloth before
placing round food items.

When putting the knives, forks, spoons and plates in position do *not* lump them all together at one end so that a cat's
cradle of guests weaves and struggles down to one end to get
their implements and maybe back again to the opposite end to

heap their plates with whatever has caught their eye. Stagger plates and all cutlery and silver in smaller, interspersing heaps between the dishes and food and from end to end. This way congestion is anyhow partially avoided.

Diagram 2

When it comes to the food, you must pre-determine, by the serving labour at your disposal, whether you have a carver for the cold roast, sucking pig, goose, baron of beef, ham or gammon, and another pair of hands to manipulate the puddings properly; or whether you serve everything *in individual portions* no matter how large the number. Let us illustrate with Turkey *Chaudfroid* (pp.147-8). Cut up the bird into neat pieces, making each one the size of a portion. Mask them with *chaudfroid*. Arrange them on the serving dish and fill the spaces in between with diced aspic or piped mayonnaise – either in advance, if refrigeration space allows, or, when space is limited, stack the ungarnished sauce-covered portions on baking sheets, refrigerate, and do the dish settings and garnish *on the day*. Bitter experience has taught us that, however distinguished our guests, they make a monumental mess of helping themselves or carving and everything looks a wreck after the first few minutes.

At this point we must admit to an error which sometimes gets us into trouble. This reached its peak when Fanny's father celebrated the publication of his hundredth novel on his eightieth birthday. This so went to Fanny's head that she produced 100 different dishes and 80 candles on his cake to celebrate. Clearly there were not 80 portions of anything, so the evening was punctuated by little moans from one or other of the 80 guests – 'I didn't get the boned quail,' or 'All that chocolate pudding was gone before I could reach it!' Where you choose a dish with something in it like oysters, which are not everyone's yen, you must obviously serve an alternative, but do not choose too many different items lest you fall into our trap!

You will see that our lists of suggestions from recipes in this book for small, medium and large buffets are in fact pruned down to a fantastic degree from the selections offered when even George V was on the throne. Here they are, and we have annotated them with preparation notes in the hope that these might be of some help to you.

A Small Buffet

Lobster Patties (vol-au-vent cases stamped out, pre-frozen, to thaw, fill and bake the day before)

Turkey *Chaudfroid* (from leftovers)

Cold Sliced Ham or Gammon (from leftovers)

Tomato (day before), Russian (two days before) and Green Salads (pick and prepare day before, toss last moment)

French Potato Salad (prepare day before, toss last moment)

Mont Blanc (purée in advance, cream at last moment)

Tipsy Cake (sponge weeks before and freeze, thaw out and finish day of service)

A Medium Buffet

Caviare Cream (keeps two days in mild refrigeration), hot
   toast and butter

Liver Pâté (keeps one week in mild refrigeration)

Pigeon Pie (freezes beautifully after cooking) with cranberry
   sauce (one week in advance)

and/or

Cold Collops of Hare (three days in mild refrigeration) with
   Cumberland Sauce (keeps several weeks)

Russian (make two days beforehand) and Windsor (assemble
   day of presentation) Salads

Tansy (two days in refrigeration) and Orange Fool (two days in
   refrigeration) with Lemon Jumballs (make seven days
   beforehand, keep in airtight tin with bag of silica gel from
   Boots to offset humidity)

A Large Buffet

Grapefruit and Orange Cocktail (sections freeze well in waxed
   cartons, assemble on the day)

Prawn or Shrimp Cocktail (mixture the day before, into individual portions on the day)

Turbot *Chaudfroid* (complete day beforehand, garnish on day
   using piped anchovy butter, mayonnaise or seasoned cream
   to mark off into individual portions for easy service)

Cold Sucking Pig (cook two days before, dress on the day) and
   Celery Salad (cut celery, refrigerate in slightly salted water,
   assemble on day)

or

Cold Roast Turkey (roast three days before) and Corn Salad
   (toss last minute)

or

Cold Roast Goose (roast three days before) and Orange Salad
   (freeze for last-minute dressing)

French Potato Salad
Our Trifle (two days before, leaving cream garnish to day)
Charlotte Russe (freezes for one month)
Frozen Christmas Pudding (freezes for three months)

CHRISTMAS DECORATIONS

CHRISTMAS DECORATIONS

'Oh, how that glitter taketh me!'

Diagram 2a

Every year we are depressed at Christmastime by the startling lack of originality in so many Christmas decorations. It always puzzles us that the average household is content to send some Christmas cards, wrap some parcels, hang a few paper chains or sprigs of evergreen and jab a piece of holly into a Christmas Pudding at an uninspired meal, which begins with too heavy a soup and ends with entirely unsuitable mince pies. There is a lack of cohesion between tradition – which we venerate – and originality – into which we impart something of our own personality. Surely a happy mean between the traditional and the original is the goal towards which every cook/hostess/wife/mum should strive. None of us could defend ourselves on the grounds of limited scope, for the potentials are almost limitless.

Yet we know one woman who possesses a vast income, buys colossal quantities of Christmas presents and roars round in a state of fantastic panic for days, despite which *not one idea, not one touch exclusive to her own mind and imagination* ever puts sparkle into her Christmas rooms. We know another who has practically no money – relatively speaking – children, insufficient help and whose house at Christmas last year was a joy to behold, though both time and money were so scarce. Charm, intelligence, thoughtfulness abounded. A call there to leave small parcels, to have a Christmas Eve sherry, was an experience not to be missed.

Let us submit one, simple illustration with mistletoe – the most conventional and traditional of Christmas decorations. With the aid of a few baubles and some ribbon we can transform it from the simple original into something much more sophisticated, which contains a bit of us in the treatment. Alternatively, we can stick to the rules, as laid down in the following quote:

> Against the Feast of Christmas every man's house, as also their parish churches, were decked with holme, ivy, bayes, and whatsoever the season of the year afforded to be green.

Mistletoe, which Virgil compares to the golden bough in Infernis, never, according to Brand, 'entered sacred edifices but by mistake, or ignorance of the sextons; for it was the heathenish or profane plant, as having been of such distinction in the pagan rites of Druidism, and it therefore had its place assigned it in kitchens, where it was hung up in great state with its white berries; and whatever female chanced to stand under it, the young man present either had a right or claimed one of saluting her, and of plucking off a berry at each kiss.'

Instead of tying a bunch '*au natur*' to (a) a chandelier, (b) an electric bulb fitment or (c) a ceiling hook, try the mistletoe ball.

THE MISTLETOE BALL

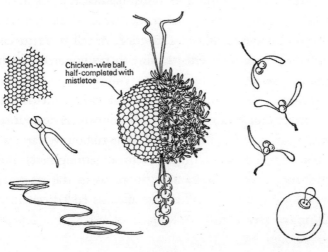

Chicken-wire ball, half-completed with mistletoe

Diagram 3

Assemble a large, small or medium piece of ½in mesh chicken wire – depending solely on the sized ball deemed suitable – several yards of very narrow white or scarlet ribbon, five, seven or nine glitter balls (scarlet only), mistletoe and a pair of pliers. Shape the chicken wire into a ball. Tie a piece of ribbon centrally to the top centre of the wire ball and affix loose ends to the ceiling – making sure that you gauge the height of your room so that the complete ball, dangles and all, is at least 6ft 9in from the floor to give head clearance to all but Goliaths.

Now stuff tufts of mistletoe through the wire until it all disappears, pinching the chicken wire where necessary to hold any wobbly tufts securely. Finally use graduated lengths of narrow scarlet ribbon to tie to the base centre of the ball. Affix a bauble to each and the job is completed. If at this point it is as clear as mud to you, turn to Diagram 3, which will, we hope, clarify your confusion.

Note: If you have a garden with fruit trees and are prepared to gamble, you *can* acquire your own mistletoe, though we do not suggest this should be attempted by what our grandparents called 'octogeraniums' as they might well be despatched to heaven before their efforts came to fruition. On Twelfth Night pick all the berries off before consigning the mistletoe to the bonfire. Climb up an apple tree with the seeds, a small blunt knife and one very sharp one indeed. In one or two crotches scrape away the bark over a small area, then with the blunt knife squash onto the prepared surface a few of the berries and work the paste in with the knife as if crushing a clove of garlic to pulp. We take the added precaution of binding the area lightly for about a month with a 2in-wide strip of polythene.

THE YULE LOG

One of the more popular explanations of the origin of the word 'Yule' is that it derived from *Juul* or *Yule* from the Hebrew word *Lile* (night). *Lile* is formed from a verb signifying to howl – 'nothing is more common (in the northern counties) than the call that melancholy barking dogs oft make in the night – yowling'. On Vigil or Even night our ancestors lit logs of wood by the fire, which were called Yule-clog or Christmas-block. These illuminated the house sufficiently in those days for the claim to be advanced that this turned night into day – see Herrick's *Hesperides* . . .

> *'Come, bring with a noise,*
> *My merrie, merrie boyes,*
> *The Christmas Log to the firing . . .'*

This is fine counsel for the few extant owners of baronial halls and adaptable in modest proportions to contemporary chimney pieces. Even in smokeless zones one log is unlikely to evoke a Disturbance of Clean Air Officials! But it is impasse for the rest who must settle for symbolism in one of two forms: either a Christmas Log Cake (see p.281) on the tea table or a Log Candle Holder, which has the two bits of symbolism together.

LOG CANDLE HOLDER

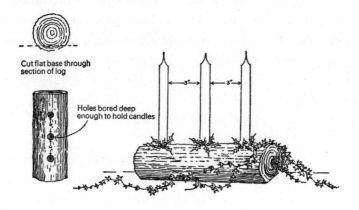

Cut flat base through section of log

Holes bored deep enough to hold candles

Diagram 4

Take a log of modest girth and of a length suitable to the position it will occupy and saw, or have sawn for you, sufficient from the underside to ensure that it rests steadily. Get the man of the house or local carpenter to bore through the upper sides, into which red candles may be inserted – not less than 3in apart or the candles will melt each other (see Diagram 4). If something goes wrong and the holes are too large, so that the candles wobble, wind single strands of Bostik-strip around the base of each before inserting; then either decorate the log with green moss and one or two slender ivy trails (traditional) or paint the log with quick-drying white paint, scatter glitter dust over liberally while the paint is still wet, and encircle the base of each candle with a tiny ring of berried holly bound with fine florists' wire. If holly is scarce, make the little rings of leaves only, and twist on artificial berries.

CHRISTMAS BOXES

When you are tying up your Christmas parcels it may amuse you to recall the origin of this antique custom of giving Christmas boxes. These trace their origin 'beyond the borderline of the earliest Roman Christianity, to the Roman Paganalia instituted by Servius Tullius'. Boxing Day is the day on which the boxes were opened and the money distributed which had been accumulated in pots set up on altars erected in the towns and villages.

HOW TO MAKE A KISSING BOUGH

A recent return to popularity has been made by the Kissing Bough, which may be used either additionally or as a substitute for the Mistletoe Ball.

Study Diagram 5 and use it in conjunction with the following instructions:

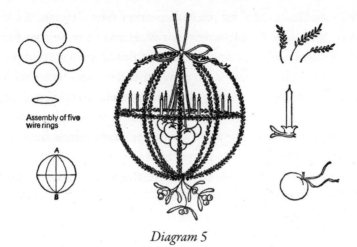

Diagram 5

Materials: Rosemary or box; strong, pliable wire; eight spiral Christmas-tree candle-holders; eight red or green or mixed Christmas-tree candles; red and green ribbons for bows, ties and strings; rosy apples; one fat bunch of well-berried mistletoe.

The bough can be as large as the room will take. Our measurements are merely given as an *aide memoire* for a small, effective size.

1 × 30in-circumference circle of pliable wire for the horizontal.

4 × 30in-circumference circles of pliable wire for the verticals.

Secure all verticals together with a piece of fine, strong wire at A and B in the diagram. Slip the horizontal over the secured verticals and bind these together centrally from top and bottom in such a way that all the verticals are an equal distance apart round the parallel and all are equidistant A from B. Now cover all finely with wire-bound sprays of box or rosemary. IF you require fairy lights as well as candles, then bind these in at this point, in such a way that the greenery conceals the wires and does not conceal the actual lights. See that you end up with the light connection at A or you will say something very rude! Cover a 6–8in piece of strong wire with box or red ribbon, thread through A on the kissing bough, secure in a loop and bring fairy-light wires to the point, ready to sling from the light fitment when completed.

To complete. Secure the spiral candle-holders midway between the horizontal and vertical meeting points. Insert the candles. Tie narrow red and green satin ribbons to the stalks of rosy apples, cut the ribbons off to equal lengths and secure to the top of the kissing bough so that the ribbon-slung apples dangle down in a cluster inside the bough. Secure the bunch of mistletoe to the base of the bough so that the berries' heads hang downwards, and fix to a light fitment where desired.

The origin of Christmas cards is debatable, as on the one hand the credit is given to Sir Henry Cole and on the other to Mr J. C. Horsley RA in 1846. Some of these early cards are now collectors' pieces and we have had the pleasure of seeing an enchanting collection, which was the property of the late Miss Eleanor Farjeon and which is now in the possession of her niece, Miss Joan Jefferson Farjeon, the painter and stage designer. Now they get duller and duller and edge farther and farther away from the theme of Christmas, so to brighten them up for the children we send them in very gay envelopes.

HOW TO MAKE CHILDREN'S CHRISTMAS CARD ENVELOPES

See Diagram 6. Unpick an envelope of the required size. Use as a pattern to cut envelope in shiny emerald-green or scarlet paper. Stick a minute Christmas tree transfer in the top

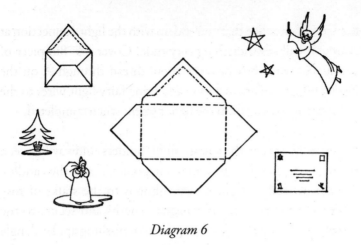

Diagram 6

left-hand corner, a similar Father Christmas in the bottom left-hand corner, an angel in the bottom-right corner and write Master This or Miss That in either green ink on red envelopes or red ink on green ones. They will be received with rapture by children of any age who still believe in Father Christmas.

THE CHRISTMAS TREE

As we have a number of suggestions to make we will start with the traditional one and build up to the Cradock eccentric when you have been sufficiently conditioned to our mad ideas! The Christmas tree appears to be traceable to the Roman saturnalia and is thought to have been imported into Germany by the conquering legions of Drusus. It is certainly portrayed hung about with toys and mannequins by Virgil (Geor. ii 389) – '*Oscilla ex alta suspendent, mollia pinu*' – and it is generally accepted that Prince Albert brought it to England after his marriage to Queen Victoria.

For a traditional evergreen tree there must be a fairy on the top, arms extended, a wand in one hand and a glittering star in her hair. There should be candles and they should be lit at the moment when the light begins to fade on Christmas afternoon, the Queen's speech is over, the needle is poised over the disc of 'Silent Night', curtains are drawn and all other illuminations extinguished. Our earliest recollections of the enactment of this ceremony included one vital and virtually extinct performer – the footman holding a long stave with a wet sponge tied to the top standing at the ready beside the glitter-ing tree, prepared to douse any recalcitrant candles lurching perilously near to a tip of evergreen, which would otherwise flare up like a Roman candle. In these days it is sad but sensible to turn our backs on tradition and buy some electrically lit fairy lights.

Similarly, few of us still maintain a couple of gardeners who can totter in with a growing tree in a tub, so in the main we fall back on the bought tree, either rootless or else fated to die because the roots have been boiled before it is offered for sale lest it survive and thereby diminish the sales thereafter. There is on sale today a splendid but costly fitment, which grips the base stem of the Christmas tree in its screw-adjusted teeth and stands on its solid metal feet without benefit of tub; failing one of these, either damp soil or damp sand must support it, tamped down vigorously in its tub or pot to ensure no untimely lurchings. The best kind of baubles are made of some sturdy substance that will dent if squeezed tightly but will not shatter into a thousand pieces on very modest impact. Except when there is a war on and everyone is in the same boat, steer clear of those gay exhortations in the humbler women's magazines to make your own gold, silver and glitter stars and crescent moons or to paint and glitter home-made baubles – they only end up looking rather tatty.

If small parcels are to be hung, these look much prettier if all the parcels are wrapped in shiny white, red or green paper and tied up with contrasting ribbons in the same three alternatives. Otherwise use all gold wrapping, all silver or mix the two together or, perhaps best of all, all wrappings white and shiny, tied with scarlet and emerald green.

If You Want to Be Different with a Plain Green Tree you can achieve effective results with cotton-wool 'snow', provided it is carefully done. Use a razor blade in a holder and 'shave' the top of the branches to the wood, *leaving all the rest.* Then cover the shaven areas with narrow strips of cotton wool and sprinkle them lavishly with glitter dust.

A very exotic effect, still using a traditional tree, was achieved by a friend of ours with whom we were spending Christmas. She asked all the women to 'bring all your glittery *costume*, not real, jewellery with you – you can have it all back after Christmas'. She slung it all, including her own, on the tree, having first wound on two sets of star-like fairy lights. With all the presents heaped below, she achieved an Aladdin's Cave result.

Whichever you choose the main thing is to make sure that your tree is absolutely laden with glitter balls, cascading with tinsel, sparkling with fairy lights or dripping with those silver strands that can be bought in packets from chain stores.

A Gold and Silver Tree

If you do not give a fig for tradition and want a tree with a difference (or an extra one), you might like to try a gold and silver tree. This is a combination of two artificial trees, one gold, one silver. Before planting, pull out all branches on both trees to one side so that the two main stems may be lashed securely together (Sellotape and gold or silver paint to cover!). Now plant in chosen pot and tamp securely using either soil or sand. Pull the branches this way and that to achieve a complete mixture of silver and gold. Then hang the branches with gold and silver baubles, fairies, crackers and fairy lights, tie the ends of the branches with gold and silver ribbon bows, alternated with emerald-green feathered birds with long, glittery, fringed tails and watch the faces of children and adults alike when they see it for the first time.

The Austrian Twin Trees

Let the children copy the Austrians. Give them two tiny real trees destined for Mum and Dad. They spray one tree silver and one tree gold and wrap all their little presents in gold for the gold tree and silver for the silver one, tying on as many gold and silver ornaments respectively as you can manage to find for them.

A Lollipop Tree is a triumph with very small squeakers. Use a tiny real or glittery make-believe tree. The main thing is to drive yourself hairless by tying on a lavish assortment of lollipops, ranging from candy walking sticks to individually wrapped and tied sweetmeats of all descriptions. We finished ours with a belly ache of jelly babies; thread a large darning needle with clean white cotton (used double) and spear yards of jelly babies through their midriffs and then festoon them over the tree. These ideas, of course, are just to start you thinking.

Incidentally, wherever it can be managed, practically for electric lights and safely for urban residents in light-fingered areas, it makes a gorgeous welcome if you can manage to put lights on a flourishing evergreen tree in the front garden.

THE HOLLY BOUGH

'The mistletoe hung in the castle hall,
The holly branch shone on the old oak wall.'

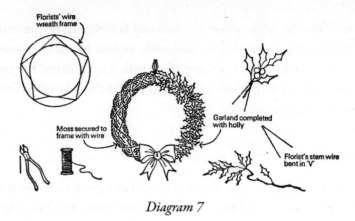

Diagram 7

We have dealt with the mistletoe bit, but we are in a quandary over the holly branch. Was it a bough just lopped off a tree and stuck up on the wall? Or was it a ball – we get enough of those already with mistletoe and box – or could it possibly have been a wreath or garland? We plump for this last as being the most probable. Hang on the wall outdoors or in. Take down pictures where necessary and remove into safe temporary storage. Choose between the traditional and the 'different' so we will start as commanded by the quote with:

The Holly Garland

It is no use deceiving ourselves – this is a synonym for a wreath, which has gloomy connotations, so we make the point and then refer to a garland! These are the very devil to make unless we have the right materials, which mercifully are not expensive, so assemble a wire frame (see Diagram 7), some dried florists' moss and fine florists' wire and well-berried holly cut into neat short sprigs (alternatively use male holly devoid of berries and cluster a few artificial ones on each sprig). You will also need some florists' stem wire, which is sold cut into convenient lengths. Begin by padding the frame with moss and binding it securely into position with fine florists' wire – plenty of it. Then push as many sprigs as possible through the moss and wire. This invariably leaves gaps so you finish by winding the centre of pieces of stem wire round individual sprigs of prepared holly. Pull the two ends of each down to make a 'V' and finally push the two wire prongs of each into the remaining spaces. Affix a narrow scarlet ribbon loop to the top from which to hang it on the wall or front-door knocker and 'finish' the base with a big shiny red satin bow, also given the wire prong treatment.

The Mixed Evergreen Garland

Follow the above instructions with available evergreens (see pp.327-8) and if the bow proves insufficient, pinch the top of a stem wire 'V' with a pair of pliers until it is narrow enough to push through the base of a scarlet glitter ball and drive a few of these into your completed evergreen garland either singly or in clusters.

Note: For either of these two when using on a wall, you may affix a slanting strip of wide scarlet ribbon from top off-centre left to bottom off-centre right, securing it to the back of the moss packing with a couple of stout pins.

For a garland with a difference, which can be used as suggested above or as the centre piece of a table arrangement, make:

A Fir-cone Garland

You will need a small, sharp saw; very strong adhesive; artificial holly berries; small and medium dried fir cones; a cardboard ring, 2in wide and 16in in diameter and either shiny gold paper or scarlet felt-finished Fablon. Cover the cardboard ring with the paper or Fablon. Saw larger fir cones into slices. This sounds crazy but stay with us because it works! Dab the back of each slice generously with adhesive and press them securely to the Fablon until the ring is completely covered except for the spaces in between the fir-cone slices. Twist artificial holly berries into little bunches. Dab the little spaces with adhesive and push into them alternate baby fir cones and holly berries. Tie to a wall or door with scarlet ribbon. Alternatively affix a rim to the back of the cardboard at the beginning so as to hang up invisibly or use as a Table Decoration (see pp.70-71). For an edible interpretation of this idea see the Garland Cake (pp.282-3).

This, like the Pom-pom Trees, is a brainchild of ours and we hold ourselves responsible if it does not win favour with you.

POM-POM TREES

The Evergreen Pom-pom Tree

This offers tremendous scope if you number patience among your virtues! You also need a garden cane, some crêpe paper cut into 1in strips and in at least two colours, fine wire, chicken wire, and holly or mistletoe, laurel or just tissue paper in one or more colours. Crunch up the chicken wire carefully to form a ball at least twice as big as a soccer ball and then secure this really firmly to the top of the cane. Twist a single narrow strip of crêpe paper up the cane from end to end so that it is completely concealed. Twist a second contrasting strip wide enough apart to show the first colour through alternately and thus candy-stripe the cane. Then stuff the wire ball with holly or mistletoe until every scrap of wire is concealed.

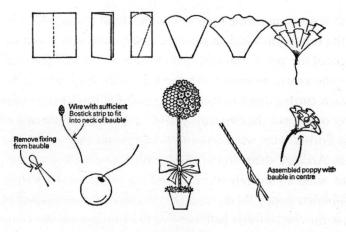

Diagram 8

Add a few strands of narrow ribbon with glitter baubles on the ends, or a prim formal bow two-thirds up the covered cane, and drive this confection into a flowerpot filled with soil or wet sand. Mask the pot with single leaves of chosen evergreen stuck on with UHU (which would stick Auntie to the floor!) and use as a standing decoration; or use un-potted to bind to the curve of a balustrade.

The Crêpe Paper Pom-pom Tree (Scarlet, Emerald or White)

This is our favourite (see Diagram 8). The basis is the same as for the Evergreen Pom-pom Tree in that you have a preferably plastic pot, a 2ft 6in cane and a chicken-wire ball, 6–8in in diameter. Then you add to your assembly scarlet crêpe paper, fine florists' wire and very small scarlet glitter balls. Pull out the fixings from these. Push a tiny pad of Bostik strip onto one end of a florists'-wire flower stem and press a little glitter ball in securely. Cut a 6½in red crêpe paper square; fold over left to right like a book with the fold on the left; round off the top with scissors; taper the right side of the 'book' from full width at the top to 1in width at the base; open out flat; pull out the edges of the 'petal' thus achieved to make it flute and then pull out the centre to round the petal. Do the same with a 5in square, cutting down to ¾in on base end. Put small petal inside large one. Twist the two narrow ends and with an 8in strand of fine florists' wire, wind one end firmly round the twist. Make four. Arrange them round the bauble-topped piece of stem wire, wind all securely together and the result will be a large, full-blown poppy. Make as many of these as are required to mask the chicken-wire ball completely, pushing each stem wire through the chicken wire and bending it round to secure. Just be careful when cutting the crêpe-paper petals to cut them with the grain of the paper running top to bottom, not across the petal. The *pull* is then in the right place when you flute and curve them; otherwise you will find out the hard way by wasting paper!

Cover the length of the cane with a 1in strip of the same red crêpe paper, winding it round and round. Drive into a high-gloss painted white pot filled with wet horticultural sand. When this dries out in a warm room, the stem is embedded as in a rock. Cover the sand with little squares of crêpe paper, twisted together exactly as for Tissue Paper Swags (pp.69–70) and pushed in securely, and 'finish' the stem with a red crêpe-paper bow as shown in Diagram 8.

THE PYRAMID

If you possess any pedestal bowls in any way similar to the one shown in Diagram 9, you can make an enormous variety of Pyramid Christmas decorations, which have the added virtue of taking up far less space than any spray arrangement.

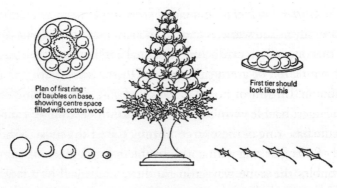

Plan of first ring
of baubles on base,
showing centre space
filled with cotton wool

First tier should
look like this

Diagram 9

Use Honesty with either minute scarlet and/or emerald-green lovers' knots made with ¼in satin baby ribbon or cut in felt; or a bunch of artificial holly berries. Fill the bowl with wet sand. Select a tall spray of honesty of a length when driven in to give you the maximum required height for your finished pyramid. Drive in sprays of diminishing length all round until you end with little 3in sprigs at the base. This will make a rather bare arrangement but, happily, dried honesty (with the outer casings of the seed pods rubbed off between finger and thumb) has the most fantastic clinging characteristics and all you have to do to fill in the gaps and achieve a beautifully balanced shape is to push in short sprigs, which will stay wherever you put them, although they are virtually suspended in mid-air. Then add bows or berries in little clusters, just pushing them in or dabbing them on, and *they will hold* without any further assistance from you.

Use Old Man's Beard exactly as described above for another Christmas Pyramid, but be sure to gather it away from main roads or, instead of being delicately silvery, it will be as grey as the cobwebs in Miss Havisham's drawing room. Finish by spraying all over with hair lacquer and sprinkling liberally with silver glitter dust. Then add bows and berries as described above.

Use Glitter Baubles of graduated sizes and either one colour or carefully mixed scarlet, emerald and silver. Study Diagram 9. For this one, take a cardboard cake base and cover completely with white, red or green shiny paper. Then, working so that a minimum 1in rim of board is left all round, dab one side of each largest bauble with UHU and press into position to form a secure base-ring of these largest baubles. Fill the centre to the level of this first ring with cotton wool and stick the next ring of baubles the same way atop the first, making this and all ensuing rings slightly smaller than its predecessor, and repeating the central pads of cotton wool as the rings mount higher and higher and the baubles get smaller and smaller. Continue until you reach the summit with one final bauble. Fill the spaces in between the baubles with varnished bay or holly leaves, being careful to use the smallest leaves at the top and the largest at the base, finishing with an encircling necklace of overlapping ones to form a base 'collar' and conceal the board-rim. Once made, this can be kept and used year after year; set against a dark background and on a dark surface, it will *blaze*.

The Holly or Evergreen Pyramid

For this one you will need to make a cone in chicken wire into which you simply prod innumerable small sprigs of holly or evergreen until the wire vanishes, finishing in this case with a small red bow at the top and streamer ends trailing downwards.

The Fir-cone Pyramid

Study the instructions for the Glitter Bauble Pyramid and copy, replacing baubles with graduated fir cones and studding the interstices of the completed pyramid with little tufts of artificial holly berries.

Whatever it is, our latest ideas are always our prime favourites so in this section we have saved the two current newcomers to our Christmas tree decoration suggestions until the last.

1. THE TWELVE DAYS OF CHRISTMAS NURSERY TREE

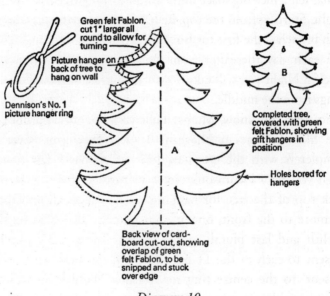

Green felt Fablon, cut 1" larger all round to allow for turning

Picture hanger on back of tree to hang on wall

Dennison's No. 1 picture hanger ring

Completed tree, covered with green felt Fablon, showing gift hangers in position

Holes bored for hangers

Back view of cardboard cut-out, showing overlap of green felt Fablon, to be snipped and stuck over edge

Diagram 10

Have a good look at Diagram 10 (B), which shows this completed tree, and then you will understand our description more easily. We are going to give you the instructions for making a wall tree for any children who still believe in Father Christmas. The tale you tell them runs something like this: 'When Father Christmas comes down the chimney with all the parcels, he sometimes brings a nursery wall tree as well. He has invented this for children because so many of them have told him in their letters, or when they meet him at parties, that they wish Christmas Day could last longer (he also understands that they are not speaking for adults!). Because of this wish he has created this kind of tree, which makes a little bit of Christmas go from Boxing Day right up until Twelfth Night when all Christmas decorations have to come down.

'He has made the tree with 11 branches (counting the one at the top), which makes one for each day except for the last, so he has left a nice big space in the middle of the tree for Twelfth Night. Starting from the top, he has put you a tiny present on each branch – the first for Boxing Day, and then so on, taking one each day thereafter from the remaining branches. On Twelfth Night you will take down the biggest and best, which hangs from the middle.'

So now you know, Mums! First you cut out a cardboard tree like the one in Diagram 10(A). Then you cover it completely with the green Fablon, which has a felt finish. Then you fix a Dennison's No. 1 picture hanger ring to the back top of the tree for hanging it onto the wall and then 11 more to the front, one at each branch. Then you fix the twelfth and last plumb in the centre. Tie a really minute present to each of the 11 branches and tie the twelfth 'best present' to the centre ring for Twelfth Night. This can be something like a 4–5in teddy bear.

2. THE CHRISTMAS-CARD TREE

After years of standing Christmas cards about and accumulating dust, of hanging them on ribbons, pinning them on streamers and generally getting the twitch over them, here is a solution that enables you to stand one small cardboard tree on a table or sideboard and get a hundred cards into it, a space

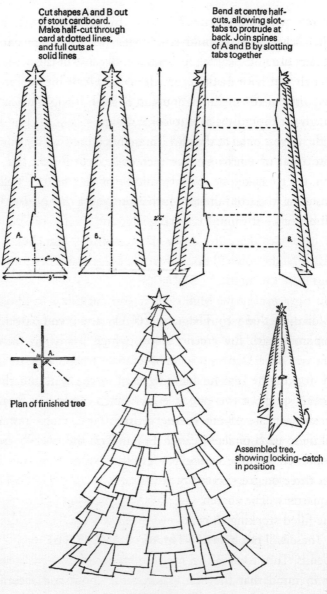

Cut shapes A and B out of stout cardboard. Make half-cut through card at dotted lines, and full cuts at solid lines

Bend at centre half-cuts, allowing slot-tabs to protrude at back. Join spines of A and B by slotting tabs together

Plan of finished tree

Assembled tree, showing locking-catch in position

Diagram 11

economy which is enhanced by the fact that the trees are in themselves very decorative. The instructions are given in Diagram 11.

When you have made it, get the best out of it. Sort your cards into small, medium and large. Push the small ones through the topmost slits, put the medium ones in the middle and the largest of all at the base. If you are one of those people whose total of Christmas cards received is still on a rising graph, try to make one extra tree either to use for this year's extras or at worst to fall back upon as something to tie on the real tree for a last-minute unexpected guest.

SWAGS

It is for these that we urged you in January (p.5) to hoard old nylon stockings. Now cut off the feet, stuff them with crumpled tissue paper and bind them together with fine wire so that each stocking makes one curved swag section. Wire together trimmed sprigs of evergreens to matching lengths and leave sufficient wire at each end to bind securely onto stocking swags until these are completely covered or, in the case of wall swags (as opposed to those wound round pillars or banisters), only cover three-quarters round each cascade, because the remaining quarter will be unseen. Use an occasional stout pin through tissue-filled stocking to make evergreen strands lie absolutely flat. These will not be seen when *in situ*. Finish with red bows and ends. Turn to pp.327-8 for your choice of evergreens and bear in mind that the best subjects are *Picea smithiana* or Weeping Spruce, *Cedrus deodara* and for a flat, more formal treatment *Laurustinus*, more especially when this has been colourless-varnished.

HOLLY BELL PULLS

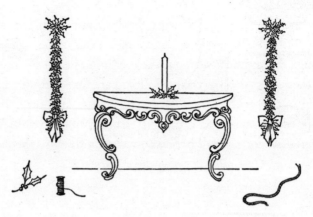

Diagram 12

These are invaluable for hanging on either side of any door or pairing on a wall left and right of a console or card-type table. To make them, take a piece of rope about 5in shorter than the desired finished length and bind short, fat sprigs of holly round the whole length with fine wire. Make a separate posy for the top of each bell pull and wire to one end of the rope, leaving a little loop of wire from which to hang each one invisibly. Thread and wind from top to bottom a strip of narrow scarlet ribbon. Finish the bare end – now the base – with a slightly smaller posy of holly sprigs, tie a bow of scarlet ribbon immediately above and let two long ends hang down as illustrated in Diagram 12.

FLAT TABLE DECORATIONS TO OCCUPY
MINIMUM SPACE

Please study Diagram 13 carefully. It shows the meandering and uneven shape which you cut to your chosen size in a piece

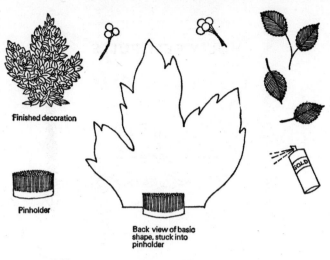

Finished decoration

Pinholder

Back view of basic
shape, stuck into
pinholder

Diagram 13

of flat, unridged cardboard. Spray this with gold paint. When dry, stick unvarnished dried beech leaves all over. When these are securely set, give short bursts with gold spray, push little twists of artificial holly berries in here and there and then drive the base of the cardboard backing at the centre into the front prongs of a fairly large pinholder. If the leaves have been stuck on well over the edges all round, the base one will conceal the pinholder completely as well as the top and sides of the cardboard backing. Pushed flat up against a light-coloured wall, these are very impressive.

A CONTAINER FOR CRACKERS

If a Christmas table is sparsely decorated, a few Christmas crackers do brighten it up, but they are a perfect pest on really pretty, well-decorated ones. We got so fed up with them that we invented a special glitter container (see Diagram 14), which looked gay on the top of a piece of wall furniture in our dining

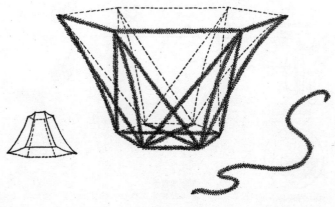

Diagram 14

room and only came into table use when the covers had been drawn and the time had come for dessert. Naturally the choice of colours is optional. Use an old lampshade frame. Cover the wires completely with tinsel – say, vivid emerald green. Criss-cross a further strand of tinsel across the top so as to form a trellis. Invert so that the top becomes base. Finally wind a few struts with your chosen tinsel so that these and the base trellis stop the crackers from slipping out. Fill with white and scarlet crackers and thus keep them out of the way during the meal.

WALL SPRAY DECORATIONS

There are two ways of doing these. In the case of walls that do not matter slap a piece of green plasticine into position and press securely. Now drive in evergreens or sprayed and glittered dried items, following some of the basic shapes in Diagram 15(A), (B), (C) and (D). When walls are precious, cut small, medium or large circles in strong cardboard. Paint white, red or green and/or spray with gold, silver or glitter dust. When dry slap plasticine onto cardboard and bore a couple of small

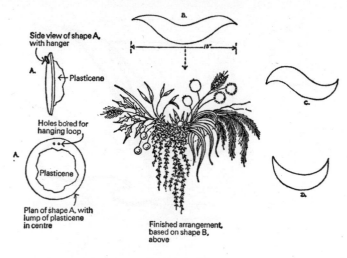

Side view of shape A, with hanger

A.

← Plasticene

Holes bored for hanging loop

A.

Plasticene

Plan of shape A, with lump of plasticene in centre

B.

18"

C.

D.

Finished arrangement, based on shape B, above

Diagram 15

holes about 1in in from the edge and 1in apart in the cardboard. Thread a short piece of wire through and twist to form an invisible hanging loop. Thus all the items suggested above, and indeed glitter balls, mistletoe and holly, can be incorporated into wall sprays, following the suggested outline shapes or inventing your own.

FLAT-BASED SET PIECE DECORATIONS

If you follow the cardboard disc and plasticine instructions given above for Wall Spray Decorations and just omit the holes and loop of hanging wire, you can work up spray or circular arrangements in just the same way by driving your chosen items into the plasticine. If you study Diagram 16, you will see that a tall candle, red, white or green, has been made the focal point of an evergreen or painted and glittered dried-item arrangement and that the position at which to affix a ribbon bow is also shown in this diagram – again just to start you thinking.

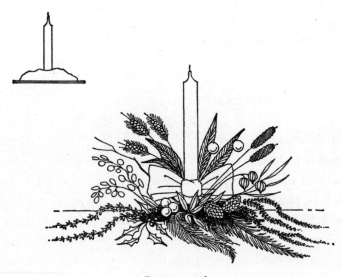

Diagram 16

To delve a little more deeply into this type of arrangement
let us assume that you want a white-and-gold table piece and
itemise some of the subjects that come together harmoniously: a backing piece of jagged edged tree bark, base-painted
white, then sprayed with gold and finally partially sprinkled
with gold glitter dust; one large fir cone, gold-painted and
glitter-dusted; three cock pheasants' feathers, gold-painted
back and front and the fronts thickly glittered; one, three or
five dried magnolia leaves, white-painted and glittered; three
white and glittered poppy heads; one or two shortish sprays
of white painted-and-glittered buddleia heads; a plume of
white and gold verbascum; several white-painted, gold-
sprayed short sprigs of honesty and a few similarly treated
wheat ears to make the arrangement look feathery, adding
perhaps a little cluster of Chinese lanterns, also white and
gold. Alternatively, the whole arrangement could be made
white, silver and silver glitter dust with perhaps a big scarlet
bow and one or two clusters of scarlet baubles of graduated

heights impaled on florists' stem wire to silhouette themselves against the solid of the bark.

PINEAPPLE DECORATION

This produces wonderfully pretty results for very little labour! Stand a pedestal dish on a circular tray about 6in wider in diameter than the top of the pedestal dish. Shape a 2in-deep circle in plasticine just wide enough in diameter to protrude about ½in all round when a whole pineapple is pressed into it in the centre of the dish. Take any number of non-drip tapering florists' candles (preferably bright green) and push them into the plasticine rim as if arranging flowers. Fill the remaining spaces with pushed-in sprigs of mistletoe and smother the base tray with either mistletoe or mixed shades of evergreen sprigs. Turn out room lights, and light the candles!

CHRISTMAS STOCKINGS

If you agree with the suggestion made in our January proposals, that adults as well as children should have large stockings full of nonsense presents at breakfast on Christmas morning, here is the method we use for the majority of ours. Take a 28in-wide, 30in-long strip of thin red, white or green felt. Cut into a stocking as shown in Diagram 17. Stitch up with a ¼in turning on the double and turn out. Then with a skewer prod holes around 3in from the top and thread through a narrow contrasting ¼in satin ribbon and finish with a bow in the centre front. Alternatively make all your stockings in white felt, edge the tops with red or green bobbly braid, cut off a few extra bobbles and sew them at random over leg and foot. With any coloured

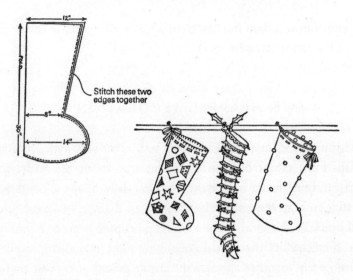

Diagram 17

felt you can stick extra squares in contrasting colours to make a patchwork decoration and sew glitter fringe around the top.

If you are looking for work and have a small girl in the family, cover a plain strong white cotton stocking with white frills and spatter with little velvet ribbon bows, or make stockings in shiny PVC and cover with transfers or cut-outs. In this context we are sure you will be pleased to know that we have found sugar mice with tails at Woolworths and one or two of these sewn by their tails to a stocking here and there is a very popular move. Do not forget a few blown-up balloons tied to the tops, a stick of barley sugar, a puzzle game, and a joke present from Davenport's, a brand-new penny and plenty of comics.

IN THE RIGHT PLACE

Whatever you choose to make, do remember the one governing factor that will determine success or failure. Consider your backgrounds. Stand and *imagine* into position whatever it is that you want to make and discard ruthlessly what your mind will confirm is unsuitable.

Oak panelling, chintz, Welsh dressers, khivers and spinning wheels would be outraged by gold and silver trees, but flattered by holly garlands and bell pulls; whereas gilt furniture and elegant pale silken papers welcome gold and silver trees. White walls form the perfect background to scarlet pom-pom trees or wall-hung fir-cone garlands, just as well as they do to gold and silver arrangements or traditional evergreens and red ribbons.

White doors inset behind white pillars look gorgeous if given holly wreaths to hang from their knockers and evergreen tresses wound slantwise around the columns. A small porch with no pillars will be much happier with a couple of tub-planted pyramid conifers tied here and there with rain-resisting scarlet bows.

Patterned wallpapers muddle mixed-glitter wall plaque decorations. In this case swag the plain banister rails instead. When making standing set-pieces in bowls do keep them *flat at the back* so that they can go flush against the walls when put in place, especially in small rooms.

CHRISTMAS TABLES

SCHEME 1

The surface of a fine polished table looks marvellous when laid with table mats of shiny white PVC. Just cut them out – no stitching is needed – and stick, alternately, artificial green leaves and artificial holly berries around the edges. Use real holly to make small garlands bound together with fine florists' wire for encircling the base of white candles in silver candlesticks or red candles in white candlesticks. Make larger garlands for the base of your chosen candlesticks. Cut a large oval, rectangular or white PVC centre mat. Edge this in the same way as the table mats and stand a holly Pom-pom (without a stem – see pp.61-2) in the centre. Affix a scarlet bow to the top centre. Let two long ends trail down onto the white mat and you have an easily achieved, simple Christmas table.

SCHEME 2

Cover your table to the floor with a scarlet cloth. This can be made by dyeing a white sheet or, in an ascending scale of grandeur, be made of scarlet satin lining fabric (sent to the cleaners thereafter and *then used as a lining!*); or you can mask your red-dyed sheet with red cotton organdy, or if you happen to possess a large red velvet curtain, use this. Use a panel of looking glass as a centre piece. Make four miniature white crêpe paper Pom-pom Trees (pp.62-3) with miniature red bauble centres and stick them in 3½in white painted flower-pots (don't forget to cover the drainage holes!) filled with wet horticultural sand. Stand them at the four corners of the looking glass; cover the edges with very short holly berry sprigs wound into strands with fine florists' wire and 'float' white water lily candles on your imitation lake. If flying high, use stark white plates and green table napkins pulled through white table napkin rings. These are made in moments from strips of Velcro covered with white 1in velvet ribbon and pressed together. Just remember to leave a ¼in overlap at each end uncovered by the velvet!

SCHEME 3

Use a plain white tablecloth or sheet and cover with a Nottingham lace bedspread. If you happen to have enough dark green pottery or china plates, team them with scarlet table napkins and fill a shallow ruby dish with *Helleborus niger* – the white ones that flower at Christmas time – for your centre piece. Use green candles in red candlesticks or red candles in green ones and pierce your arrangement of white flowers with both green and red long, slim flower candles to achieve height and width without obstruction. These are non-drip so will do no harm to your bedspread.

SCHEME 4

Cover the table to the floor with green windproof lining. This has a very special sheen on it. Place a panel of looking glass in the centre and a Holly Garland (pp.59-60) cross-gartered with narrow scarlet ribbons in the centre of the glass. Cluster three, ideally silver, candlesticks together inside the garland, with red candles, of course. Make four miniature holly Pom-pom Trees (pp.61-2) in 3½in red flowerpots and make fine strands of mistletoe by binding the tufts together with florists' wire to lay over the edges of the glass.

SCHEME 5 (FOR A CIRCULAR TABLE)

Cover completely with red-and-white checked gingham or very coarse white linen. Make a slender central pyramid of holly on an emerald-green shiny-paper-covered cake base. Tie six yard-long strips of ½in red and green satin ribbons to the top. Conceal the knots with a double red-and-green satin bow. Pull the ribbon ends out alternately red/green like a maypole and to form a circle. Pin each to the cloth and place a minute holly garland on top. Use green table napkins and stand six short, fat red candles in the smallest possible green holders in between the sections of the ribbon maypole, where the garlands form the circumference of the centre circle of decoration.

SCHEME 6

Go crazy with a silver scheme. Cover the tabletop and legs completely with smoothed-out kitchen foil so that it looks like a giant silver parcel on legs. Scrumple up crimson net to make the base of your centre piece and push sprigs of holly and mistletoe alternately through the base edges. See that the stems are very short or these will show through. Scatter the peaks and billows of the crumpled net with tiny bows of bright green

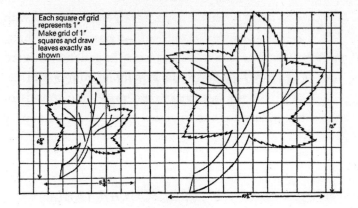

Each square of grid represents 1″
Make grid of 1″ squares and draw leaves exactly as shown

Diagram 18

velvet ribbon. Put alternate red and green candles into six to eight short silver (or silvered) candlesticks and push them round the edges of the billowing net so that they appear to be rising up from it. Cut a place mat in the shape of a giant vine leaf (Diagram 18) in several folds of green tissue paper for each cover. Hold these together with a minute smear of UHU and then UHU them securely to the foil table covering. Make water lilies in kitchen foil and scatter them around the centre arrangement to contain chocolates, crystallised fruits, almonds, raisins and any other similar items chosen for dessert.

SUGGESTIONS TO STIMULATE THE CREATIVE

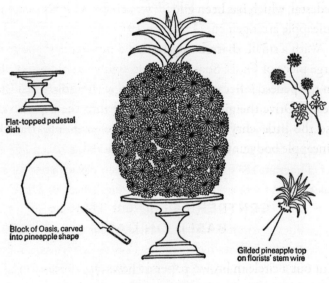

Flat-topped pedestal dish

Block of Oasis, carved into pineapple shape

Gilded pineapple top on florists' stem wire

Diagram 19

DECORATIONS BASED ON OASIS

This gift to flower arrangers is sold in various shapes – corks, squares and brick-like rectangles – of a green polystyrene substance. It can be used as purchased or the large pieces can be cut, shaped, literally sculpted by the neat-fingered, into far more decorative base shapes.

A typical example is 'The Pineapple'

We have a rather tatty but very profuse December blooming red-brown chrysanthemum, which grows in a sheltered corner; the blooms are small and we cut them off with a maximum 1½in stem. We then gild the green sprouting top saved from a pineapple that has been demolished much earlier in the year. With these two unlikely items and a small, old cast-iron pedestal, which has been gilded, we achieve a highly decorative pineapple arrangement (Diagram 19).

With a small, sharp knife, 'sculpt' a pineapple shape from a large piece of Oasis. Soak very thoroughly in cold water. Place on the pedestal. Because it is weighted with water, it will stand steady. Drive the gilded pineapple tuft into the top and then use the little chrysanthemum heads to stuff into the Oasis pineapple body until it is completely masked.

CENTREPIECES FOR TABLES
BASED ON OASIS

Cut out a circle in brown paper or newspaper measuring 12in, 14in, 16in, 18in or 20in in diameter according to the size of your Christmas table. Cut a 10in, 12in, 14in, 16in or 18in circle from the centre of whichever size you choose, leaving a 2in-wide ring. Mark off in sections of 2½–3in spacings. Number the sections and cut them up. Using these as patterns, cut 1in-thick slices from a block of Oasis. Soak thoroughly and assemble these into a ring on a flat dish or on a matching ring base cut from three to four layer-thick pieces of kitchen foil. Position on a dish or on foil on the table and you have a garland or ring into which you can arrange all or any short stems of evergreens, holly, mistletoe, etc. Turn to pp.327-30 and make your selection from Christmas Decoration Material.

With chosen candles in their candlesticks grouped artistically in the centre of this ring, you have a decorative centrepiece for a Christmas table. Furthermore, the Oasis ring sections can be cut and assembled months ahead and stored ready for use at the last moment.

Wet Sand Is an Ideal Medium for Live Christmas Decorations

Line the base and sides of painted flowerpots or jars, bowls and vases with kitchen foil. Fill with sand and just moisten with water sufficiently for any stems to hold positions when driven in. Make your arrangements in these containers. If done shortly before Christmas, the sand will dry out and grip the items like concrete, thus enabling you to achieve very original shapes in the completed arrangements. If wanting to do well in advance, use dried or everlasting instead of fresh material and they will literally 'hold' until they look like Miss Havisham's drawing room.

If You Have Enormous Patience

Make giant wall swags or miniature tablecloth swags in red, white and green tissue paper (see Diagram 20). The finished width of these swags is solely dependent upon the size of the squares (millions of them) that you cut initially in the tissue paper. The only other item that you need is fine florists' wire of the type sold in reels. You then prepare the squares for wiring. Put one square centrally over a fingertip and push down with the opposite hand for about ½in. Ease off the finger, twist lightly from the centre for about ½in and you should have the corners standing up like a posy on a small stumpy end. Take the end of the wire, wind tightly round the stumpy end and repeat this process, winding prepared squares on very closely together to any required length so that the finished strands look like miniature or giant tissue-paper boas. If you work with 1½in squares in scarlet or green, you can pin these strands in swags to the sides of a white tablecloth and pin them in arches to delineate each cover at the table. If you work with 6in squares of tissue paper, you will obtain fat feather-boa-like wall swags 'finished' with contrasting tissue-paper bows and ends.

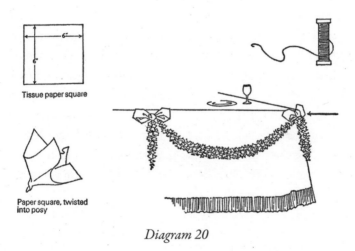

Tissue paper square

Paper square, twisted
into posy

Diagram 20

Two Suggestions for Napkins for the Christmas Table

(1) If large scarlet or emerald-green paper table napkins are re-cut into circles, they can be made into highly decorative additions to the Christmas table. First, copy the size of an ordinary table napkin ring in matching-width, fairly stiff grosgrain or Petersham ribbon, white or green. Then cluster with little twisted tufts of artificial holly berries and either sew or stick with UHU onto the rings. Lay each circular table napkin flat,

pick up the centre and pull this through the ring, thus making a 'stem' at one end and a fan-shaped chou of scarlet or emerald at the other. Set 'stem' ends towards the edge of the table on white side plates.

(2) Fold red table napkins (paper or otherwise) into narrow, flat rectangles not more than 3in wide. Encircle centrally with plaited green and white ½in ribbon. Tie into a bow and ends. Flatten down. Thread small glitter balls with fine wire and affix to the top centre of the bow tie and twist a wired-on place label around the neck of the little glitter ball.

CHRISTMAS RECIPES

We are grateful to the Gas Council for providing the following chart showing comparative temperatures:

Gas Mark	Approx. Electrical Temp (Fahrenheit)	Approx. Electrical Temp (Celsius)
¼	240°	115°
½	265°	130°
1	290°	145°
2	310°	155°
3	335°	170°
4	355°	180°
5	380°	195°
6	400°	205°
7	425°	220°
8	445°	230°
9	470°	245°

1 eggspoon is approximately 1 level teaspoon
1 saltspoon is approximately ¼ teaspoon

FOREWORD TO
RECIPE SECTION

It is possible that there are still some Scrooges among us who hate not only Christmas, but also fairy stories, but even so they are at most a sad minority so we make no apologies for beginning this recipe section with both a potted version of a fairy story, which is absolutely true, and a statement, which, though it too may sound like a fairy tale, is equally factual.

Many years ago, while Queen Victoria reigned over our forebears and we were a world power, London was a centre of the gastronomic world. Great chefs, superb waiters and profoundly knowledgeable *sommeliers* came here eagerly to cook, wait at table, serve wines classically and commit their great knowledge to publications.

During this heyday a slender and very beautiful woman whose origins are now unknown opened a school of cookery (1884) and wrote a number of cookery books, which we think remain unequalled in modern English. Her name was Agnes Bertha Marshall. She is almost totally forgotten by older generations and unheard of by the young. A stained-glass window to her memory may be found in the parish church, Pinner. She was given a magnificent diamond necklace by her adoring pupils and although, happily for us two, we did not find it out until the mid-1950s, *she cooked before audiences almost exactly as we have done since 1951.* We respectfully submit that she was the greatest English woman cook who ever lived. Her knowledge of French and French gastronomic literature was astounding and in her early years, by her own testimony, she worked and studied with many of the greatest Continental *maîtres chefs de cuisine* of the time. In the foreword to her first publication, she wrote: 'No apology is, I think, needed for adding this to the already long array of cookery books, as it is published at the repeated solicitations of some thousands of my old pupils, to whom . . . I dedicate this volume, *assuring them that every recipe in it has been successfully carried out by myself*.'

We, not she, have italicised her last phrase because we have found this *essential* author/cooks' assurance to be conspicuous by its absence in almost every cookery book written in modern English.

Therefore we now assure you that this Christmas book of ours, written over 60 years later, has been produced at the request of many of the millions of our television viewers; many hundreds of thousands of our stage audiences to whom we have cooked as elaborately dressed as Agnes Bertha Marshall herself and those for whom we have written in national newspapers, magazines and books. So it is with pride that we re-echo her '*nothing published which is not tested*'.

Even so mistakes occur, like the time we published a soufflé recipe in the *Daily Telegraph* with the method for using the egg whites given and the egg whites completely omitted from the ingredients; or the time on BBC Television when not one of our team of colleagues spotted the printer's error in the supporting booklet, which read seven instead of two egg whites in a recipe for leftovers!

We also fall over backwards in our all-out efforts to render unto Caesar by crediting whomsoever is the creator of a recipe that we quote. The greatest of us all, Georges Auguste Escoffier, wrote in the foreword to his masterpiece *A Guide to Modern Cookery* the following words: '. . . *the chef has absolutely no redress for plagiarism on his work . . . he may have forfeited his recreation and his night's rest . . . and as a reward, he finds himself compelled, morally at least, to convey the result of his study to the first person who asks, and who, very often, subsequently claims the invention of the recipe – to the detriment of the real author's chances and reputation'.*

At least we can assure you that we shall *never* plagiarise as someone did to a friend of ours, that fine cook/author, Mrs Gretel Beer. She made just such a typing error as we have explained above; she had it drawn to her notice after the publication of her excellent *Austrian Cooking* and she subsequently amended it in her next edition. In the interim she had the dubious pleasure of reading the recipe elsewhere *as the creation of someone else, errata and all!*

THE CHRISTMAS FEAST

'Now thrice welcome, Christmas,
Which brings us good cheer,
   Minced-pies and plumb-porrage,
Good ale and strong beer;
With pig, goose, and capon,
The best that may be,
So well doth the weather
And our stomachs agree.'

Poor Robin's Almanack for 1695

The great traditional dish for our ancestors was The Boar's Head bedecked with bay and rosemary and with a rosy apple in the mouth. Our forebears were also goose addicts and while both of these are known to us today, we are somewhat less familiar with Plum Porrage, Frumenty, Christmas Pye, roasted swan, peacock and bustard. These last three appeared before our ancestors re-feathered, either with gilded beaks or with their beaks holding scraps of sponge soaked in alcohol so that flames spurted out as the servitors bore them shoulder-high to table. So eminently suitable for small twentieth-century houses or town flats!

It was fine for Gay to rhyme for his contemporaries:

'Sometimes with oysters we combine,
Sometimes assist the savry chine;
From the low peasant to the lord,
The turkey smokes on every board.'

But for his forebears turkeys were NOT. They were not known in England until 1542 when they were brought from Mexico. Sixty-eight years later Norwich alone were sending close on a thousand turkeys to the London markets each Christmas.

The bustard, which became extinct in this country in the early nineteenth century (approximately 1838, according to our researches), was an exceedingly popular table bird as far back as the fifteenth century; while the heron was the poor man's main Christmas dish with perhaps a crane or spoonbill as well.

Swan featured in far grander bills of fare. We have served it in mediaeval style, all feathers replaced after roasting. Alas, it is the only item recorded in our menu books that is annotated 'a total failure'. After every venturesome guest had sampled it, nine-tenths was left upon each plate. We endorsed this rejection because the sickly sweet, predominantly fishy flavour is repellent to most modern palates – certainly to those of ourselves and our friends.

Henry VIII was a great one for 'Bull Bird' or Norfolk bittern, whose 'booming' is familiar today to anyone raised near the reed and marsh areas of the Norfolk broads; but of course the great status symbol among the table birds eaten by our forebears was the peacock, borne aloft by servitors to an accompanying rousing fanfare from the trumpeters.

The evolution of the Christmas Pudding as we know it today could almost merit a Pudding Tree based upon Mr Darwin's amoeba/man tree. The earliest methods read as revoltingly as the antique antidote for tuberculosis, which was actually told to us by an old gardener who had learnt it from a second footman . . . Swallow a frog live and whole and you will never have it (tuberculosis) . . . and we would be the last to agree that 'he who discovered the new star in Cassiopeia . . . deserves not half so much to be remembered as he who first married minced meat and raisins together'.

There has been plum pudding, plumb pudding and a sort of dogs' dinner, plum porrage – a mess of raisins, spices, bread-crumbs, wines and fruit juice, frequently containing meat as well. At one time and another in our chequered culinary careers we have made many hundreds of different kinds ourselves, and then in 1949 in an unpublished ledger compiled by Georges Auguste Escoffier – discovered in the vaults of the Bank of England where it had lain for over 40 years – we found what we consider to be the *ne plus ultra*. Escoffier called it *Le Pouding des Rois Mages* and made it in a special log-shaped mould. This we did also at the Royal Albert Hall before 7,000 people but a rose is just as sweet . . . so Escoffier's Christmas Pudding is what we call it, having rendered unto Caesar. Whether steamed in an ordinary pudding basin, or in a ring savarin mould with brandy flames quivering in the centre, it has no peer in our opinion. This has been endorsed by millions, and if it is as yet unknown to you, we beg you to try it, for, if you follow the instructions exactly, you will be rewarded with a pudding that is tradition-ally dark and rich but very untraditionally featherweight. Indeed, many who have eaten it with us, first declaring they dislike all Christmas Pudding intensely, have come back for seconds and even thirds and thus become converted.

Mince pies began in Shakespeare's England as pies made of mince. They gradually evolved to the excellent if rather broad instructions that we reproduce here for your amusement:

TO MAKE MINCE PIES THE BEST WAY (1777)

Take three pounds of Sewet shred very fine, and chopped as fmall as poffible, two Pounds of Raifins ftoned, and chopped as fine as poffible, two pounds of Currants nicely picked, wafhed, rubbed and dried at the Fire, Half a Hundred of fine Pippins, pared, cored and chopped fmall, Half a Pound of fine sugar pounded fine, a Quarter of an Ounce of Mace, a Quarter of an Ounce of Cloves, two large Nutmegs, all beat fine; put all together into a great pan, and mix it well together with half a pint of Brandy, and Half a Pint of Sack; put it down clofe in a Stone-pot, and it will keep good four Months. When you make your pies, take a little Difh, fomething bigger than Soop-plate, lay a very thin crust all over it, lay a thin Layer of Meat, and then a thin layer of Citron cut very thin, then a layer of Mince Meat, and a thin Layer of Orange-peel cut thin, over that a little meat, fqueeze half the Juice of a fine *Seville* Orange or Lemon, and pour in three Spoonfuls of Red Wine; lay on your Cruft, and bake it nicely. Thefe Pies eat finely cold. If you make them in little patties, mixt your Meat and Sweet Meats accordingly. If you chufe your Meat in your Pies, parboil a Neat's Tongue, peel it, and chop the meat as fine as poffible, and mix with the reft; or two pounds of the infide of a Surloin of Beef boiled.

Footnote: The original mince pie was something of a generic really, for some were made of eggs and some even of meats (ox tongue).

Quite magnificent, if a little intimidating by modern standards, is the thought of a Christmas Pye. We have a fourteenth-century record, which instructs us:

Take: two partridges, one hare, one pheasant, one capon, two pigeon, two coney and a bustard. These we must bone, fill with stuffing, mould with paste into the 'Forme of a Byrde' and after baking send to table 'mightily decorated' with the tail feathers of the birds!

Yet this is really quite reasonable if we compare it with the pie we made under the title *Croute Lucullus* for a very special party.

For it, we boned a turkey and filled it with a boned capon, this with a boned pheasant, this with a boned pigeon, this with a boned spring chicken, this with a boned quail, filling the interstices with *foie gras*, marinaded lambs' tongues and – of course – truffles! Wrapped in puff pastry, this was baked in a raised pie container and cut in slices with great ease. It was also eaten without complaint. A nice economical dish for everyday use in purse-constricted households.

Even as the modern Christmas Pudding is remote indeed from its original conception, so is the modern art of carving, from *The Booke of Kervynge* written by Sir Wynkyn de Worde in the fifteenth century. If we think of how the contemporary cook whips egg whites in moments by switching on an electric whisk against how the eleventh-century cook attempted the same task with a bunch of goose feathers, we have some concept of what kervynge was like in the 'good old days.' Then there was a separate term for the dismembering and slicing of fish, fowl and good red herring and no kerver was deemed worth his salt unless and until he was capable of obeying the master cook's instructions for each individual item. We append a very short set of examples of these terms for your entertainment:

Brake that dere	Lyft that swanne
Rere that goose	Sauce that capon
Speyle that henne	Fresshe that chekque
Unbrace that malarde	Unlace that cony
Dysmember that heron	Dysplaye that crane
Dysfigure that pecocke	Wynge that partridge, quayle
Mynce that plover	Barbe that lobster
Tayme that crabbe	Ilye that pegyon, woodcocke

Turn to p.19 for contemporary information.

HORS D'OEUVRE

In the matter of hors d'oeuvre there are two salient points, which must have equal consideration: you must ask yourselves if you want to fill up your guests and family before the main course or stimulate their taste buds for what is to follow. In Ali-Bab, one of our culinary bibles, and by us in translation, we learn that originally the hors d'oeuvre were put upon the table at the disposal of the guests to serve as a distraction or *frivolité* between the different courses. They were for amusement, and although today they are served at the beginning of a meal, after the soup at a dinner, they still constitute an introduction, the lifting of the curtains, the overture to a gastronomic opera, a flirtation . . . mere bagatelles. Their role remains unchanged in that they are intended to excite the appetite without imposing any great strain upon the stomach.

This is as colourful a description as the one we cherish of a certain pudding or *entremet* as given by one of the greatest living gastronomes, M. Claud Terrail, owner of Paris's oldest restaurant *Le Tour d'Argent*. He ruled, 'This delicate pudding should really be no more than a gastronomic kiss upon the throat.'

Such high-falutin' dictates are rarely for the very young and almost never for members of the American nation; but if we are to align ourselves with Ali-Bab and M. Terrail, we must draw a firm line between the delicate and the filling when choosing from the recipes in this chapter. Further – we must reflect upon the quality of the wines to follow and if they are of any consequence, we must automatically exclude (even for Christmas Dinner) anything which contains vinegar (cruel to fine wines) and of course those lethal dunking sauces, which cause total paralysis to the taste buds.

We can also cut down on the size of the portions which we serve. Give small quantities if you want your Christmas-tide hospitality to be for *gourmets* rather than for *gourmands*. Bearing this in the forefront of our minds, we can then turn for suitable suggestions to a number of the items included in the Fish chapter (pp.120-32) as well as in this one.

AVOCADOS WITH MADEIRA
(Avocate au Madère)

This is the method used in Madeira and accepted with alacrity by our guests many times over the years since we first visited Madeira. It is absurdly simple but subtle, and a modest opener to the Christmas Dinner Gorge, which places little strain either on cook or on anyone's digestion.

Halve ripe avocados, remove the stones and score the flesh with *a silver knife*. Moisten carefully and thoroughly with Madeira, chill and serve.

CAVIARE CREAM
(Crème de Caviar)

This is a very simple invention of our own, which, with a little careful presentation and a lot of crustless toast in a white table napkin, becomes very luxurious and leads quite a lot of people into thinking that they are eating real caviare at a minimum £10 per pound when they are really eating black Danish cod's roe, unblushingly sold by many grocers as caviare! For one 1¾oz pot allow 8fl oz of double cream whipped to a light peak, the strained juice of 1 small lemon and 2–3 pinches of freshly milled black peppercorns.

Fold the 'caviare' into the cream with a fork and add lemon juice and pepper, being careful to work gently as the action of these last two ingredients tends to thicken the mixture, which, if whipped, would not end up the consistency of thickly whipped cream but just butter and whey. Copy our presentation if you like. We pile the mixture into a rough pyramid in a crystal bowl and we inset this bowl in an outer one, the sides thickly packed with ice so that it is very well chilled when spread, icily cold, on piping-hot toast and eaten in the fingers like bread and jam.

CRABMEAT AVOCADO
(Avocat au Crabe)

Unless you have all the time in the world, buy the required amount of crabmeat by the ounce, making sure that you have an equal quantity of both brown and white meats. Place the two in a bowl with, to every 4oz, 1 shake from a Tabasco bottle, 2 teaspoons strained lemon juice, 1 generous pinch black pepper, 1 teaspoon cooking sherry and 1 heaped dessertspoon stiffly whipped cream. Mix well together. Heap into cavities in halved avocados and 'finish' the centre of each mound with either a small crab claw or, when it is not available, a wooden cocktail stick driven through a stuffed olive, a cocktail onion and a radish flower.

FOR THOSE WHO MUST DUNK

Those who must dunk at Christmas parties will need to assemble all or any of the following items:

Slim, long heads of chicory with absolutely no green on them (just yellow at the tips and otherwise white), quartered and divided again into eighths.

Carefully picked sprigs of corn salad (*romaine*).

Trimmed inner well-washed celery stalks.

Divided inner cos lettuce leaves.

Cauliflower hearts cut through into very small raw sprigs.

Cleaned radishes with tufts of green left on for easy handling.

Long, thin slivers of carefully peeled carrot, or these can be made very effective if large, peeled carrots are sliced very thinly on a cucumber cutter or Mandoline, and then rolled up and pierced with a cocktail stick. This also enables dunking to be done easily and without peril to fingertips.

Strips cut lengthwise from top to tail halved green, red and yellow pimentos, all pith and pips removed before slicing.

Young stems of sea kale if you like the slightly bitter flavour.

Heart of lettuce leaves.

Trimmed endive and watercress sprigs.

Trimmed spring onions.

Because they are unsuitable for anything else that we know of, we will keep your four suggested dunking sauces here and not in the general, adaptable sauce section.

(1) *Bagna Cauda*. For this hot dunking sauce you will need a fondue or other suitable pot over a hot plate, spirit stove or nightlight.

Ingredients: ½ pint olive oil; 6 peeled halved garlic cloves; 1 smallish tin of chopped anchovy fillets; a generous thread of saffron; 1 small flat teaspoon freshly milled black peppercorns.

Method: Mix all together in the pot, heat until it bubbles and carry to a side table with the dunking ingredients arranged in bowls and tumblers in an encircling garland.

(2) A cold dunking sauce may seem odd coming from us, and we do not know how we ever discovered it, but certainly nowadays when we have the young to feed in large numbers, we

make it up and give them some mixed wine brew to drink, because of course like all dunking mixtures it is lethal to good wine. Empty a tin of unsweetened milk into a bowl, have a test dunking item beside you for sampling and whip in French mustard by the teaspoon. You will find that as you do, the texture will change completely. Do it gradually and stop when the flavour is strong enough. Do not just empty a pot of mustard in regardless!

(3) Place a quarter of a batch of Oxford Sauce (pp.184-5) in a bowl and whip in gradually 1 flat eggspoon powdered ginger, strained juice of 1 small orange and a thread of lemon juice. In fact, this *can* be served hot as well as cold.

(4) *Ingredients*: 1 packet *demi sel* cheese; 1 teaspoon well-shaken Worcestershire sauce; ¼ pint single or coffee cream; 1 flat tablespoon milled beechnuts and 1 large or 2 small finely chopped gherkins.

Method: Whip all together until absolutely smooth except for the gherkin bits. Refrigerate until moment of service.

GIRONDE OYSTERS AND SAUSAGES
(Les Huitres et Saucissons au façon de la Gironde)

This most agreeable hot/cold appetiser originated in the Bordeaux area where, as a family recipe, not as a caterer's, it became an hors d'oeuvre dish served on all special occasions in the most modest and the most imposing households. The Arcachon oysters were used together with the white wine sausage of the Bordeaux.

A simple English version is to use oysters on the deep shell (so that the liquor is conserved) and arrange these on a platter with piping-hot chipolatas in a napkin fold inside a central bowl. It is implicit that the oysters are freshly opened, and that each is loosened with a silver knife just before serving – otherwise the unfortunate guest will suck . . . and suck . . .! At the table use a fork for the oysters, *provided* you do not go driving the fork into the unfortunate bivalve. The true oyster lover, to whom even a drop of lemon juice is the thin edge of the wedge of heresy, sucks the oysters directly from the shell and never uses a fork.

GRAPEFRUIT AND ORANGE COCKTAILS

Allow one thin-skinned grapefruit to every two thin-skinned oranges. Peel the required quantity in such a way that skin and pith are cut away together, leaving the flesh of both fruits exposed, which automatically ensures that you can see the dividing hair lines of skin that separate each segment from its neighbour. With a very sharp knife indeed cut against the first bit of skin segment and then on the opposing side make a second so that the fruit flesh segment comes away absolutely cleanly. After you have cut away the first two or three you will find that it becomes quite easy, if the knife is really sharp, to drive it down on the one side, turn the blade slightly and jerk the segment out all in one movement. For each serving take a sundae dish or large claret glass, dip the rim in a saucer of cold water and immediately into castor sugar. Then mix the flesh in a bowl with sifted icing sugar to taste and a drop or two of maraschino. Heap into the prepared glasses and refrigerate until the moment of service. This 'starter' is ideal as a palate cleanser before serving a very rich main course like goose.

HOT BAKED GRAPEFRUIT
(Pamplemousses Chaudes)

Halve large, firm, thin-skinned grapefruit and cut them prop-erly with a grapefruit cutter, running a sharp knife between the flesh and skin of each segment. Turn halves upside down in a deepish container and leave them for 30 minutes so that surplus juices drain away. (Drink the juices.) Invert grapefruit halves, cover each with soft brown (pieces) sugar and sprinkle lightly with powdered cinnamon and nutmeg. Dot several small flakes of butter on the tops and bake for 15 minutes one shelf above centre at Gas Mark 5. Serve immediately.

Note: These can be served plain but are greatly improved for dinner by the addition of a teaspoonful of Marsala or Bual or Malmsey Madeira to each grapefruit half before baking.

INDIVIDUAL MUSSEL MOULDS
(Rémoulade de Moules)

This is a delightfully different hors d'oeuvre with which to preface the arrival of the Christmas bird. The mixture will keep in large or small individual moulds for several days in refrigeration. Play for safety and say three.

Ingredients (for six individual moulds): 1 pint mayonnaise (pp.182-3); 5fl oz double cream; 1oz gelatine; 5fl oz real consommé or melted, undiluted tinned consommé; 1lb coarse oatmeal; 4 pints mussels; ½ pint white wine; 1½ pints water; 1 sprig parsley stalk; 2 peppercorns; 1 sliced onion.

Method: Place the mussels, unwashed, in a bucket, cover with the oatmeal and leave in a dark place overnight. The mussels will clean themselves, gorge the oatmeal and be twice the size and twice as easy to clean the next day. This is when you tug away the little pendant 'beards' from each mussel and scrub with great thoroughness in plenty of cold water. Place in a pan with the water, wine, parsley, onion and peppercorns, cover with a lid, bring to a fierce boil and maintain for a slow count of 60. Remove the lid. The mussels will now soon be open. Discard any that are not. Remove them from their shells when they are cold enough to handle. When completely cold, fold into the mayonnaise. Add the cream. Add consommé in which the gelatine has been dissolved. Stir swiftly and turn into very small basins well burnished with olive oil. Unmould when required. Sprinkle with parsley.

LIVER PATE
(Pâté Familial)

Ingredients: ½lb pig's or calves' liver; ½lb lean veal; ½lb raw unsalted pork fat; 6 anchovy fillets; 1 medium onion; 1 crushed garlic clove (optional); 2 rounded dessertspoons flour; 2 standard eggs; ½ level teaspoon salt; 1 level eggspoon black pepper; 3½fl oz double cream; butter.

Method: Butter a classic terrine or other lidded earthenware or heat-resistant glass container very liberally indeed. Mince chosen liver with the veal, onion, pork fat, anchovy fillets and crushed garlic clove. Re-mince mixture. Place in a roomy bowl. Sprinkle on the flour and stir thoroughly. Beat in the eggs singly and finally add the cream and seasonings. Blend well, turn the mixture into the buttered container, level off the top, cover lightly with butter paper, then foil or lid. Place in a meat baking tin one-quarter filled with hot water. Bake on centre shelf, Gas Mark 4, for 1 hour.

Note: The use of weights during cooling time is purely optional.

MELON BOATS
(Barquettes de Melon)

Cut chosen melon into usual portions, remove all pips and pulp and then with a very sharp knife cut the entire flesh away as close to the skin as possible from tip to tip *in one piece*. Hold the skin and flesh together firmly with one hand (keeping fingers out of the way of the knife) and make seven or nine equidistant cuts across the severed flesh from tip to tip. Then push each one the opposite way to its neighbour, so that the finished boats look like galleons with the oars sticking out alternately. Serve plainly with castor sugar, or with sifted icing sugar mixed with powdered ginger, or, if wanting a slightly different flavour of Italian origin, cut fine small strips from leaf-thin slices of Parma ham, roll them up into tiny little cylinders and stick them into the spaces left by the alternate projection of each slice of melon.

PORK PATE
(Pâté de Porc)

This is a recipe for an everyday one of the kind you and we can justify making fairly regularly and keeping in mild refrigeration. Always take out and leave to moderate its coldness before serving. Take this recipe as a pattern for *pâtés* and use your own variants therefrom. Every housewife should reach the point, as all Frenchwomen do, where she has her own particular *pâté*, which bears the hallmark of her individuality.

Ingredients: 1lb minced, lean pork; ½lb minced pork fat; 2 pork kidneys; 2 garlic cloves (can be omitted); salt and pepper; a small sprig of tarragon; 4 rashers of streaky bacon; 2 eggs; 2fl oz cooking sherry; 2 medium onions.

Method: Line a small earthenware terrine or casserole pot with the bacon. Re-mince the pork and pork fat with the onions, garlic and tarragon. Season, beat in the eggs singly, stir in the sherry and spread half this mixture over the bacon in the terrine. Cut the kidneys lengthwise in halves, cut in quarters and lay over the bed of *pâté*. Cover with the remainder. Cover with buttered papers, or with aluminium foil. Stand in an outer, shallow baking tin half filled with hot water. Cook at Gas Mark 4 for about 1 hour. *Serve hot.*

Note: This is the great speciality of a small, now-famous little Norman restaurant at Orbec, Le Caneton. Alternatively, leave until cold, store in mild refrigeration and serve cold. Ideally, put a wedge of butter and a yard or so of French bread on the table.

PORK PATE IN PASTRY
(Pâté de Porc en Croûte)

You can fill the Pork Pâté mixture (pp.105-6) into a pastry case and bake slowly, in a small buttered and floured bread tin or long pork pie tin, so that it comes out cake, or panel pork pie, shape to be cut in slices for serving. Bake on centre shelf at Gas Mark 4 for 1 hour.

The Pastry: 10oz sifted flour; 3¾fl oz water; 3oz pure pork fat (dissolved over hot water and allowed to re-firm before using).

Method: Bring pork fat and water to the boil together in a small saucepan. Pour into a hollow in the middle of the flour in a basin and work up rapidly with the fingertips. Place on a lightly floured wooden surface, knead well until smooth and place in the prepared container and mould with fingertips across base and up sides, treating it as if it was extra-malleable plasticine. Trim off surplus and keep in a warm place in a clean cloth until you are ready to roll it out for the lid.

POTTED SHRIMPS
(Crevettes conservées)

This is the kind of information that can never be specific in terms of quantity: the amount of ingredients depends upon the size of the stone pot and of course on the number to whom it is to be served. As an *aide memoire* we say it is extravagant on butter, exhausting to prepare, absolutely useless with frozen shrimps, and absolutely wonderful if done correctly.

Ingredients (to every pint of very carefully shelled shrimps): ½lb softened butter; 4 or 5 black peppercorns; the thinly peeled rind of lemon; 2 bay leaves.

Method: Soften the butter very slowly in a thick pan over a low heat. Place shrimps in one large pot or a series of small ones, with the peel of the lemon and the black peppercorns. Strain on the butter. Slip a bay leaf down the centre for every ½ pint of shrimps. Cover with foil; store in refrigeration. Allow the first chill to pass before serving.

PRAWN OR SHRIMP COCKTAIL
(Cocktail d'Ecrevisses ou de Crevettes)

Ingredients for 1 serving: 6 stalked sprigs fresh watercress; 2oz shelled, diced prawns (or whole shrimps) and 1 extra prawn unshelled: 1 tablespoon mayonnaise; 1oz diced, cooked potato; 1oz unskinned, diced cucumber and 1 slice (thin); 1 dessertspoon thick cream; 1 small teaspoon lemon juice and 1 thin slice lemon; paprika powder; 2–3 drops Tabasco; 1 scant level eggspoon concentrated tomato purée.

Method: Line a glass coupe or individual dish with all but 1 sprig of watercress. Mix together in a bowl diced prawns or shrimps, cream, mayonnaise, potato, diced cucumber, lemon juice, Tabasco and tomato purée. Place in a mound in a watercress-based coupe. Sprinkle the top with paprika powder. Shell the remaining prawn from tail to neck, leaving the head attached. Press into the top centre of the mound. Split the cucumber and lemon slices in one place to centre, twist and hang on opposite sides of the coupe. Split the remaining watercress sprig and press in left and right of the whole prawn. Serve well chilled.

SAUSAGE IN PUFF PASTRY
(Saucisson Feuilleté)

You have enormous licence as to the type of sausage you use. One of the best for this purpose is a small, whole garlic sausage of the kind readily obtained from delicatessen in this country today. Roll out bought or home-made puff pastry into a rectangular panel. Skin the garlic sausage and proceed as you would for a sausage roll. Brush with raw beaten egg or *anglaise* (pp.129-30). Bake one shelf above centre at Gas Mark 7½. Serve either hot or cold, cut in slices as for Swiss roll. It is also quite delicious if made with a *boudin*, but as this is not so easily available, it is a less practical suggestion.

SNAILS IN PUFF PASTRY
(Escargots Feuilleté)

Created by us for the party which celebrated the publication of the late Sir Philip Joubert's cookery book.

Ingredients: Garlic Butter (p.266); snails; bought or home-made puff pastry; raw beaten egg (or *anglaise*, pp.129-30).

Method: Roll out puff pastry thinly and cut into 2½in squares. Moisten the edges with raw beaten egg. Coat each snail in garlic butter. Set in the centre of each pastry square, wrap up, brush with raw beaten egg and bake one shelf above centre at Gas Mark 7½ for about 10–12 minutes. Serve piping hot in folded linen napkins.

SOUPS

Although we have recommended in the menu section the service of soups for Christmas Dinner, it is a moot point as to whether they are as useful here as in the meals which precede and follow the traditional feast. Turtle is the great Christmas soup, but we have an uneasy feeling that while we, the Mansion House and possibly Mr Nubar Gulbenkian might perhaps become involved either personally or by delegation in the three-day ritual of making real turtle soup, the majority of the inhabitants of this island would be more likely to open a tin and dilute it with either stock and wine or that culinary downfall of the British race – tap water!

If we survey the field as displayed in this soup section, there are a great many that would advisedly be left at the post for Christmas dinner. The onion soups are too filling, like the Tomato and Red Cabbage Soup and Cock-a-Leekie. The three using Brussels sprouts and/or chestnuts would have to go if either item were chosen to accompany the bird and the three-bone and carcase ones are attendant upon the demolition of the flesh, but the *Bortsch* would be delicious and palate-clearing and would stimulate the digestive juices. In an entirely different way iced *Vichyssoise* could fulfil the same function. Oysters always stimulate because, as Saki has it, oysters are more controversial than religion and therefore opinion would have to be canvassed in advance lest there were an incidence of oyster-haters among the intended company. For the rest, the soups with artichoke, shrimp, mushroom, almond and pistachio are all delicate enough to justify a place if served piping hot in bowls which have been, ideally, swilled with boiling water for a moment or two before service. In the matter of soup plates we are fanatical and while to us a toast rack is a draught with wires round, so a soup plate is a device for chilling soup.

ALMOND SOUP
(Crème aux Amandes)

Norman in origin, adapted.

Ingredients: 4oz sweet almonds, milled finely; 1½ pints milk; ½ pint ideally double, alternatively single, cream; 1oz flour; 1oz butter; 1 small stick celery; 1 small onion or shallot; salt; pepper; 1 level teaspoon castor sugar.

Method: Place the hot milk, whole onion, celery head and milled almonds in the top of a double saucepan over hot water and poach for 1½ hours. Remove celery head and onion. Season liquid. Dissolve butter in a pan, add flour and stir until blended. Add liquor gradually, stirring carefully between each addition; add cream, stirring equally carefully; stir in sugar, correct seasoning, and serve.

ARTICHOKE SOUP
(Crème aux Topinambours)

Substitute peeled Jerusalem artichokes for Brussels sprouts and proceed exactly as instructed for Brussels Sprouts Soup (p.112).

BEETROOT SOUP
(Bortsch)

Ingredients: 3 large raw beet; 4 small raw turnips; ¼ medium-size white cabbage heart; 1 head celery; 1 large raw Spanish onion; 1 Faggot of Herbs (p.160); 2lb breast of beef; 2 quarts good beef stock; 1 tumbler cold water; 1 heaped tablespoon milled fresh parsley; sour cream (optional, to be handed separately.)

Method: Coarse grate the beetroot, turnips, cabbage heart and onion. Chop the celery finely and grate the stump. Place all in stockpot with the herb faggot and breast of beef. Add the stock, bring to the boil, skim carefully, add cold water, raise to a steady simmer and maintain for 2½ hours. Strain thoroughly – the liquor should now be the colour of thin red wine – place in a clean pan, bring to the boil and simmer to two-thirds of its present bulk, i.e. 40–45fl oz. Taste, correct seasoning with salt and pepper, add parsley and serve either piping hot or icily chilled with sour cream on the side.

Note: When available, a dessertspoonful of finely chopped fresh chervil is also added.

BRUSSELS SPROUTS AND CHESTNUT CREAM SOUP
(Crème de Noël)

Ingredients: 1½lb steamed Brussels sprouts; ½lb cooked, skinned chestnuts (p.171); 2 pints milk; ¼ pint ideally double, alternatively single, cream; salt and pepper to season; 1oz butter; 1oz flour; 2 heaped tablespoon milled parsley.

Method: Rub both sprouts and chestnuts through a sieve or emulsify with a quarter of the milk and then sieve. Dissolve the butter in a thick pan, work in the flour and dilute gradually with 1 pint of the milk. Then fold in the sieved mixture gradually, alternating with additions from the remaining milk. Taste, correct seasoning with salt and pepper. Turn into the top of a double pan, cover with a wetted circle of greaseproof paper and refrigerate. When required, reheat over hot water over very low heat. Remove the greaseproof paper. Add the parsley and finally cream. If a thinner soup than the above is desired, dilute with milk when reheating as the mixture has a tendency to thicken up during the refrigeration period.

BRUSSELS SPROUTS SOUP
(Crème aux Choux de Bruxelles)

We have never been given this anywhere outside our own home! Why?

Ingredients: 1 raw grated onion; 2lb small, tight Brussels sprouts; 3oz butter; 1½oz flour; 5fl oz dry white wine; 1½ pints milk; 5fl oz cream, ideally double, alternatively single; salt, pepper and oregano to season.

Method: Steam the sprouts until tender. Place them in the milk with the onion pulp, bring to the boil, simmer for 3 minutes, rub through a sieve and return to the pan. Dissolve 1½oz butter in a separate pan, add the flour, stir to a soft ball, add the wine and stir until smooth and thick. Add the milk purée gradually, stirring well between each addition. Correct the seasoning with salt, pepper and oregano. Finish by running the remaining 1½oz softened butter through fingers onto soup and thereafter stir in the cream. Reheat in the top of a double saucepan over hot water when required.

CHESTNUT SOUP
(Crème aux Marrons)

Substitute par-cooked, peeled chestnuts for pistachio nuts in Cream of Pistachio Nuts (below); otherwise proceed as instructed.

COCK-A-LEEKIE
(Potage Cocky-Leeky)

Ingredients: 2–3lb trimmed, cleaned leeks chopped into 1in lengths; 1 cockerel; salt and pepper; stock.

Method: Place leeks in clear, cold water, bring to the boil, simmer for 10 minutes, drain thoroughly and place in large, thick pot with the fowl, salt, pepper and sufficient good white bone stock (fowl or flesh) to cover liberally. Bring to the boil, skim carefully, throw in a tumbler of ice-cold water, bring once again to the boil and maintain at a gentle simmer for at least 3 hours. Remove all flesh from the fowl, dice neatly, return to the pot, and correct the seasoning with more salt and pepper if necessary.

Note: A dozen whole primes may be added with the stock if desired.

CREAM OF PISTACHIO NUTS
(Crème aux Pistaches)

This is a most luxurious and costly soup, very little known in England.

Ingredients: A little more than 1 quart of impeccable chicken or veal consommé; 1 pint ideally double, alternatively single, cream; 1lb pistachio nuts; salt and pepper to season; 2 table-spoons brandy.

Method: Simmer the nuts in the consommé until they are quite soft. Strain them. Measure the remaining consommé and make up to 1 quart again. Bring to boiling point once more and sieve the pistachio nuts, letting the purée fall back into the liquid. Stir in the cream, correct the seasoning, add the brandy and reheat in the top of a double saucepan over hot water.

Note: If a thicker soup is required, add to the above soup 3 lightly beaten egg yolks. Pour the reheated soup onto the yolks and pour back and forth three or four times. Re-warm in the *bain marie* pan, but on no account allow the soup to boil or the yolks in it will now cause it to curdle.

LEEK AND POTATO SOUP
(Vichyssoise)

Ingredients: 2lb trimmed leeks; 2lb peeled potatoes; good, cleared stock; 1–1½ pints milk; ½ pint ideally double, alternatively single, cream; salt and pepper; chopped chives or spring onion heads.

Method: Put finely sliced leeks and rough-cut potatoes into a roomy, thick pan and cover with stock. Simmer steadily until all is very tender. Rub through a sieve. Return to a clean pan. Add the milk, then cream. The amount of milk *does* depend on the consistency you want, but it should be fairly thick. Season to taste with salt and pepper. Serve either icy cold or very hot. Sprinkle each serving with chopped chives. If not available, use very finely cut strips of spring onion.

MUSHROOM SOUP
(Crème Forestière)

Served to M. Andre L. Simon on May 2nd, 1949, when he first dubbed Fanny 'Cordon Bleu'.

Ingredients: 1lb finely chopped mushrooms (skins and stalks included); ¼lb finely chopped shallots; 1 small, crushed garlic clove; 1½oz butter; 1½oz flour; 1½fl oz pure olive oil; 2 pints veal stock; ½ pint dry white wine; salt, pepper and nutmeg to season; ½ pint ideally double, alternatively single, cream.

Method: Heat the oil and butter together in a thick pan. Cook the shallots gently for 3 minutes, then add the mushrooms and garlic and continue gently cooking until all are tender but not even fractionally browned! Stir in the flour and work to a rough paste with the back of a wooden spoon. Add wine gradually, stirring between each addition. Then add heated stock gradually. Season to taste with salt, pepper and nutmeg. Stir in the cream, turn into the top of a double saucepan over hot water and reheat when required.

ONION SOUP
(Soupe à l'Oignon)

Ingredients: 2lb finely sliced onions; 1 crushed garlic clove (optional); 1½oz flour; 1 rounded teaspoon dry English mustard; salt and pepper to season; 1 Faggot of Herbs (p.160); 3 pints good, cleared bone stock; 1 pint white wine; 2oz butter; 2fl oz olive oil; Gruyère cheese; French bread.

Method: Heat the oil and butter together and soft-fry the onions until tender *but not browned*. Stir in the flour and mustard, work to a rough pulp, add the wine gradually, stirring between each addition, add ½ pint of the stock and stir again until thickened. Then tip from the frying pan into the saucepan. Add the remaining stock and faggot of herbs and simmer for at least 30 minutes. Remove the herbs. Toast 4in pieces of French bread split lengthwise in two. Butter these and heap them with grated Gruyère cheese. Set in the bottom of large soup bowls or soup plates. Pour the soup on top. When the cheese toast floats to the top, scatter on a little more cheese and brown lightly under a quick grill.

ONION SOUP WITH PORT
(Soupe à l'Oignon Oporto)

Prepare Onion Soup as instructed above. Rub through a sieve and reheat when serving. Whip 4 eggs in a soup tureen and pour on 6fl oz port. Whip again and continue whipping while someone else pours on the heated soup. Stir and serve immediately.

OYSTER SOUP
(Crème aux Huitres)

Follow the instructions for Shrimp Soup (see below), deleting shrimps and replacing with oysters in the following manner. Allow minimum 1 dozen, maximum 2 dozen small cooking oysters. Open or have opened for you over a bowl lined with muslin so that the oyster liquor is strained into the container. Add the liquor to the soup just before adding cream, then add the oysters. Reheat immediately and serve. This soup cannot be made overnight. Make sure that each serving (6 modest portions) contains minimum 2, maximum 4 oysters.

SHRIMP SOUP
(Crème de Crevettes)

Ingredients: 1¼ pints milk; 1½oz butter; 1½oz flour; ¼ pint dry white wine; ¼ pint single cream or top of the milk; 2oz shelled shrimps; 8oz shelled shrimps; ½oz butter; pepper to season; 1oz milled parsley heads.

Method: Melt 1½oz butter in a thick pan, add the flour and stir over a low heat to form a smooth, soft ball. Add the wine gradually, beating well between each addition. Then add the milk gradually, beating well between each addition. Add 8oz finely chopped shrimps and allow to cook for 15 minutes over a mere thread of heat, stirring at intervals. Taste and correct the seasoning with pepper (no salt should be needed but this is a matter of choice). Remove from the heat and blend the cream in thoroughly. Pour into a basin, cover with a fitting circle of wetted greaseproof paper and refrigerate overnight for service on Christmas Day. Reheat in the top of a double saucepan over hot water – a process which needs no attention. Just before service remove the paper, stir thoroughly and stir in ½oz butter to give the soup a good sheen. Pour into heated bowls and scatter one or two shrimps and parsley over surface.

SOUP FROM A GOOSE CARCASE
(Purée d'Oie)

Ingredients: 1 goose carcase divided neatly; thinly peeled rind of 1 lemon; 2 quartered, unpeeled cooking apples; 1 swede, peeled and cut into small pieces; 1 Faggot of Herbs (p.160); salt and pepper to season; 5fl oz cream, ideally double, alternatively single (or top of the milk); stock.

Method: Place goose pieces, lemon rind, apples, swede and herb faggot in stockpot and cover with stock. Simmer for about 4 hours. Lift out the goose pieces, lemon peel and herb faggot and allow to chill. Take off the top crust of grease. Reheat and rub through a sieve. Reheat before serving. At the moment of service, correct the seasoning and stir in the cream.

SOUP FROM A HAM BONE
(Potage Saint Germain)

Ingredients: 1lb dried peas; 1 rounded teaspoon dried basil; 1 ham bone; approx. 6 pints stock; 1oz butter; any available bacon rinds; 4–6 crustless slices of bread cut into small dice; oil to fry bread; ½ pint milk; salt and pepper to season.

Method: Soak peas overnight. Drain and place in stockpot with ham bone, basil and bacon rinds. Cover with stock. Simmer for about 3 hours. Remove ham bone and bacon rinds; then rub mixture through a sieve. Return to a saucepan and reduce, by simmering, to approx. 4 pints, stirring to ensure thickening purée does not catch. Add ½ pint milk, correct seasoning and stir in the butter. Reheat before serving. Fry the bread squares in a little hot oil until well browned and crisp. Put a spoonful into each bowl or soup plate at the moment of service.

SOUP FROM A TURKEY CARCASE
(Potage de Restes)

Ingredients: 1 turkey carcase; outside stems of a head of celery; 1 onion, chopped small; 1 large carrot, chopped small; ¼ medium tight white cabbage, chopped small; 1 dozen bacon rinds; 2 parsley stalks; stock; ¼lb broken spaghetti.

Method: Place all ingredients, except the stock and spaghetti, in a large stock pot. Cover with stock and allow to simmer very gently for about 4 hours. Lift out the turkey carcase and the bacon rinds. Pass the remainder through a sieve, chop the sieve contents finely, return with the liquor to a clean pan and bring to a steady rolling boil. Add the broken spaghetti and simmer for the few moments required for it to become tender. Reheat when required. This is when you correct the seasoning.

Note: Not essential, but so valuable when possible, are two additions to this soup: 1oz butter in small, soft fragments slipped into the purée before reheating and 5fl oz cream – ideally double, alternatively single (or top of the milk) – stirred in just before service.

TOMATO AND RED CABBAGE SOUP
(Potage Familial)

Ingredients: – 1st stage: ¼lb shredded raw red cabbage; ¼lb finely chopped raw onion; 2 bay leaves; 2 pints stock or water.

Ingredients: – 2nd stage: 6 ripe chopped tomatoes with skins on; 12fl oz stock.

Ingredients: – 3rd stage: 1oz dripping; 1 finely chopped medium-sized onion; 1 rasher of bacon, diced small; 1 crushed garlic clove; 1 level dessertspoon finely chopped fresh mint; salt and pepper to season.

Method: Place first-stage ingredients in a pan, bring to the boil, simmer for 1 hour and strain. Place second-stage ingredients in another pan and simmer for 15 minutes. Rub through the strainer into the strained first mixture. Now heat the dripping, given in the third-stage ingredients, and fry the bacon with the garlic clove and onion. When tender, stir into the sieved mixture, season with salt and pepper and add the mint. Serve straight away or reheat when required.

FISH

The use of fish as a preceding course to the chosen bird and its many accompaniments at Christmas dinner is not prevalent today, for reasons of both purse and capacity. Nevertheless, it would be totally untraditional to omit such items as whitebait or the four smoked fish items – salmon, eel, trout and buckling. We have however chosen as carefully as possible dishes that will earn their keep far more frequently for buffet entertaining over the Christmas period.

On the more sophisticated level the *Brandade de Morue*, or French aristocrat with cod, makes a superb hot item, together with Mme Melanie's lobster. The buffet turbot and the lobster patties are on the same level, although cold. All the smoked fish items, hot and cold, lend themselves to slightly less grandiose buffet service, as does *Coulibiac*, which uses frozen salmon.

On whichever day any of these are to be served, it must be remembered that none of these lend themselves to really advanced pre-preparation. At the very most, items may be pre-prepared up to 24 hours beforehand. Stale fish is dangerous and therefore it looks very much to us in terms of menu decisions as though the fish is either bought on Christmas Eve for Christmas Day or bought on December 30th for serving at a New Year's party. In this respect fish is very valuable indeed because the plethora of poultry ensures added enjoyment of something that strikes an entirely different note.

Finally, in the interests of your health and safety, you might like to refresh your memory in the matter of choosing fish so that you may not be fobbed off with something that is not absolutely fresh. Mutter when you buy: 'Fresh fish have bright scales, firm gills and clear eyes'; brainwash yourself that dull-scaled, bleary-eyed fish are stale. Insist that all mussels are tightly closed; those with their shells gaping are no longer with us – they are dead! – and fish poisoning is exceedingly disagreeable.

Bear in mind that fresh shrimps and prawns, as we said in our *Cook's Book*, will pop their shells apart when you stretch out the tails and then press head and tails together sharply, working the poor things like little concertinas. When these small shellfish are stale, their juices wither and dry up; consequently the shells stick to the flesh and will not part with one another.

When buying lobsters, demand hens. If you are not afraid of being ever so slightly conspicuous, line them up with their tails tucked under and behinds facing towards you. The slim behinds are male and are for rejecting, except when cutting lobster *medaillons* and wanting to avoid the incidence of eggs or coral. For all other uses choose the wide behinds, which are indisputably female. They contain the precious coral.

For future reference, if you do not know already, the rule runs . . . hen lobsters–cock crabs.

AN EASY DISH OF SOLE

Ingredients for 6 persons: 6 fillets of sole; 12 unshelled prawns; 6 fl oz strongly reduced fish stock (see Lobster Patties, pp.123-4) *or* 3 fl oz fish stock and 3 fl oz dry white wine; 3 fl oz single cream or top of the milk; salt and pepper to season; 2 rounded tablespoons freshly milled parsley heads; butter.

Method: Line a meat baking tin with turkey-width kitchen foil, leaving sufficient of foil to overlap the tin so that the ends can be brought up into a loose parcel. Coil each fish fillet round three fingers. Butter the base of the foil. Place the coiled fillets on the base, stuff 2 prawns, head uppermost, into the centre of each coil, swill with stock or stock and wine, then cream, season, scatter overall with parsley and refrigerate open. Bring the edges up to form a loose parcel just before baking at Gas Mark 5, one shelf above centre, for 20–25 minutes depending on the size of the fillets.

For Simple Service: Either place individual portions on heated plates and spoon the liquor over, or do the same on a large dish.

For More Elaborate Service: Arrange the fillets on a serving dish, reduce the sauce to a thick, syrupy consistency by simmering fast in a small, thick pan, spoon carefully over each portion and surround with crescents of *anglaise*-brushed, fairly thick, stamped-out, bought or home-made puff pastry (pp.249-50).

A VERY ARISTOCRATIC DISH OF COD
(Brandade de Morue)

An aristocrat among cod recipes.

Ingredients: 1 pint lukewarm olive oil; about ¼ pint lukewarm milk; 2lb steamed, skinned, boned cod; 1 large or 2 small garlic cloves; salt and pepper to season.

Method: There are in fact two methods: the old and the new. For the former the cooked cod is pounded in a mortar with a pestle until it forms a paste. Then the milk and oil, from two separate containers, are added to the mixture slowly and carefully while pounding, so that at no time do the liquids separate, and the crushed garlic is added gradually. The trick is to add as much oil and milk in the ratio 1 part milk to 4 parts oil as the mixture will 'hold'. We have, however, discovered that the same job can be done with a fraction of the skill or labour by using a slow beat on an electric mixer. This makes a perfect *brandade* and absorbs plenty of milk and oil. The finished article should be smooth, soft and creamy. Season to taste with salt and pepper. Serve on a fancy dish surrounded by fancy shaped bread croûtons fried in olive oil, or turn into a puff pastry case, decorate with parsley and cover with a puff pastry lid.

FRIED MUSSELS
(Moules Frites)

Ingredients: 1 quart mussels; boiling water; 2 heaped table-spoons fresh, milled parsley; 2 lemons; 4oz butter; 1 raw beaten egg; flour; soft fine breadcrumbs; pepper.

Method: Place carefully cleaned bearded mussels in a steamer over boiling water, set over a strong heat, bring to the boil, and remove as soon as all shells have opened (about 2 mins). Turn off the heat. Strain the mussels, take from the shell and, when cold, pass first through the flour and then through the raw egg and finally through the breadcrumbs. Heat the butter in a large, shallow pan. Fry the mussels until golden over a fairly strong heat. Heap onto a d'oyley-covered dish, sprinkle with parsley and hand with cut lemon and very thinly cut buttered brown bread, denuded of crusts and rolled into little cylinders.

LOBSTER PATTIES
(Bouchées d'Homard)

The Cases: Use bought or home-made puff pastry for cases. Roll out to a minimum ¾in depth. Stamp with plain or fluted cutters 3in in diameter for the outers and 2½in plain cutters for the inners. Dip each cutter for each time of using into boiling water and shake off drops before cutting. This facilitates the puffing of the pastry during baking. When stamping inners in the same manner, be equally careful to press down so as to leave a thin base layer uncut. Brush incised centres and fluted edges with strained raw beaten egg (1 egg, 1 flat teaspoon salt to give high glaze) without allowing the egg wash to run into the inner incision or it will seal it up during baking and make it difficult to ease off the little lids thus formed. Place on baking sheets, which have been rinsed under a cold tap (never flour or flour and butter). Bake one shelf above centre, Gas Mark 7½, until well risen and only a pale golden brown. Take from the oven and remove the little inner lids carefully. Hollow out the central surplus 'goo', if any, and return the cases to the same position in the oven to dry out for a further 5 minutes at Gas Mark 2.

The Filling: Ingredients: 1½oz butter; 1½oz flour; ¼ pint dry white wine; ¼ pint strongly reduced fish stock (recipe below); ¼ pint single cream or top of the milk; extra ½oz butter; 1 tablespoon brandy (optional); 1¼lb hen lobster; 3oz finely diced unskinned mushrooms or their stalks.

Method: Split the lobster centrally from head to opposite end, being careful to fold the tail underneath before cutting; thus, as it were, cutting the rear end through on the double. Remove and discard the small split pouch below the head on each half. Take out all the flesh, separating the 'coral' (the strips of bright pink, tight-packed eggs) before dicing the remainder.

Smash down all lobster shell roughly. Place in a pan with 1lb sole or plaice bones, skin and trimmings, 1 bay leaf, torn into three pieces, 1 large leaf lemon peel, 2 peppercorns and 2 or 3 parsley stalks. Bring to the boil, simmer steadily for 30 minutes, strain into a clean pan and reduce by further simmering to ¼ pint fish stock.

Dissolve 1½oz butter in a thick pan and work in the flour to a smooth soft ball. Add the white wine, gradually beating between each addition, then add the stock with regular beating, then the brandy, and cook this mixture for a few moments over a moderate heat. Then add the cream/milk gradually and diced mushrooms. Simmer for 5 minutes and fold in the lobster. 'Finish' with ½oz butter to give a fine sheen and either fill immediately into the prepared cases or bake the cases to pale biscuit colour only, foil-wrap when cold and store until needed. Turn the made mixture into a basin, cover with a wetted circle of greaseproof paper, refrigerate for last-minute assembly and reheat at Gas Mark 1 until piping hot.

LOBSTER MELANIE
(Homard Mélanie)

We submit that this is the most beautiful hot lobster dish of all. It does not require a recipe but just a method of preparation and assembly. It can be prepared in the morning and refrigerated, uncovered, during the day for service at night. If serving as a main course dish use 1¼lb hen lobsters; if intended as a fish course only, use 1lb lobsters. Split these in halves and remove the 'pouches' or request your fishmonger to do the job for you. Remove all flesh and large claws. Remove the claw meat. Place the half-shells closely together in an ordinary meat baking tin or heat-resistant serving dish. Dice the lobster meat small and pack into the half-shells. Have ready grated Parmesan cheese, dry white wine, milled black peppercorns, milled parsley heads, fine soft white breadcrumbs and double, preferably Jersey, cream. Moisten each filled half-shell with the wine, sprinkle with crumbs, then cheese, then parsley, then pepper and moisten with cream, being careful with both wine and cream to let some splash into the container. Repeat from wine to cream, by which time the base of the container should be covered to about ¼in before putting into the oven, but do not cover while refrigerating. When baking, cover with foil and place one shelf above centre at Gas Mark 6 for 15–16 minutes. Serve with extra spoonsful of the pan mixture over each portion.

POACHED SALMON
(Saumon poché)

This can be done with either individual salmon steaks or a piece of any size of middle cut (*darne*) of salmon. Whichever is chosen, cut or tear the requisite sized pieces of kitchen foil to enable a whole piece or individual steaks to be wrapped into loose parcels. Butter the inner surface of each piece. Set the salmon in position. Brush the top surface with more melted butter, sprinkle with salt and pepper and wrap up loosely. Sink 'parcels' into a shallow container of slightly shivering hot water – please remember that this must not be allowed to boil – 'Fine Fish Is Never Boiled'. Allow 10–15 minutes for steaks depending upon thickness, 30–40 minutes for a *darne* or middle cut depending upon thickness. Remove 'parcels', allow surplus moisture to drain away, unwrap carefully and slide with interior juices onto a heated dish. Serve with Mousseline Sauce (pp.183-4).

RUSSIAN FISH AND RICE DISH
(Coulibiac)

Ingredients: 1½–2lb puff pastry; ¾lb par-cooked, grain-separate rice; 1–1½lb skinned, boned Pacific salmon cut into fingers; 4oz melted butter; 3 heaped tablespoons freshly milled parsley; 4–6 finely chopped hard-boiled eggs; salt and pepper to season; optional ¼lb thinly sliced mushrooms; raw beaten egg.

Method: Roll pastry out into a 14in by 10in rectangle. Make a central panel with one-third rice, then one-third salmon, season with salt and pepper, cover with one-third chopped eggs, sprinkle with 1 tablespoon of parsley, add an optional layer of mushrooms, re-season, moisten with one-third melted butter and repeat until all ingredients are absorbed. Brush the raw pastry edges with raw beaten egg, bring up the long sides to overlap centrally, pinch the edges securely, hide the join with a pastry 'plait', brush overall with egg-wash, bake one shelf above centre at Gas Mark 6 to a rich golden brown. Serve hot and hand a sauce boat separately of melted butter.

Note: A lush and optional addition to this dish is to top each serving with a leaf-thin slice of smoked salmon.

SEAFOOD PLATTER

This is a presentation and not a recipe. Take, according to numbers, one or more of the largest available platters. Cover the base with (a) seaweed when available or (b) green salad leaves as a substitute. Count heads and drive an equal number of large-headed pins into corks from wine bottles (well washed). Set a small, rimmed container (we use a ruby goblet) in the centre of each platter. Hook prawns uniformly around the top edge of the container, fill the centre with parsley and fill the remainder of the dish with all or any of the following seafoods – Christmas selection will depend solely upon purse!

Cooked cockles, mussels, brown shrimps (unshelled), crayfish, winkles, split baby lobsters, oysters opened onto the deep shell.

Serve with hot bread or hot Garlic Bread (pp.265-6) and butter on the side. Decorate dish with plain or decoratively cut lemon and let everyone help themselves.

Note: It is self-evident that the incidence of finger eating in this dish creates the absolute necessity for finger bowls!

SMOKED EEL
(The Presentation of)

Smoked eels are currently sold whole and unskinned (the best) or in small, slender fillets (less flavour). The fillets present no problem as they are merely arranged on a base of lettuce-heart leaves with lemon on the side and black pepper handed separately, but experience has taught us it is worth mentioning that whole eels are not cut into finger lengths with the skins still on. First, the skin should be loosened with a pointed knife just below the gills and then peeled back so that the flesh is exposed all over; heads and tails are then discarded and the skinned finger lengths served individually as with fillet but on the bone, or – for buffet presentation – the whole eels are skinned with the heads on, served on a platter, coiled round and with a sprig of parsley pushed into the teeth of each head.

SMOKED EEL IN PUFF PASTRY
(Anguilles fumées en feuilleté)

This is a hot first course dish for which a fat eel must be topped, tailed, skinned as explained above and the whole spine bone removed, leaving the four long strips of flesh ready for reassembly. For a 1lb eel place the following in a bowl: 4oz soft white breadcrumbs; 1 standard egg; 1oz fresh milled parsley heads; generous pinch of black pepper; pinch of salt and 1oz ground almonds; pour on 1oz melted butter and work up to a paste. Shape this paste into a thin sausage the length of the eel fillet and use as a replacement for the spine bone, pressing the four fillets onto and around the stuffing sausage. Place this on a fairly thinly rolled strip of puff pastry. Brush the edges with cold water, roll up like a giant Swiss roll, lay on a wetted baking sheet, brush with *Anglaise* (see below) and bake at Gas Mark 7, one shelf above centre, to a rich golden brown, approximately 20 minutes. Hand cut lemon separately.

SMOKED SALMON ROLLS
(Saumon fumé en feuilleté)

Owing to the high cost of smoked salmon and acting upon the recommendation of a friend, we wrote for and obtained on the date specified a 2lb piece of Irish smoked salmon, which cost us 35*s.* but do not hold us to that exact figure. Prices change! Part of this we used to cut leaf-thin into slices for Smoked Salmon Rolls. We also used bought puff pastry.

Roll out the pastry as thinly as possible and cut into rectangles approximately 5in wide and 6in long. Brush the rectangles all over with melted butter, cover each with a thin rectangle of smoked salmon, moisten with strained lemon juice, give each a *soupçon* of cayenne pepper (do not be heavy handed with this, please) and roll into cylinders. Place on a wetted baking sheet, brush with raw beaten strained *Anglaise* and bake one shelf above centre at Gas Mark 7 to a good golden brown and serve immediately.

Note 1: These make an excellent light first course or can be made smaller, impaled with wooden cocktail sticks and handed as finger food.

Note 2: Anglaise is the classic term for a savoury egg wash: to every standard egg allow 1 teaspoon olive oil, ½ level eggspoon salt, ¼ level eggspoon white pepper; beat all together thoroughly, strain and use.

SMOKED TROUT OR BUCKLING

To Serve Either Fish Cold: Remove skin, as instructed for eel, on both sides of each fish from below gills to the beginning of the tail. Serve on heart of lettuce leaves either as a general assembly or individually. Garnish with cut lemon and hand Horseradish Sauce (pp.181-2) separately.

To Serve Hot: Brush the skinned chosen fish all over with melted butter, place in a shallow buttered heat-resistant container, bake on the middle shelf of the oven for 10 minutes at Gas Mark 4, and serve with cut lemon.

THE TUNA RICE BOWL

Simple, filling food for a teenage buffet.

Ingredients: 12 peeled black olives; 24 whole green olives; 1lb rice; grated rind and strained juice of 1 lemon; ½ pint French dressing (pp.180-81); 4 sliced, hard-boiled eggs; 2 halved, de-pithed, de-pipped, thinly sliced pimentos; 7½oz tin tuna fish, broken into small pieces; 1 lettuce or endive.

Method: Cook rice in plenty of fast-boiling, slightly salted water for 11½ minutes, strain and chill. When cold, stir in lemon rind and juice and then pimento strips. Wash and tear lettuce or endive. Line into (preferably) wooden salad bowl. Turn rice mixture onto the salad bed. Arrange the pieces of tuna on the rice. Intersperse with green and black olives and at the moment of service pour on French dressing. Serve with hot garlic bread (pp.265-6).

TURBOT FOR A BUFFET
(Turbot en Chaudfroid)

Ingredients: 1 whole turbot (and 1 large fish kettle in which to poach it, or do not go on with this recipe!); butter; salt; pepper; fresh or dried fennel (substitute bay leaves and parsley stalks if necessary).

Method: Oil a sheet of turkey-width foil, enough to enclose the turbot completely and *loosely*. Rub the dull side of the foil liberally with butter. Lay on a sprig of fennel, or a parsley stalk and 2 bay leaves. Sprinkle with salt and pepper and lay down the turbot. Rub the top surface of the fish liberally with butter. Lay on a sprig of fennel, or 2 bay leaves and a parsley stalk. Season with salt and pepper and enclose, curling the foil edges very tightly indeed over each other but keeping the actual parcel loose. Immerse in a fish kettle containing sufficient cold water to cover. Bring to a gentle simmer and poach with extreme gentleness for about 20 minutes to ½ hour depending on the size of the fish. Lift out, uncover, take off the top skin and lay the largest possible dish upside down just above the turbot while someone else levers up the fish with two slices. Then, as your assistant presses upwards, press down with the dish and the pair of you turn the fish over! This is the way we get a whole hot fish onto its garnishing site without breakage. Rehearse it dummy first with a board instead of the fish. Now you can remove the underside of the foil and skin the fish.

From this moment onwards, presentation is a matter of employing each garnish effectively. One of the easiest ways of obtaining a very good appearance is to brush the surface of the turbot, when cold, with aspic that is at the syrupy stage. Allow this to set and then trim off a clean line all round where the aspic has slipped onto the border of the dish. Scrape the trimmings back into a bowl, re-melt and stir into an equal quantity of mayonnaise (pp.182-3). This mixture can then be piped through a nylon icing bag in a diagonal trellis with about 2in spaces between each line.

Start at the head and work diagonally right down to the tail, just drawing straight lines with the pipe 2in apart. Then reverse and cross these lines with another set of lines 2in apart. The centre of each diamond can be decorated with a tiny tuft of parsley, a slice of stuffed olive or merely a rosette of mayonnaise. Then fork up aspic which has been allowed to set, arrange a narrow edging of this froth around the fish to define its outline and stick a tuft of parsley in its mouth.

WHITEBAIT
(Blanchailles)

These are an excellent forerunner to the Christmas bird. There are just a few simple rules to be remembered. The little fishes are not topped and tailed! They are fried '*entier*' after passing through flour and lightly shaking off the surplus. Do *not* dip the fish in flour until you are ready to fry them. The oil for frying must be hot enough (where a thermometer is available, 390–400°F) to sizzle away angrily from a scrap of dipped-in raw potato. Only a few whitebait may be fried at a time, unless a cloggy mass is desired. A frying basket should be thinly lined out with the floured fish. They only take a few moments to fry. As soon as they turn colour they are ready. Do not over-fry.

If you remember these things, 10 minutes will suffice to fry enough for 6–8 persons. Heap them onto a paper d'oyley on a warmed dish. Serve with cayenne pepper, cut lemon and crustless, leaf-thin brown bread and butter.

MEAT, GAME AND POULTRY

The trouble with buying today is that the simple basic knowledge of what is 'quality' and what is *not* has become desperately complicated by the existence of so many additional deceitful practices. These constitute extra pitfalls for the unwary.

Most of us know that a thick, short fat ham is a far better buy than a long thin one and that it is better to buy two small legs of lamb than one large one. The little chaps have a succulence and sweetness of flavour advantage over the big ones.

Similarly it is pretty common knowledge that beef must be well hung, clear bright red, *fringed*, not streaked, with clear light-coloured fat. It only remains to establish that you know when making any of these purchases and chuck the ball right into the butcher's court. If he replies, 'Oh yes, madam,' to the query, 'Has this beef been sufficiently "hung"?' you can then storm back with an offending tough slice and demand explanation and compensation. Make him taste it if it is tough – a nice practical conversion of the 'eating his own words' phrase!

But – and we know the rhetorical question is sloppy and only plead for it in this instance as *absolutely essential* – does everyone know when buying poultry and game if the birds have been in the deep freeze? We wonder! We present our case and then we leave the rest to you.

You can go along to your poulterer, choose from the array above your head, but still you may never know whether that bird is fresh or 'fresh frozen'. Indeed you may not care.

However, if you do, you may as well realise that many birds are bulk frozen dangling from bars and left hanging in their freezing chamber until the time comes to thaw them and re-hang them in the shop.

So ask straight out: 'Is this bird fresh or frozen?' for you need not fear an untrue reply from any reputable poulterer.

Because of dehydration the answer to this question affects the cooking. We recommend busy housewives to use the natural sauce that is drawn from a turkey cooked in foil.

Some birds will yield a far higher quantity of natural sauce than others, but the larger quantity is not always the best in flavour. A fresh turkey, hung in normal storage through the normal lines of communication from producer to vendor, will have dehydrated. Therefore it will make less, though possibly more highly flavoured, natural sauce than one which is wrapped, sealed and then frozen, partly because the process eliminates the period of exposure and partly because these birds are washed before wrapping and sealing.

Where dehydration has occurred (bulk freezing 'on the hook' or slow transportation unfrozen) we have found that very liberal buttering before foil wrapping helps the moistening process.

Where a bird is very moist, we use very little butter and reduce the natural sauce by a few minutes' simmering after the bird has been dished up and the liquor transferred to a small pan.

In the case of frozen birds pre-treatment is essential. We allow a minimum of three days before cooking a bird that arrives in its frozen state. Unless you are very experienced at the thawing game, rip off any wrapping immediately and then leave the bird for 24 hours in ordinary domestic refrigeration. Remove to the kitchen and leave for a further 24 hours. Remove the polythene bag of liver, neck and so on, prepare for the oven and cook the next day.

Remember, too, that the flavour of a 6lb bird is entirely different from that of a 20lb turkey; that the large bird yields a better balance of brown to white meat; and that a big, well-fattened bird can be full of flavour if he has put on weight *fast*, whereas a big-boned fellow of considerable weight is sometimes suspect as being too elderly to cook really well.

The springing, pliable breastbone is always indicative of youthfulness. Young turkeys have smooth, black legs; those of old ones are rough and reddish. Freshly killed turkeys have bright eyes.

Norfolk ones are still rated highest, but whichever you buy ask for it to be delivered plucked, drawn and trussed.

HOW TO JUDGE POULTRY, GAME AND MEAT

Young Fowls – the cocks should have short spurs, smooth black legs and close dark vents. Young hens should have smooth legs and smooth combs. The young tender bird has a flexible tip to the breastbone.

Young Geese and Ducks should be free from hairs and have pliable yellow feet and yellow bills.

Young Pigeon should have supple feet and firm vents. Any discoloration is evidence that the bird is stale.

Rabbits and Hares – look for a narrow cleft in the lip, a stiff young body and smooth, sharp claws. Just be sure to turn the claws sideways. If they are young these claws will crack. Young ears are supple and easily bent. If the forepaws break easily, they are sure to be tender. Knees should be large; necks should be stumpy.

Meat – remember always that the younger the animal, the lighter the flesh; the older the animal, the darker the flesh. Fine quality beef is a good red. Old cow meat is dark in colour, coarse grained and cased in a mean layer of yellow fat. On good beef the fat is light, butter coloured and ½in or more in thickness.

Sucking Pig should be between eight and ten weeks old.

THE SOAKING OF HAMS AND GAMMON

This is a controversial matter. Bacon experts stress that six hours is enough for such cuts as gammon, corner gammon, collar, forehock, etc. and this we know to be perfectly correct, *if* you like slightly salty bacon. We do not, therefore we insist on a very long soaking indeed for either bacon or ham. Our experience is that the taste develops in opposite ratio to the incidence of salt, but we must leave you to choose whether you want it 'sweet' or not. When you have soaked whatever piece you have chosen, proceed with any of the bacon recipes as given on pp.148-50.

TRUSSING

Two things are needed: a skewer (wooden is best) and a length of thin, strong string. For a 4–6lb bird use 1¾ yards of string, increasing proportionately to the increased bulk of the bird.

Place the bird on the table, breast uppermost, neck end nearest to you. Pull the legs towards you and down as far as possible. Drive the point of the skewer through the fat upper flesh on the right-hand leg, then through the skin between wing and wing tip, then through the bird, through the skin between wing and wing tip of the left-hand wing and finally through the down-drawn left leg. By this one skewering, wings and legs are held firmly in position.

Now take the string, turn the bird round and tie the leg tips securely together in the centre of the string so that two equal lengths remain left and right. Work with these simultaneously. Turn the bird over. Cross the string round the parson's nose so that it is firmly held; draw the string tightly to the protruding left and right ends of the skewer. Wrap the string with one firm turn round each skewer as close to the bird as possible. Draw tightly across the bird's base and tie securely. Turn the bird over and you will find that it is as neat as a pin and perfectly secure. Always remember to pull the string tightly. Loose string means an untidy and insecure truss. Tight string means a clean truss and a firmly held bird.

OPEN OVEN ROASTING

Beef. In pursuance of the policy which serves the majority – under-done beef with a crisp edge – and still leaves something for the odd bod who likes beef well done (synonym ruined), we have found that the most successful method is to heat a thick iron pan until white hot and sear every scrap of exterior of chosen piece so that the juices thus become sealed in. At this point we assume that you have invested in a little inexpensive meat thermometer – you really do need it. Place the seared beef in a meat baking tin, which has just been brushed on the base with some clean fat. Roast one shelf above centre at Gas Mark 6 and after the first 45 minutes shove the thermometer through the centre. The dial will faithfully record for you rare or under-done, medium or overdone or ruined. Now relax.

Ducks. A good-sized duck: centre shelf, Gas Mark 5, 85 minutes. A young duckling: centre shelf, Gas Mark 5, 55–60 minutes.

Geese. See pp.159-60.

Roast Leg of Pork with proper crackling. This is the exception to all other rules. We have found it infallible; the end product is crackling that flies, and exquisitely tender, well-cooked meat – pork should never be eaten under-done. This is really little more than a hard and fast set of rules. (1) Pork should be properly and deeply scored; each rind section should measure little more than ¼in. (2) Pork should then be rubbed vigorously with handfuls of coarse salt. (3) When the upper surface is completely serrated with little salt ridges, place in a meat baking tin without fat. (4) Place on the centre shelf at preheated Gas Mark 4 and allow 2¾ hours for a good family-sized leg of pork or 3¼ hours for a really large one. (5) Then baste thoroughly with the fat that will have accumulated. If your oven permits, raise the shelf to the next height up, return the pork to the oven, raise the setting to Gas Mark 8. Leave for 15 minutes, baste again, return to the same position and temperature for a further 20 minutes. Now see the crackling fly, even when the pork is cold.

Turkey. Fifteen minutes to the pound after an initial 30 minutes for the first pound. Gas Mark 4/5. Always remember to cover the upper breast of the bird with a piece of kitchen foil after the first 30 minutes of roasting and until the last 15 minutes of roasting.

It is implicit that all open roasting will include basting.

WHEN YOU CARVE

See that you have a long, slim-handled French knife, which must not only be extremely sharp when the first slice is cut with it but must be kept so by frequent re-sharpenings even during the carving session. Study a professional carver at work in a contemporary restaurant.

Mr Edwards at the Savoy is a great and classic exponent of the Modern Art of Carving. Count how often during one session he re-sharpens knives which were sharpened to 'musicians' absolute pitch' (or whatever is the carving equivalent) before the session began. Then copy Mr Edwards, who would never dream of handicapping himself from the onset by working with inadequate tools.

A certain basic knowledge of the anatomy of the bird or joint is essential. If the carver is unaware of *where* the bones will be encountered and where the bone joints lie, he or she will be in just about the same mess as the surgeon who does not know where the appendix lies and so slashes about at random, thereby depriving his victim of any further chance of gastronomic orgies!

Start understanding the art of carving by settling down with a raw bird and articulating the wings and legs, doing a little braille work with the fingertips over the carcase, until from wishbone to parson's nose the bone structure has become properly familiar. Do the same with joints. Understand the lie of the bone on a saddle. Learn the shape so that your knife understands it when you stand up with a flourish and the vegetables begin to cool. Then you will reduce time-waste and ensure settling to a hot plateful yourself. *Remember those bones are quite unyielding*. Indeed, the policy of a carver is in inverse ratio to our policy of living. In life you go slap up to an obstacle and force your way through it. To go round is to double the size of the obstacle next time. In carving *you must go round*. You simply learn the shortest way and the one closest to the bone or obstacle.

The real trouble of course lies not in any refusal to learn, nor in any lack of intelligence. It is part of the same racial complex which inhibits the British from asking 'abroad', lest they make fools of themselves anywhere. As in foreign countries the British remain silent rather than run the risk, so they are reluctant to 'waste the butcher's time' or 'bother him with my ignorance' – quite losing sight of the fact that all of us adore showing someone else something we know really well ourselves. It flatters the ego – so go and flatter your butcher's and poultryman's ego, and enable yourself thereafter to get the best out of your meat, game and poultry.

The following small points may help to make the overall job easier:

1. Remove all skewers and trussing string.
2. Cut through the skin that holds the legs to the breast. Drive the prongs of a fork in from the breast side outwards and force the legs out until, as they bend away from the carcase, they disclose the base joint, which can then be cut through cleanly. Lay this severed leg on the flat and cut through at the joint. This reduces leg and

thigh to two portions. Thereafter this meat may be sliced off comfortably from the legs of a large bird. In a small one each provides part of a portion to which breast slices should be added.

3. Cut off the wings to left and right of the wishbone flesh, so that a small crescent of white meat is attached to each wing and the wishbone is left free. Divide these wings, separating wing from *aileron* or wing tip. In the case of a small bird, set aside the *ailerons* for the stock pot. In large birds these again constitute part-portions to which breast meat must be added.

4. Remove the parson's nose (regarded in our family as carver's perquisite!).

5. You are now left with a limbless carcase from which it is child's play to take easy, even slices, provided that knife of yours is still really sharp. We do not carve thin slices from the breast ever, because we cut all game and poultry in the French style, but feel this traditional season is not the time for forcing our taste upon you.

6. Once the limbs have gone, it is comparatively simple to remove the stuffings from either end of the bird without extraordinary contortions, wangling a spoon into the cavity via intruding legs and wings.

7. Do the carving in the kitchen. Then reassemble the Christmas bird. Re-warm under foil and send to table for Instant Service in a large household and a hot portion for Pa.

ON ROASTING YOUR CHRISTMAS BIRD

Let no one delude anyone that there is a replacement to equal flavour for the good old-fashioned spit-roasted, well-basted

bird, or for the oven-roasted one, which is regularly and liberally basted with the very best butter at decently short intervals.
These two methods represent the counsel of perfection, easy
enough to achieve in France in the good old days when Grand-
mère sat in her rocker, ladle in hand, and within easy reach of
the oven door!

There are substitutes of course. Some of them are very good.
Among the best is foil roasting, provided that it is done properly. Totally inaccurate information was widely disseminated
some years ago when foil roasting was little known in Britain.
Canada had it years before us. English cookery writers rushed
into print, warning their readers that all foil-roasted birds
would be pallid and uncoloured on top unless the foil was
completely removed for the last 15 to 20 minutes of baking.

All this was poppycock, which a little proper testing before
writing would have proved.

The facts are as follows:

Items of meat, game or poultry to be roasted in foil (which
    method enables the cook to dispense with basting) *must be
    wrapped very loosely indeed.* If meat, game or poultry are
    tightly enclosed in foil they will be insulated from the heat
    for such a very long time and so effectively that a bird can
    remain practically raw in a hot oven for a considerable
    period.
A tight wrapping of foil ensures insulation.
A loose wrapping of foil enables the heat to penetrate.
If meat, game and poultry are not properly prepared for oven
    roasting in foil, the results may well be disappointing.
Rub the turkey liberally with coarse salt and coarsely ground
    pepper. Rub with softened butter. Wrap up loosely in the
    foil. Bake at between Gas Mark 4 and 5 and allow 40 minutes
    for the first pound and 20 minutes for every pound thereaf-

ter, whereas a lesser time is allowed per pound for open roasting.

Note. Please do not be offended – but do remember the butter goes on the *bird* and not on the *foil*. We hesitate to point this out, but we have been asked, 'Do I put the butter inside or outside the foil?'

Here is the scale to which we have worked for a number of years:

All poultry up to 14lb: 30 minutes for first pound, 20 minutes per pound thereafter. For every additional pound between 15 and 20, 15 minutes per pound. For every additional pound between 20 and 25, 10 minutes per pound.

HOW TO CARVE A COLD TURKEY

When hosts and hostesses are the working staff, we regard it as wasteful to spend time carving when we could be talking to our friends, so we carve the bird in advance, restore its shape and leave everyone to help themselves.

Method: With a pair of game scissors for the fortunate, or a pair of gardening secateurs for the inventive, cut the whole of the breast cage of the bird away, starting at the neck end and cutting round level with the parson's nose so that when the top is completely severed, the base shell is a hollow one ready to receive the carved meat. Attach home-made pie frills to the unsightly leg bones. Carve all the breast meat and carve an equal quantity of any cold, cooked meat such as ham, tongue, salami or liver sausage. Replace the carved meat in the central cavity in layers, set vertically, 1 ham, 1 tongue, 1 stuffing, 1 turkey – so that when all is replaced the top of the bird is rebuilt by the tops of assorted slices.

BOILED TURKEY

There is an old adage which says 'a turkey boiled is a turkey spoiled'. Like most generalisations, this one has its exceptions! To achieve a very edible boiled turkey first bone the bird, which means, for the average cook, get the poulterer to do the job. Just make sure he *knows* what he is doing and bones out from the neck end without any incisions across the breast!

Cover the base of the boned interior with French stuffing, lay in a cooked, skinned tongue and finally fill up with more stuffing until the original bird-shape is restored. Remember that the tongue must only be cooked *firm* and not 'tender', otherwise it will be overcooked at the finish. Thrust stemless, unskinned, open mushrooms between the skin and the flesh, or, if means and taste allow, do this with thinly sliced truffles. Salt and pepper the bird liberally. Wrap in butter papers, wrap in clean linen, enclose in a sheet of kitchen foil and sink into good stock. Simmer until tender. Dissolve 1½oz butter in a sauce saucepan, stir in 1½oz flour and, when the mixture forms a soft ball in the pan, add a large wineglassful of Madeira. Stir in, add small quantities of the stock in which the turkey was cooked, stirring well between each addition, and so continue until the sauce is just a shade too thick. Correct the seasoning and 'finish' with about 5–7½fl oz double cream. Dish the bird on a bed of mixed, diced, steamed vegetables, and remember to carve across in slices exactly as if you were dealing with a Swiss roll. Thus each portion will be turkey meat enclosing forcemeat and tongue. Ladle the sauce over, and set vegetables at the side.

The mixed vegetables can be diced carrots, turnips, potato, or small artichokes, potatoes, turnips and carrots steamed separately, or artichoke bottoms heaped with mixed diced vegetables.

CURRIED TURKEY
(Dinde au Kari)

This follows the method of an authentic Goa Lamb Curry, replacing the lamb with pieces of the brown meat from a turkey.

Method: Put 5 tablespoons of olive oil (in lieu of Ghee?) in a thick, shallow pan. Add 3–4 sliced medium onions and a crushed garlic clove. Cook gently till fairly soft. Sprinkle on a small handful of grated fresh (or desiccated) coconut and work in 1–2 tablespoons of Masala paste. Add a small ladleful of stock and work up; continue doing so until the mixture is of the required consistency. This should be fairly thick. Fold in the meat (allowing 2 teacupsful) at the last, as it has already been cooked, and just give it time to get really hot. Serve with plain rice – 1lb fast boiled for 11½ minutes in slightly salted water, strained and that is it – plus two side dishes: one of halved, lengthwise-split, buttered-fried bananas and one of leaf-thin slices of fresh coconut, also fried in butter.

GRANDMAMA'S ROAST TURKEY
(La Dinde de Madame Sortain-Hancock 1896)

'It was a turkey! He could never have stood upon his legs, that bird. He would have snapped 'em off short in a minute, like sticks of sealing-wax.'

Charles Dickens

Fill the belly of a home-fed turkey with peeled raw potatoes, the thinly peeled zest of 2 lemons and 2 oranges and a large sprig of rosemary that these may sweat during the roasting time and thus infuse the flesh with their fragrance and with their moisture as they steam inside.

Tuck very fine slices of black truffles beneath the skin of all the breast so that the flesh is wholly and neatly covered.

Set the bird upon a bed of chopped pork fat and cover completely with pig's caul [as used for making faggots, F. & J.C.]. Be sure to baste well after the caul has 'shed' its fat. Remove the caul for the last 20 minutes of roasting. See that the oven is mild and even. [Gas Mark 4, F. & J.C.].

SOUTH AMERICAN TURKEY
(Dinde Sud-Americain)

This is an acquired taste! It certainly is different.

Marinade Ingredients: 2–4 peeled garlic cloves; 1 large red or green pimento, split, de-pithed and de-seeded; 2 large Spanish onions; 2–3 bay leaves; 2 rounded tablespoon milled parsley; strained juice of 6 lemons; 6fl oz wine vinegar; 35fl oz inexpensive dry white wine.

Method: Mince or emulsify the garlic, pimento, onions and bay, mix with the liquids and work well into the bird's interior and exterior. Set the bird in a deep container as near its own size as possible. Cover with the marinade and turn frequently for 14 hours.

Stuffing Ingredients (for vent end): 14oz peeled, cooked chestnuts, chopped roughly; 3 finely chopped hard-boiled eggs; 8oz soaked, stoned, chopped prunes; 1 large, raw grated onion; 4oz butter; 4fl oz olive oil; 15oz manioc flour.

Method: Heat the oil and butter together and fry the onions gently until soft but not browned. Stir in the prunes, chestnuts and eggs, and gradually as these fry sprinkle on the manioc flour, working it in with the back of a wooden spoon until all is absorbed. Fill into the bird.

Stuffing Ingredients (for neck end): ½lb peeled, chopped Spanish olives; 8oz minced gammon or ham; scraped turkey liver; minced heart and gizzard; 2oz butter; 2fl oz olive oil; 1 finely chopped onion; 1 tablespoon finely chopped or milled parsley; 1lb manioc flour; 2 eggs.

Method: Soften the butter, add the oil and all remaining dry ingredients, and work in one or two eggs according to their size. Stuff into the neck end of the bird.

Cover the bird with strips of unsalted pork fat. Set in a baking tin containing the remainder of the marinade and roast one shelf below centre at Gas Mark 4, basting frequently.

TURKEY CHAUDFROID

This is merely cold turkey, or any other cold, cooked bird, cut into very neat slices or sections and masked with Chaudfroid Sauce. This is in fact aspic softened to the syrupy stage in equal parts with the following smooth white sauce:

Dissolve 1½oz butter in a small pan and stir in 1½oz flour. When the mixture forms a soft ball in the pan, leaving the sides and base cleanly, pour on 5fl oz of white wine and allow the mixture to boil. Then beat until very smooth and in small quantities add ¾ pint of milk, beating very thoroughly between each addition. If well made, this sauce will be as smooth as silk and *glistening*. Add an equal quantity of aspic to this, beat well and allow to cool down to just above blood heat, which is the point at which you spoon it over the chosen meat.

If working with neat, meaty portions, set these fairly wide apart on a rack above an absolutely spotless shallow dish (to catch the drips so that you can use them again!). Spoon the *chaudfroid* over the portions, scoop up those (clean) drips, return them to the pan, re-soften the *chaudfroid* for a moment or two and give a second coat for a faultless finish. When set, trim with a small pair of scissors. Set on a dish and either arrange forked aspic between the portions, or pipe coloured creamed potato decoratively or – and this is more ambitious – make a further batch of aspic and mask the entire dish with a light coat of pale golden aspic before garnishing with scraps of parsley, pimento, etc. The alternative, simpler method is to arrange a design of sliced meat on a large dish overlapping the slices until they resemble a flat fish – a kind of headless turbot shape. Then this can be covered in one swoop with *Sauce Chaudfroid*, masked with aspic and only the outer rim garnished.

ALABAMA GAMMON

Ingredients: 3–4lb gammon joint; 8oz soft brown (pieces) sugar; 1 large or 2 small eggs; 1½ pints apple cider vinegar; 1 level tablespoon dry mustard; 12 prunes.

Method: Soak the prunes and the gammon for 48 hours in cold water, or when feeling lavish replace water with 50% rough cider. Place in a pan and *almost* cover with the water or water and cider mixture. Add ½ pint of the vinegar, bring to the boil and simmer, allowing 20 minutes to every 1lb. Lift out, cool sufficiently to handle, remove skin and place in a dry baking tin. Mix the egg, mustard and sugar in a basin. Coat the gammon with this paste. Pour the remaining vinegar around the gammon and bake for 50 minutes at Gas Mark 6, basting every 15 minutes. Lift the gammon onto a flat, oval dish. Surround with pan liquor when skimmed, simmered down to a good flavour and thickened with potato flour mixed with a little cider or water. Decorate with stoned prunes, leaves of chicory, potato baskets of potato puffs, pineapple rings and glacé cherries.

Note: The remaining liquor should be chilled, skimmed meticulously and reduced as a base for a family soup. When reduced to the degree that gives a good flavour when tasted, soak ¼lb split peas to every quart of liquor. The next day cook, with a faggot of herbs and outside stems of a celery head, and add in a slice or two of rough-cut gammon trimming. Emulsify or sieve, correct seasoning and serve with plenty of diced croûtons.

FLEMISH GAMMON OR HAM IN BEER

Soak chosen cut for 36 hours in cold water. Drain and set in a deep container just large enough to take the meat. Cover with draught ale and water in the proportions 1 part ale to 3 parts water. Turn regularly in this liquor for 3 days. Then simmer in this liquor until just tender. Do not remove until cold.

GAMMON BAKED IN A CRUST
(Le Bacon en croute)

This is an old country method of considerable merit. It calls for dried raspberry leaves so please make a point of storing some in the early autumn. Select unblemished leaves, bunch and tie and hang upside down in a draught until absolutely dry. Then tie up in black tissue paper to conserve flavour and protect from dust. The method is then simple:

Soak for 36 hours (if you like it sweet) and simmer the gammon in stock or water till almost tender. Chill and skin it. Cover the fat upper surface completely with raspberry leaves. Prepare a thick flour and water pastry; stir but do not beat it, or the pastry will surely crack during baking. Roll out the pastry without violent pressure to avoid giving it elasticity. Cover the centre with raspberry leaves. Set the gammon on this. Wrap up loosely in the pastry. Seal the edges well together with more water and bake one shelf above centre at Gas Mark 6 for 1 hour. Break off the crust and send the gammon immediately to table.

Note: There is no French word for 'Bacon' and mediaeval French references abound for 'Le Grand Bacon'.

SWEET SOUR HAM
(Jambon Aigre-Doux)

This method is equally applicable to gammon.

Soak a ham for 24 hours in cold water. Place in a large pan and cover with cider. Add 1lb unsoaked prunes, 4oz sultanas, 1 Faggot of Herbs (p.160) and turn twice daily in this mixture for 3 days. Cook in the marinade until tender. Remove, skin and keep warm. Strain the liquor and set the prunes (removing stones) and sultanas around the ham on a warm dish. Reduce the liquor by simmering to 1 quart. Thicken with a little potato flour blended with 2½fl oz sherry and stirred into the liquor – this thickens it clearly and fast; or thicken with 4 egg yolks beaten with 8fl oz double cream and stirred into the liquor (do not continue cooking the liquor at all with this method or the eggs will surely curdle). Pour the liquor over the ham or as much as will glaze it, and send to table with the remainder in a sauce boat.

THE BARON OF BEEF
(Un Grand Aloyan de Boeuf)

Henry VIII, so the story runs, was so delighted with the appearance of what the French term '*un grand aloyau de boeuf*' that he promptly dubbed it. Thus it became a baron or sir-loin! Today in France a 'saddle' of mutton or of lamb is also called '*Un baron d'agneau ou de mouton*'.

Treatment is simple. Insist upon well-hung meat, which has never had the remotest contact with deep, quick or any other kind of freeze. Allow to rest in the room in which it will be cooked for 24 hours beforehand. Spit roast whenever possible; or, placing a small piece of raw beef suet above and below the meat in the pan, roast high up in the oven at Gas Mark 8 for 15 minutes and then reduce the heat to Gas Mark 4. Use a meat thermometer to test for medium, rare or 'ruined' (well done right through). Do *not* put dripping or any other fat into the pan. Just cover the bottom with cold water. Baste after the first 50 minutes, and then baste every 15 minutes. Treat with profound respect – remember the French adage, '*Les chefs sont faits; les rôtisseurs sont nés*' – or 'Chefs are made – roasters are born'.

BEEFSTEAK AND KIDNEY PUDDING (AND PIE)

We cannot subscribe to the method which requires the cook to place raw meat in a prepared suet crust and steam both together. Sorry!

Ingredients for Beefsteak and Kidney Mixture: 3lb diced, lean stewing steak; 1lb diced ox kidney; 1lb small-diced carrots; 1lb very thinly sliced onions; seasoned flour; 1 teaspoon Worcestershire sauce; 1 level dessertspoon concentrated tomato purée; either stock to cover or, when feeling extravagant, 8fl oz inexpensive red cooking-type wine and the balance in stock to cover.

Method: Mix all prepared meat and vegetables in a large bowl, sprinkle seasoned flour over all and turn until all are thoroughly coated. Turn into a roomy casserole, add the remaining ingredients, stir, cover and cook one shelf below centre at Gas Mark 4 for at least 1¼ hours or until the carrots are just firm to the teeth when tested. Cool.

Note 1. The quantities given for the above filling are sufficient to make one pie (inside measurements of the dish 7¼in ×

11in × 3½in) and one pudding (8½in diameter pudding basin).

Note 2. Prepare seasoned flour by sifting together 2½oz flour, 1 rounded teaspoon salt, 1 rounded teaspoon dry English mustard, 1 rounded teaspoon powdered paprika; 1 rounded eggspoon freshly milled black pepper; 1 level teaspoon dried oregano and 1 level teaspoon dried basil.

To Make Beefsteak and Kidney Pudding

Ingredients for Suet Crust: 15oz sifted flour; 7½oz suet; 1 scant level teaspoon salt; cold water to bind.

Method: Mix all dry ingredients together in a roomy bowl. Add water gradually and work up with a knife to form a smooth dough of pastry consistency. Turn onto a floured surface and roll out into a large rough circle just over ¼in in thickness. Roll up on a rolling pin, unroll over your chosen, buttered, floured basin and press into the base and sides. Cut off surplus at the top edge with a knife. Fill to within 1in of the top with the cold meat mixture. Draw the edges of the pastry over the mixture. Roll out the trimmings to form a lid, wet the edges of the pastry surfaces, press the lid on top, trim off the edges and press down all round to secure. Cover with a circle of foil cut large enough to allow you to make a generous 1in pleated fold in the centre. This will open out as you press foil round the sides and thus allow room for expansion. Place in a steamer and steam without allowing water to come off the boil for 2 hours.

To Make Beefsteak and Kidney Pie

Place the remaining meat mixture in a pie dish. Press a pie funnel down into the centre. Roll out bought or home-made puff pastry to ¼in thickness, cover to the rim of the pie dish, pinch the edges neatly. Make a hole in the centre so that air can escape through the funnel. Decorate with a few pastry 'leaves', brush with egg wash (pp.129-30) and bake at Gas Mark 6, middle shelf, to a rich golden brown. Serve either hot or cold.

Note 1. Before putting on the pastry crust, the cooked, cooled meat mixture may be covered with 1 dozen oysters and their juices. Prod them down gently, add 4 quartered (lengthwise) hard-boiled eggs and then put on the crust. The oysters – inevitably – are optional!

Note 2. Any surplus meat liquor may be handed separately in a sauceboat.

BEER AND BONES

Get the butcher to cut good beef bones into convenient lengths and remind him forcefully you only want the ones with plenty of marrow in them. Brush the cut ends with made English mustard, cover with a thick paste of flour and water. Wrap in cloths, tie up and sink in fast-boiling water to cook for 40–45 minutes. Serve with plenty of hot crustless toast, salt and pepper. The marrow is dug out with old-fashioned silver marrow scoops or lobster prongs and spread onto the toast. Both are washed down with generous libations of cold (not English luke-warm) beer.

BURGUNDIAN YORKSHIRE PUDDING
(La Gougère Bourguignonne)

Ingredients: Scant 5fl oz milk; 1oz butter; 1 eggspoon salt; 2½oz flour; 2 eggs; 1oz diced Gruyère; ½oz grated Gruyère; 1 small raw, beaten egg; ½oz diced Gruyère.

Method: Place the milk, butter and salt in a small, thick pan. Bring to the boil. Toss in the flour; let this seethe for a moment, then turn out the gas and beat well. Beat the eggs in singly. Stir in 1oz diced Gruyère. Spread into a well-buttered shallow cooking tin (a Victoria sponge tin is best). Cover the surface with beaten, raw egg. Dot with ½oz diced Gruyère. Sprinkle with grated Gruyèré. Bake in a preheated oven one shelf above centre at Gas Mark 8 for 25 minutes.

CHESTNUTS FOR GOOSE
(Les Marrons Normande)

This is Norman, shatteringly fattening and highly indigestible, but almost indivisible from our concept of the perfect Christmas Goose.

Nick, boil and skin chestnuts, remembering to boil a good many more than you will need as the incidence of breakage is very high.* Dissolve lots of butter very slowly in a small pan. Pack the chestnuts with great care into a heat-resistant container and completely smother them with melted butter and cover lightly with foil. Place them on the floor of the oven at Gas Mark 4 and let them cook slowly until they are like little chestnut sponges. Then, when you bite a piece, the butter runs down your chin as with the best crumpets!

* Use broken pieces for Brussels Sprouts with Chestnuts (pp.188-9).

CHICKEN IN THE MANNER OF LYONS, FRANCE
(Poulet Demi-deuil)

Ingredients: 1 large prime roasting fowl; at least 1 gallon of good clear white stock; 1lb mushroom cups; 6 small or 8 large quartered carrots; 12 shallots or very smallest onions; salt and pepper to season; 1 Faggot of Herbs (p.160).

Method: This dish is cooked on top of the stove in a lidded container, which must be deep enough to allow you to invert a stone jam jar or heat-resistant pudding basin on the base and stand the prepared chicken on a heat-resistant plate on top of it. Place the jar or basin in a pan, pour on the stock and add the carrots, onions and faggot of herbs. Stalk the mushrooms, chop the stalks finely and add them to the liquor. Then working from the neck end of the bird, run your fingers gently and carefully between the upper skin and the upper flesh so that you can finally pass your hand underneath from end to end. You can facilitate this if you pinch the skin all over the upper part of the bird to loosen it first. Then push the mushroom cups, white side uppermost, between skin and flesh until the bird's figure looks somewhat remarkable but all mushrooms are tucked inside. Remember that the more skin you can loosen, the more mushrooms you can tuck in down the sides as well as the breast. Sprinkle the layered bird lightly with salt and pepper. Place on the heat-resistant plate, stand on the inverted basin or jar, cover with a lid and simmer until the bird is tender and the carrots and onions are cooked, by which time you will understand the meaning of the French phrase 'demi-deuil' or half-mourning. The only difference is that the French use sliced truffles; these are known in France as the black diamonds of French gastronomy and are almost as costly in England!

To Dish Up. Place the bird on a heated serving dish, surround neatly with the strained vegetables and keep warm in the oven. Bring the remaining liquor to the boil, maintain until reduced by 1 pint, strain, taste, correct seasoning with salt and pepper, ladle enough over the bird and vegetables to moisten, hand the rest separately and provide soup plates rather than ordinary meat plates, as we suppose you also do for boiled beef and carrots.

Note: Do not worry if you find yourself with surplus liquor on your hand; it is merely a residue of ready-to-serve soup when you have reheated it.

COLD COLLOPS OF HARE
(Medaillons de Lièvre froid)

The large hare yields two splendid collops of meat down either side of his backbone and it is from this meat that we can make an excellent cold dish. One should not forget, however, that hare is a lean meat with a tendency to being a dry one if insufficiently nourished during cooking. Therefore the collops should be darned with strips of pork fat in and out every inch and these strips cut off to tuft ½in above the flesh till each collop looks like an elongated porcupine. There is a special needle for this job. When it is done, the collops are placed in the following marinade for 2 days.

Marinade: 1 breakfastcupful olive oil; 1 tumbler of strong red wine; 1 sliced onion; 2–3 parsley stalks; 12 peeled green olives; a few peppercorns; a blade of mace; 2 bay leaves; thinly peeled rind of a small lemon. Mix all together, pour over the collops in a casserole and turn twice daily. After 2 days add 5fl oz of both red wine and stock, cover closely and cook slowly one shelf above centre at Gas Mark 3 until the collops are tender. Strain off the marinade and reduce by relentless simmering to a meat glaze about 5–6 tablespoonfuls all told. Place the two cooked collops lengthwise down a long narrow dish. When absolutely cold mask with the meat glaze. Encircle with any available green herbs and hand Oxford Sauce and Cumberland Sauce separately.

P.S. Of course you *can* have redcurrant jelly, but isn't it rather a pity?

COLD FILLET OF BEEF
(Filet de Boeuf au jus de viande)

Treat exactly as for Cold Collops of Hare (p.156), except that the mace is deleted from the marinade and 2 tablespoons of brandy with ½lb thinly sliced mushrooms added to it. Cooking is identical. After cooking and cooling, the fillet is laid down a long narrow dish and the strained liquor simmered down to 5–6 tablespoons of meat glaze. When the meat glaze masks the fillet, stamp a number of crescents from rolled-out puff pastry (pp.249-50), bake to a good, golden brown and set in lines down either side of the finished fillet. Arrange a large sprig of watercress at each end and serve with Duke of Windsor Salad or Salamagundy (p.205).

COLD GREEN OMELETTE
(Torta di Bleia)

This is the old French/Italian mountain border peasants' omelette. They used to clap slices between wedges of bread to take with them and eat at noon in the shade of the olive groves. '*Omelette Verte*' is Madame Baudoin's name for the sophisticated and urbane version which she serves in her *Caravane* of Hors d'Oeuvre at her famous *La Bonne Auberge* restaurant. In the Midi, *Bleia* is used. We substitute spinach for the grim reason we can rarely obtain *Bleia*, even in rather grand shops, and have been forced to bring seed from the border and raise it in our own garden.

Ingredients: To every 6 eggs take: 3oz grated Parmesan cheese; 1 teacupful dry, sieved, cooked spinach purée; 4oz finely minced veal; salt and pepper to season.

Method: Butter a straight-sided earthenware or heat-resistant container *very thickly indeed*. Whip up your eggs, add the remaining ingredients and stir them in slowly and not too thoroughly. Turn into the pot, cover with a lid and cook on the middle shelf at Gas Mark 2 until set. Leave until cold. The omelette will shrink away slightly from the sides of the pot. Turn onto a flat dish – it now resembles nothing so much as a round crusted cheese. Serve cold in slices like a cake or galantine.

COLD OXTAIL IN ASPIC
(Queue de Boeuf en gelee)

Ingredients: 2 large oxtails, home- or butcher-divided into 2–2. in sections; 1 rounded teaspoon each of milled parsley and salt; 1 rounded eggspoon milled black peppercorns; 2 bay leaves; 6fl oz cooking sherry; stock; 2 tablespoons wine vinegar; 2 separated egg whites; 2 crushed eggshells; lard or clarified meat or poultry fat; 1lb carrots, diced fine; 1.lb onions, diced fine; gelatine.

Method: Fry oxtail pieces briskly in your chosen fat. When well browned, layer into a casserole with carrots and onions. Add parsley, salt, pepper and bay leaves. Just cover meanly with stock, then with a lid or kitchen foil and cook at Gas Mark 3 in a position which depends upon the shape of the casserole. Reckon to allow a 4–5in clearance from the inside top of the oven. When the flesh is *really* tender (2.–3 hours), lift out the meat and set aside to cool. Strain the casserole contents into a roomy bowl. Either chill and remove the fat crust or do so immediately with pieces of kitchen paper towed across the top. Measure the cleared liquor. Simmer down to half the quantity. Add the sherry, wine vinegar, unbeaten egg whites and crushed eggshells, from which you have carefully removed the inner skins. Set the pan over a moderate heat and whip relentlessly until the mixture reaches boiling point, when a revolting scum will form, completely obscuring the liquor below. Remove the whisk, reduce the heat to absolute minimum, leave for 30 minutes, turn off the heat, then very slowly and carefully pour through a sieve lined with four folds of muslin. The result should be a golden to straw-coloured crystal-clear fluid. For every .pint of this fluid, allow .oz gelatine dissolved in 3–4 tablespoons cold water. When clear and syrupy, stir into clarified stock and allow to chill sufficiently for it to be of a heavy, syrupy consistency. Meanwhile arrange the cold oxtail pieces cut side uppermost in a panel on a long narrow dish or in a ring on a circular one. Pick all over the carrot and onion residue from first straining and remove any scraps of bay leaf which are adhering. Arrange in the centre panel of a narrow dish or fill in the ring made by the oxtail pieces on a round one. Pour syrupy aspic over all. If any remains, leave to set, whip with a fork and arrange as a foamy border outside the oxtail pieces on the narrow dish or around the outer side of the oxtail ring on the round one.

EASILY DIGESTIBLE ROAST GOOSE
(Oie Rôti sans graisse)

'There never was such a goose.'
Charles Dickens

Rub the bird all over with salt and milled black peppercorns, stand on a grill pan rack in a large, deep baking tin and then prick all over, *violently* and *thoroughly*, with a fine-pronged fork. *Then* the excessive fattiness will run during roasting time, thereby doing the basting for you. In the case of an excessively fatty bird it may well be necessary to pour off some of the accumulated fat at about half-time. Bake at Gas Mark 4 – allowing approximately 20 minutes per pound overall.

Note 1. By the above method the skin should be richly browned and quite crisp.

Note 2. The accumulated goose fat is perfectly splendid for making Raised Pie Pastry (p.167).

Note 3. If you want to cut the richness with a tart, refreshing flavour, peel and remove the central core from a number of the sharpest, smallest cooking apples obtainable, dip each one into melted butter and stuff them into the cavity of the bird. Withdraw the apples when dishing up, encircle the bird with them and at the moment of service scatter with finely grated orange rind and stick a bay leaf in the top of each.

THE FAGGOT OF HERBS
(Bouquet Garni)

Now that we have a proper herb garden, we have a great orgy in summer and muslin bags are put up with various blendings for use throughout the remainder of the year. While the season permits, we take our herbs from the plants, bushes, trees and shrubs. This is a question of opportunity so we offer a mixture for general use, which can be assembled at the lean end of the year (Christmas).

Ingredients: 1 trimmed outside stick celery; 2 dried bay leaves; 1 sprig dried thyme; 1 or 2 parsley stalks (when possible include a scrap of parsley root); 1 brown onion skin (all dry and crackling); 3–4 peppercorns; a blade of mace; IF you are lucky enough to corner and reserve some, a wisp of clean and fragrant hay.

Method: Tie all in a scrap of muslin. Affix a long string. *Then* you can immerse the bag but loop the string around the handle of the container. This eliminates all that frantic fishing about in a large pot from which you wish to remove your 'faggot'!

FRIED SANDWICHES

Ingredients: Sad, stale party sandwiches (filled with any savoury spreading mixture); 2 egg whites; 3oz sifted flour; 3fl oz cold water; frying oil; salt.

Method: Press the sandwiches firmly together. Whip the flour, water and a generous pinch of salt in a bowl to make a smooth paste. Beat well. Whip the egg whites stiffly, into a paste. Dip the sandwiches in this batter, deep-fry in slightly smoking hot oil, and serve with any sauce which is complementary to the sandwich-filling.

MRS MARSHALL'S FRIED SANDWICHES

Ingredients: Puff pastry; 1lb cold cooked game or poultry; 1 egg yolk and another egg to brush pastry; salt; pepper; 1 rounded dessertspoon milled parsley; a few drops of sherry and cream (or thick white sauce) to moisten; oil for cooking; raw, beaten egg; fine soft breadcrumbs.

Method: Stamp out two ovals of fairly thinly rolled puff pastry for each sandwich. Mince the game or poultry, add the egg yolk, parsley, salt and pepper to season, and moisten with a few drops of sherry and cream or thick white sauce. Keep the mixture firm enough to pat it out to just under ½in thickness on a lightly floured surface. Brush surfaces of all pastry discs with raw beaten egg. Stamp out matching ovals of the filling to fit on half the pastry ovals. Cover with the remaining pastry ovals, press neatly together, dip in raw beaten egg and coat with breadcrumbs. Chill in the refrigerator until required. Fry in slightly smoking oil.

MUM'S BANGERS
(Les Saucissons de Maman)

'The skins are so repellent' – thus Fanny's mama, who solved the problem to her own satisfaction in the following manner: skin, or shape up from sausage meat, the requisite number of chipolata-sized sausages. Roll first in flour, then in strained, raw, beaten egg and finally in fine, soft white or brown breadcrumbs. Place in a meat baking tin with a very little, very clear dripping, or better still, lard, and shake for a few moments over a fair heat.

Bake thereafter at Gas Mark 4, turning to ensure even colouration (approximately 20 minutes one shelf above centre).

Note: These are splendid either impaled on little wooden sticks (never plastic, which tastes like the smell of disinfectant) or as an accompaniment to any game, bird or poultry.

NORMANDY DUCK
(Caneton Ma Pomme)

Ingredients: 1 sandwich loaf; olive oil to fry; 2 prime ducklings or 1 prime duck; salt, pepper; butter; 8–12 small, sharp cooking apples (in season cider apples are gorgeous for this dish); ½ pint cider; 2 tablespoons calvados; ½ pint double cream; 2 egg yolks.

Method: Cut all the crusts from a sandwich loaf. Hollow out the crumbs from the centre to make a rectangular case. Deep fry in hot olive oil until golden brown. Rub the duck or ducklings with butter lavishly. Sprinkle with salt and pepper, place with the peeled apples in a deep heat-resistant dish, add the cider, cover and cook one shelf above centre at Gas Mark 4 until the ducks are tender. From this point there are two treatments: one with the ducklings remaining whole, one with them divided into portions. Whichever is done, the birds are removed and kept warm. The apples are removed and half are set in the bread case and half around a heated dish. The liquor from the ducks is strained and placed in a pan, the calvados is added and the pan tipped to a fierce flame to ignite. Use more calvados if you wish of course (we do!). When the flames have burned out the greasiness (the prime function), leaving only flavour, add all but two tablespoons of the cream and simmer for reduction. When well reduced, correct the seasoning, stir in the egg yolks previously mixed with the remaining 2 tablespoons of cream. For divided-bird presentation heap some of the sections over the apples in the bread case, arrange the rest with apples around the case on the heated dish and pour the sauce over all, adding a few sprigs of well-picked watercress at the moment of service. For whole ducks set one each side of the case *lengthwise* down a heated dish, pour some of the sauce into the bread case until it is filled level and the sauce sinks into the spaces between the apples, and hand the remainder in a sauce boat. Again, use watercress to 'dress' the dish.

PANCAKES WITH GAME OR POULTRY LEFTOVERS
(Crêpes farcies au Jambon ou Dinde)

Ingredients: 16 thin pancakes; 3oz butter; 3oz flour; ¾ pint strongly reduced turkey stock (from the carcase); salt and pepper to season; 2oz finely grated Parmesan cheese and extra 1½oz; 1 dozen transparently thin leaves of Gruyère cheese and extra 1½oz; ¾ pint milk; ¼ pint single or coffee cream; 1 large breakfast cup diced brown and white turkey meat; 1 large teacup diced lean and fat of cooked ham; optional ¼lb thinly sliced mushrooms cooked into sauce.

Method: Butter the base and sides of a shallow rectangular heat-resistant dish. Dissolve the butter over a moderate heat, add the flour, stir to a smooth paste; add stock, beating well between each addition. Add milk gradually. Cover with a circle of wetted greaseproof paper and store in refrigeration (if desired).

On the day of service divide the sauce into just over and just under half quantities; fold in diced turkey and ham, 2oz Parmesan, 1½oz Gruyère and the optional mushrooms into the larger amount of sauce, heated and beaten well in the top of a double pan over hot water. Taste and correct seasoning. Spread the mixture over all the pancakes, roll up and set in the prepared container. Dilute the remaining sauce with cream, 1½oz Parmesan and a little additional milk if the sauce is considered too thick. Pour over all, cover with the Gruyère leaves, dot with a few additional flakes of butter and refrigerate until required. Reheat one shelf above centre, Gas Mark 5, until the top is bubbling golden brown (approx. 25 to 30 minutes).

PEKIN DUCK
(Canard Oriental)

This is a modern presentation of an old Chinese recipe. Hang your chosen duck or goose (the treatment applies equally well to either) in a slight draught for 48 hours before cooking, so that the skin becomes dry. Rub liberally with salt and pepper. Try whenever possible to use *real* French kitchen salt and *real* black peppercorns ground in a little mill. Then smear the whole bird with thin honey; you must use your hands, so this is messy to do but essential! Stand the bird on a rack (we use the rack from a grill pan) in a dry baking tin and bake as instructed on pp.159-60. There is no cause for alarm at the rich, dark chestnut brown colour of the skin. This is how it should be.

PHEASANT WITH FOIE GRAS
(Faisan Souvaroff)

Ingredients: 1 plump hen pheasant; 5fl oz dry Madeira *and* 2½fl oz dry Madeira; 5fl oz strongly reduced white stock *and* 2½fl oz heavily reduced stock or game liquor, which has been simmered to syrupy stage; 4 rounded tablespoons truffle trimmings 7oz *pâté de foie gras* or substitute *pâté*; 6–8 de-rinded No. 3 cut rashers best back bacon; 2 tablespoons brandy or Armagnac; 1lb any flour and some cold water to bind to a firm paste.

Method: Begin by putting 5fl oz Madeira and 5fl oz stock into a small pan with truffle trimmings. Simmer for 3 minutes. Strain the liquor away into another small pan. Strew truffle trimmings over the base of a lidded copper or earthenware terrine. Dice the *foie gras* or substitute, simmer for 1 minute in the Madeira mixture, drain again, add about 1 tablespoon to the truffles in the pot and slip the remainder into a plump hen pheasant. Wrap the bird completely in bacon. Swill with Madeira liquor. Cook at Gas Mark 6 one shelf above centre for 25 minutes. Remove from the oven, add the second lot of Madeira and the very strong special stock with the brandy or Armagnac and replace the lid. Now make a fat sausage from stiffish flour and water pastry. Roll the pastry sausage out to about 1in thickness and long enough to go right round the lid. Place it in position so that contents are thus hermetically sealed. Step up the heat to Gas Mark 7 and cook one shelf above centre for 25–35 minutes depending on the size of the bird.

Warning: After affixing raw flour and water pastry, the dish must be returned immediately to the hot oven, otherwise raw dough will seep into the lid's join and defy you when you try to cut round it with a knife at table in order to remove the lid and release a fabulous cloud of aromatic fumes.

PIGEON PIE

Ingredients: 4 pigeon; 2lb rump steak; 4 hard-boiled eggs; 2 large onions; 1 rounded tablespoon milled parsley; seasoned flour; 12 peeled, French olives; 6fl oz Beaujolais; stock; bought or home-made puff pastry to cover; pure lard or *very* clear dripping.

Method: Divide the pigeon into neat portions (4 from each bird), cut the rump steak into thin fingers and slice the onions thinly. Turn the steak, pigeon and onions in seasoned flour. Fry briskly in your chosen fat and pack into a large pie dish, with the olives and hard-boiled eggs. Sprinkle with parsley; add wine and sufficient stock to cover. Cook, covered, at Gas Mark 3, middle shelf, until nearly tender. When cold, cover with a pastry lid and bake one shelf above centre at Gas Mark 7½ for 30–35 minutes.

PITT-Y-PANNA

A wonderful way of using up leftovers.

Ingredients: 8oz stale brown or white bread; 8oz cold boiled potatoes; 8oz any cold cooked meat; oil or butter; salt; pepper; 2 medium onions; 4 egg yolks; milled parsley (optional).

Method: Dice the bread, potatoes and meat into small pieces. Just cover the base of a thick frying pan with oil or butter. Fry grated onion until golden brown. Add the meat, potatoes and bread and fry, adding a little more oil or butter if required. When all are lightly browned, turn into small bowls, press the egg yolks in their half-shells into the centres of the mixture and, if liked, sprinkle with milled parsley. At table, each person tips the yolk over the hot mixture and stirs well with a fork *thus* saucing it as the heat cooks the stirred egg immediately.

PORK SPARE RIBS

Ingredients: 5lb pork spare ribs, cut into strips; 1½ pints *and* ½ pint cold water; 8 tablespoons soy sauce; 2 level teaspoons salt; 8 tablespoons sherry; 4 heaped teaspoons soft brown sugar; 4oz pineapple pulp; 3 scant rounded tablespoons potato flour or arrowroot, 6 tablespoons wine vinegar.

Method: Place the spare ribs with 1½ pints water, soy sauce and salt in a thick, deep pan. Let the liquid boil, cover, reduce to a simmer and maintain for 1 hour, stirring occasionally. Remove the lid, add the sugar and turn over a stronger heat until all the ribs are well impregnated. Add the sherry, pineapple and wine vinegar and continue turning and bubbling for a few moments. Stir your chosen thickening agent into ½ pint cold water, pour on, stir quickly and vigorously and bubble again until the liquid is very strongly reduced and quite clear.

RAISED PIE PASTRY WITH GOOSE FAT

Follow the Raised Pie Pastry recipe on p.168 but instead of using lard, use clarified goose fat, which has been refrigerated until it is quite firm.

To Clarify: Place the 'set' goose fat in a very large bowl, cover completely with boiling water, stir well and leave in refrigeration until the fat rises to the top and sets. Cut out the fat in sections and scrape away all impurities, which will have attached themselves firmly to the underside.

RAISED RABBIT PIE

Proceed exactly as for Veal and Ham Pie below for the pastry crust, the case making and the method – only the filling is different.

The filling
Ingredients: 1½lb jointed rabbit pieces; ½lb sliced onions; 2 peeled, sliced tomatoes; 1 finely diced carrot; 2 hard-boiled eggs, split lengthwise; 1 pint strong cleared stock; 5fl oz dry white cooking wine; a generous pinch of nutmeg; 1 level dessertspoonful paprika; salt and pepper to season; 4 de-rinded rashers streaky bacon; ¾oz powdered gelatine.

Method: Cut the flesh carefully from the rabbit pieces and dice neatly. Mix with the onions, tomatoes, carrot, eggs, nutmeg and paprika, season with salt and pepper and lay half the mixture in the raw, raised pastry case. Lay down two of the bacon rashers. Repeat, finish with the remaining bacon rashers, swill with the white wine, cover with the lid, decorate with the tassel, brush with the egg mixture and bake as instructed in the recipe for Veal and Ham Pie. Fill with the stock and gelatine after baking and leave until cold before cutting.

RAISED VEAL AND HAM PIE

'When an eating housekeeper sets down afore his customers and deliberately eats one of his own Weal pies, no man can refuse confidence.'

Simmons, 1858

Ingredients for Pastry Case: 10oz sifted flour; 3¾fl oz milk and water mixed together in equal proportions; 3oz lard.

Ingredients for filling: 3lb neck pork neatly diced; ½lb gammon neatly diced; 2 small shallots, cut thinly; 2 hard-boiled eggs split lengthwise; 2 small bay leaves; a generous grating of milled black pepper; 1 small wineglassful cooking sherry.

Ingredients for jelly: 1 pint strong, cleared pork and ham stock; ¾oz powdered gelatine; 1 tablespoon cooking sherry.

Method: Bring the milk and water to the boil with the lard and, when dissolved, pour into a well in the centre of the flour and work up very gently and swiftly with the fingertips. Please keep this warm while working up. Take off three-quarters of the dough and work with your fingers until it forms a case. *The wall will hold.* Place a pie funnel in the centre. Mix the gammon, pork and shallots lightly together and season with the pepper. Lay into the pastry case, with the egg halves between the bay leaves. Moisten with sherry. Use the remaining quarter of dough to press out into a neat lid. Wet the pastry case edges and pinch together firmly with the lid. Make a hole in the centre to release the head of the funnel. Trim off any surplus, roll into a narrow strip, slash finely into a 'fringe', roll up into a tassel and bake separately at given temperatures until a good golden brown. Brush the top and sides with strained, raw, beaten egg mixed with a little salt. Bake on the middle shelf, Gas Mark 6, for 20 minutes, reduce the heat to Gas Mark 3 and cook for a further 1 hour 20 minutes.

Meanwhile add hot stock to the gelatine and sherry, strain and place in a jug. Pour slowly into the central cavity until filled. Insert the tassel and leave until perfectly cold.

ROAST SADDLE OF VENISON
(Selle de Venaison rôtie)

Make sure that your butcher gives you a small saddle, not a large one (it is never so good), and that the meat has been really well hung. Take off all the skin and remove the sinews (if you cannot, get your butcher to do this for you). If you have no larding needle with which, ideally, the saddle should be darned using strips of raw unsalted pork fat, then, as a second-best method, wrap the entire piece in thin pork fat. Set the prepared saddle in a baking tin on a bed of sliced onions and carrots. Add a few flakes of butter and cook for the first 20 minutes, middle shelf, at Gas Mark 7. Reduce the heat to Gas Mark 4/5, allowing 2¼ hours overall for a 6lb piece for the average taste; increase the time a little for the folk who like everything over-done. Serve with Cherry Sauce (p.178) or redcurrant jelly.

SAUSAGE ROLLS
(Les Saucisses en feuilleté)

We only insert this because there are always new crops of young people who have been taught by ignorant cookery teachers to make sausage rolls singly.

Roll out pork sausage meat into long cylinders of the thickness suitable to sausage rolls – about 1in in diameter. Roll out strips of pastry of matching lengths 3in wide and a little less than ½in in thickness. Brush one edge of each strip with water. Lay down a length of sausage meat centrally. Roll up and over so that the join is now underneath. Prick along whole length with the prongs of a fork about every inch, brush with raw, beaten, strained egg, chop off desired lengths, lay fairly widely spaced on lightly floured baking sheets and bake one shelf above centre at Gas Mark 6 until a good golden brown, for approximately 20–25 minutes.

TO COOK SAUSAGES WITHOUT
FEAR OF SPLITTING

Unplait the strands, lay undivided in a meat baking tin, which has been rubbed (base and sides) with butter or *impeccably clean* dripping! Bake, *unpricked*, one shelf above centre at Gas Mark 5 (turning when slightly browned on the upper parts). Overall time about 45 minutes, depending on the brownness required. Then divide.

THE SUCKING PIG
(Le petit Cochon au lait)

Cook: Either on a modern spit, as we always do, or in an oven. For either you must baste to obtain the really crisp skin, which should be as light as paper and very highly pork-flavoured, from the regular basting with the natural juices as they flow.

Cooking Temperature: Gas Mark 8 for 10 minutes, then turn down to Gas Mark 4/5 for about 2 hours. These times and temperatures have been checked on 10–12-week-old pigs.

Prepare by first seasoning the interior with crushed garlic, French *gros sel* and butter or with ordinary kitchen salt and butter or oil. Stuff with Traditional Sucking Pig Stuffing (pp.173-4). Sew up the openings, or use – please do not be horrified – surgical clips, which are as good for piggy as for our tums! Score very lightly with an extremely sharp, small kitchen knife. Now rub the skin violently all over with rough salt, and remind yourself while basting that *ca vaut la peine*, the little pig will be so tender that you can slice him with a plate as is done in a famous restaurant in Toledo.

APPLE STUFFING

For duck or goose.

Ingredients: 1lb peeled, quartered, minced cooking apples; 1lb peeled, minced shallots; 1lb fine, soft brown breadcrumbs; 6oz suet; grated rind of 1 lemon or orange; salt and pepper to season; 1 teaspoon each of sage, thyme, parsley and oregano; 1 egg to bind.

Method: Mix all the ingredients together to form a malleable mixture. Stuff into the chosen bird.

Note: The addition of 1 peeled, minced quince gives a superb flavour to this stuffing.

CHESTNUT STUFFING

For turkey or pheasant.

Ingredients: 2lb chestnuts; 1lb cooked, sieved, dried potato purée (p.195); salt and pepper; the grated rind of 1 orange; 6oz ground almonds; 1 raw, beaten egg; 2fl oz rich Madeira or sherry (brown, milk, cream).

Method: Nick the chestnuts and boil until tender. Skin, sieve and work up with the remaining ingredients.

FORCEMEAT BALLS

Ingredients: ½lb lean veal; ½lb suet; 2oz bacon fat (cut finely); 2 heaped tablespoonsful fine, white breadcrumbs; 1 dessert-spoonful finely chopped parsley; 1 rounded teaspoon finely chopped onion or shallot; 2 eggs; a pinch of powdered mace; a pinch of powdered nutmeg; 1 level eggspoon milled black pepper; 1 level teaspoonful salt.

Method: Mince the veal finely. Then, for perfection, pound it in a pestle and mortar, but this is not essential.

Mix the veal with all the remaining dry ingredients. Work in the raw eggs thoroughly. Shape into small balls, place in the top of a steamer over hot water and steam for 20 minutes. Just before serving, place in a frying basket, immerse in slightly smoking oil and cook fast to colour and crisp.

FRENCH STUFFING

For pheasant or a small turkey.

Ingredients: 1 slim, stale stick of French bread (*baton*); red cooking wine; 2 pig's kidneys and the liver of the bird; 2 tablespoons fresh, chopped parsley; 1 tablespoon rubbed thyme; 1lb finely chopped fatty bacon; 1lb small diced lean veal; pepper to season; 2 finely crushed juniper berries; 3–4 finely grated shallots; 2–3 egg yolks.

Method: Soak the sliced bread in sufficient wine to make a pap. Wring this pap out in muslin, turn into a bowl and add the diced pig's kidneys, scraped bird's liver and all other remaining ingredients. Work well together and use.

LIVER STUFFING

For turkey, duck or goose.

Ingredients: 1lb chickens' livers; the bird's liver; 1lb soft brown breadcrumbs; 1 raw grated onion; 1 crushed garlic clove (optional); ¾lb minced fatty bacon; salt and pepper to season; 1 large or 2 small raw, beaten eggs.

Method: Mince the chickens' livers and the bird's liver. Work up all remaining ingredients in a bowl. Stuff into your chosen bird.

MUSHROOM STUFFING

Particularly good with chicken but can be used with almost any bird.

Ingredients: ¾lb mushrooms (with stalks and skin, please); 1 large onion; 6oz fatty bacon; pepper to season; 2 tablespoons milled parsley; 1 celery heart, minced finely; strained juice and grated rind of 1 orange; 1 egg; 2 tablespoons brandy; 12oz soft brown breadcrumbs.

Method: Mix all together and use with any bird.

OYSTER FORCEMEAT

Ingredients: 12 bearded oysters; 8oz fine brown breadcrumbs; grated rind of ½ lemon; 1½oz melted butter; 1 rounded teaspoon freshly milled parsley; 1 pinch of nutmeg; 1 pinch cayenne pepper; 1 pinch salt; 1 egg yolk; the carefully saved oyster liquor; extra crumbs; white stock.

Method: Chop the oysters finely with a silver knife and mix with the crumbs, melted butter, lemon rind, parsley, seasonings, 8oz crumbs and egg yolk. Finally add the oyster juice, keeping the mixture to a firm consistency by adding a few extra crumbs if necessary. Shape the mixture into small balls. Have ready a medium pan half filled with carefully strained white stock (or water). When boiling, slide in the little balls and allow them to poach gently. Alternatively, stuff forcemeat into your chosen bird as explained on p.290 1 hour before completion of roasting.

TRADITIONAL SUCKING PIG STUFFING
(Farce pour un cochon en lait)

Ingredients: 1lb sausage meat; 8oz soft white breadcrumbs; 1 dessertspoon chopped sage and parsley, mixed; 2 finely chopped onions; 4oz minced fatty bacon; 1 raw beaten egg.

Method: Mix all together and use.

Note: It is permissible to add a small ladleful of good stock to the above stuffing, if desired.

TURKEY STUFFING No. 1

Ingredients: 1lb finely rubbed soft brown breadcrumbs; scraped liver of the bird; grated rind of 1 lemon; 5oz suet; ½lb raw, grated Spanish onion; 6oz minced raw gammon; 3oz sultanas; 2oz chopped walnuts; 1 or 2 eggs to bind; 1 scant flat teaspoon black pepper.

Method: Mix together and use.

TURKEY STUFFING No. 2

Ingredients: 2lb pork sausage meat; 2 raw, grated medium-sized Spanish onions; 1 level tablespoon each of milled sage, thyme, parsley, chives (whenever possible); 1 level tablespoon chopped hazelnuts; salt and pepper to season.

Method: Roll out the sausage meat on a floured surface. Mix the remaining ingredients together. Spread over the rolled-out sausage meat. Shape into a ball, re-roll, re-shape and stuff into the bird at the vent end. Fill the neck end with Chestnut Stuffing (p.171).

TURKEY STUFFING No. 3

Ingredients: 4 pork kidneys; 1 batch Liver Stuffing (p.172); 8 rashers back-bacon, No. 3 cut.

Method: Skin and halve the kidneys. Cut each half in two lengthwise. Wrap each one in half a bacon rasher. Line the base interior of the bird with half the Liver Stuffing. Lay down the kidney/bacon rolls on top. Fill up with the remaining Liver Stuffing. If a very large bird, add a quarter, half or twice as much again.

SAVOURY SAUCES

As we all know, the art of saucing is the finest and the most subtle of all the culinary arts, but we know equally well the traditional British Christmas is without doubt the most un-gastronomic period in our culinary year. In consequence, while there are classic sauces in this section it is not in the main an amalgam of the subtle and the *recherché*. No really great sauce is unkind to wine and it is fair to say that Oxford, Cumberland and Horseradish Sauces are not merely unkind, they are brutal; yet they fulfil a very definite and important function by supporting some of the traditional Christmas items whose absence from this book would invoke shrieks of fury from traditional British Christmas-makers! Indeed, redcurrant jelly is to jugged hare what cold roast sirloin is to horseradish, even as cold gammon demands Oxford Sauce, so this is not an apologia – it is just an explanation.

APPLE COMPOTE
(Compôte de Pommes)

Poach ½lb peeled, cored, sliced apples and 1lb peeled, cored, sliced quinces in the minimum of clear white stock. Do this in the oven at Gas Mark 1, until collapsed and fluffy (a saucer-covered stone jar does very well). Then rub through a sieve and stir in 1, 2 or 3 tablespoons of mint jelly. The quantity must not be arbitrary because no two persons agree on the sweetness they like in this sauce.

BASIC BROWN SAUCE
(Sauce Espagnole)

Ingredients: 2oz flour; 2oz butter; 32fl oz good clear meat stock; salt and pepper to season; 1oz finely diced pork or bacon fat; 2oz diced carrots; 1oz diced onion; 1 small, crushed bay leaf; 1 eggspoon thyme leaf; 1 teaspoon chopped parsley; 1 extra oz butter.

Method: Melt the 2oz butter in a small, thick pan, add the flour and stir until the mixture forms a soft ball and leaves the base and sides of the pan clean. Add the stock gradually, beating well between each addition. Simmer over the lowest possible heat for 30 minutes. Meanwhile dissolve the pork fat and extra butter in a separate pan. Add the herbs and vegetables and fry until nicely browned. Then add the basic sauce to them gradually, simmering until the vegetables are perfectly tender. Rub through a sieve and correct the seasoning to taste with salt and pepper.

BASIC WHITE SAUCE
(Sauce Béchamel)

Ingredients: 1½oz butter; 1½oz flour; 15fl oz milk; salt and pepper to season.

Method: Soften the butter over a low heat, stir in the flour and work up until the mixture forms a soft ball that leaves the sides and base of the pan clean. Add a little milk, allow to come to the boil and beat very thoroughly indeed. Continue in this way, adding the milk gradually and beating between each addition, until all the milk is absorbed. Draw to the side of a very low heat and simmer for 30 minutes, stirring from time to time. If using as a basic sauce, do not season. Try not to use (seasoned) as a completed sauce – very dull and flat!

BREAD SAUCE

Rather than have you write and tell us that we have forgotten this, we make so bold as to confess we think it so horrible and such a ruination to all upon which it imposes itself that we will not be associated with it. But we do use it for poultices! Alas, you will find it in almost every English cookery book. Impenitently, Fanny and Johnnie Cradock.

BURGUNDY SAUCE
(Sauce Bourguignonne)

Ingredients: 1oz butter; 1 rounded tablespoon finely grated shallot or onion; 8¾fl oz modest red Burgundy; salt and freshly milled black pepper to season; 1 Faggot of Herbs (p.160); 5fl oz Basic Brown Sauce (p.176); 1 extra oz butter.

Method: Dissolve 1oz butter in a small pan, add the onion and allow to simmer gently until it is soft but not coloured. Reduce the heat to minimum. Pour in the red wine. Season with salt and pepper. Add the faggot of herbs and allow to simmer gently until reduced to a scant 4½fl oz. Stir in the brown sauce. Rub through the finest available sieve. Reheat in a clean pan, adding the extra ounce of butter in very small flakes. Taste and adjust seasonings if necessary.

CHEESE SAUCE
(Sauce Mornay)

Ingredients: 1 pint Sauce Béchamel (pp.176-7); 3oz finely grated Parmesan cheese; ½oz butter; salt and pepper to season.

Method: Stir the cheese into the hot Béchamel and add the butter gradually in small flakes, beating well between each addition. Taste and correct the seasoning.

CHERRY SAUCE

No. 1 – Classic
Ingredients: 1 tin of black cherries; ½ pint Basic Brown Sauce (Sauce Espagnole) (p.176); strained juice and grated rind of 1 lemon; 1 liqueur-glassful cherry brandy; 1 tablespoon brandy; 4 tablespoons cherry syrup; pinch pepper; pinch salt; 1 table-spoon water; 1 meanly rounded dessertspoon potato flour (*fécule de pommes*).

Method: Place the sauce and cherry syrup in a pan and bring to the boil. Add the cherry brandy and allow to reboil. Dissolve the potato flour in the lemon juice and water, add to the pan mixture, stir until thickened, add lemon rind and brandy, simmer for 4 minutes; add the stoned cherries and pour over the bird.

No. 2 – Emergency
Ingredients: ½ tin consommé or julienne soup; strained juice 1 lemon; 1 tablespoon cherry brandy; 1 teacupful tinned stoned black cherries with their liquor; salt and pepper.

Method: Heat the soup, lemon juice, cherry brandy and cherries thoroughly. Season to taste with salt and pepper. If not thick enough, add ½ teaspoon potato flour dissolved in a little cold water and stir well.

CHESTNUT PURÉE

Nick 1½lb chestnuts. Place under a mild grill until the skins split explosively. Remove every particle of outer and inner skins and simmer until the nuts are tender, in either consommé or a clear strong stock, adding 2 small sticks of celery. Strain, rub through a sieve and mix with ¾lb of made Duchess Potatoes (p.191). When thoroughly blended finish the completed purée with 1 tablespoon of double cream and 1–2 dessertspoons Madeira. Season with pepper to taste.

CRANBERRY SAUCE

Ingredients: 1lb cranberries; water to cover; 5fl oz dry white cooking wine; 1 small stick cinnamon.

Method: Place the cranberries, water and cinnamon in a saucepan. Cover with a lid, bring to the boil and simmer gently until tender and the water is considerably reduced. Remove the cinnamon stick. Rub through a sieve. Stir in the wine and set aside to reheat when required in hot water (*au bain marie*), or put hot water into the base pan of a double saucepan and put above the mixture into the upper pan.

CUMBERLAND SAUCE

To serve with cold ham, beef, gammon, etc.

Ingredients: 4 rounded tablespoons redcurrant jelly; 4fl oz port; 1 teaspoon finely chopped shallots (which have been covered with cold water, brought to the boil, simmered 1 minute and pressed in a scrap of muslin); 1 teaspoon each of orange and lemon peel cut into thin strips; strained juice of 1 orange and ½ a lemon; generous pinch cayenne pepper; generous pinch powdered ginger.

Method: Place all the ingredients, except the orange and lemon peel, in a small pan, allow to dissolve, bring to a slow rolling boil, maintain for 1 minute and remove from heat. Meanwhile place the peel strips in a separate pan, cover with cold water, bring to the boil, maintain for 2 minutes, strain and stir into the sauce.

EDWARDIAN DEVIL PASTE
('Le Diable')

Ingredients: 1 rounded teaspoon dry English mustard; 1 teaspoon Worcestershire sauce; 1 teaspoon anchovy purée; 2 generous teaspoons olive oil; ½ level teaspoon powdered paprika.

Method: Work up all the ingredients to a smooth paste. Spread on turkey or other fowl drumsticks and leave for a while to infuse before warming through in a well-buttered, lidded casserole. Ideal temperature Gas Mark 1 until just piping hot, say 15–20 minutes.

FRENCH DRESSING
(Sauce Vinaigrette)

When this basic French salad-sauce is made with olive oil, it can be stored (in a bottle with a cork or screw top) for at least four weeks at normal room temperature* and without the benefit of refrigeration, thus obviating the necessity of making at the moment of dressing and serving salads.

Just remember this sauce should never be poured over salads until the moment of service. Made as advised here, you just shake the bottle well to redistribute the wine vinegar and seasonings and then use as required.

Ingredients: 15fl oz olive oil; 1 rounded teaspoon salt; 3fl oz wine vinegar; ½ eggspoon freshly milled black peppercorns; ½ teaspoon made French mustard *or* dry English mustard.

*Except in very hot weather.

Method: Mix the salt, pepper and your chosen mustard together with sufficient olive oil to make a thick, smooth paste. Add a few drops of wine vinegar and continue adding oil and vinegar until both are used up. Pour into a bottle and use as instructed.

FRENCH DRESSING WITH GRAPES

Peel ½lb of modest white grapes into a sieve over a small bowl and leave in refrigeration overnight. Mix together in a separate bowl a flat teaspoon of salt, a scant flat eggspoon of freshly milled black peppercorns, a flat coffeespoon of dry English mustard and work up to a smooth paste with a few drops from a measured ¼ pint of pure olive oil. Once the mixture is smooth, work in about a fifth of the oil and then a splash from the accumulated grape juice and continue quickly either with a wooden spoon in a bowl or with a mortar in a pestle, working in the oil and splashes of the grape juice until all are smoothly blended. Add the grapes and set aside out of refrigeration for a maximum 24 hours before serving, remembering to work up again at the last moment.

HORSERADISH SAUCE

There are innumerable fancy ways of making this mixture, but experience has taught us that only initiated palates prefer them to this most simple of all.

Grate 2 breakfastcupsful fresh horseradish finely. Spread out on a shallow dish. Sprinkle with the strained juice of ½ lemon and leave for 15 minutes. Drain well and fold in ¼ pint lightly whipped cream. If liked, this may be lightly seasoned with freshly milled black peppercorns.

Note: The introduction of vinegar, even *real* vinegar made with wine, is lethal!

INDIA SAUCE

For cold cuts.

Ingredients: 2 hard-boiled egg yolks, sieved; 1 flat teaspoon curry paste (Masala paste); 8fl oz olive oil; 2fl oz tarragon wine vinegar; 1 quick shake of Tabasco.

Method: Work the sieved yolks with the curry paste, incorporating the olive oil very gradually and cutting as you work, with small splashes of the vinegar. When absolutely smooth and thoroughly blended, beat in the Tabasco.

MADEIRA SAUCE

Ingredients: 1 pint Basic Brown Sauce (p.176); 1 Faggot of Herbs (p.160); salt and pepper to season; 4fl oz fairly dry Madeira; 1 generous tablespoon cooking-type brandy (optional).

Method: Place the Brown Sauce in a thick pan with the faggot of herbs and allow to come to a gentle simmer. Continue simmering for 5 minutes, remove the herbs, add the Madeira, simmer for 3 minutes, taste, correct seasoning and, if liked, stir in the brandy. This, however, is optional, as is the last piece of classic instruction, which we have slightly rephrased into . . . when you come into a fortune, add 1 large black truffle diced extremely finely.

MAYONNAISE

Ingredients: 4 egg yolks; ½ pint oil; 1 scant teaspoon salt; 1 scant level eggspoon pepper; 1 rounded teaspoon mustard;

2 dessertspoons strained lemon or orange juice or 2 scant dessertspoons vinegar.

Method: Place the egg yolks in a basin and whip with a rotary whisk, loop whisk or ideally with an electric mixer until the yolks are thick and creamy . . . 5 minutes by hand, 2½ minutes by electric mixer. Beat in the oil gradually, beating well between each addition until ¼ pint has been absorbed into the mixture. Add all seasonings, 1 dessertspoon vinegar or citrus juice and continue beating in the remainder of the oil. Add the remaining citrus juice or vinegar. Store in mild refrigeration.

MINT JELLY

Ingredients: 8oz bruised mint leaves and stems (from the plant tips); 2 teacups wine vinegar; 2 teacups cold water; strained juice 2 lemons; 6 heaped teacups castor sugar.

Method: Cover the mint with water, boil and then simmer very gently for maximum 5 minutes. Strain, with gentle pressure from the back of a wooden spoon. Add lemon juice and wine vinegar. Bring to the boil again, add sugar, melt carefully and then re-simmer until jellied. Pot and tie down.

MOUSSELINE SAUCE
(Sauce Mousseline)

Ingredients: ¾lb butter; 3 egg yolks; pinch of black pepper; ⅛oz salt; 1½ tablespoons wine vinegar; 1½ tablespoons cold water; ¼ pint stiffly whipped double cream; ½ teaspoon strained lemon juice.

Method: Place the salt, pepper, vinegar and water in a very small pan and simmer until reduced to a scant 1 tablespoonful. Turn the heat to a mere thread, draw the saucepan to the side, add an extra dessertspoonful of cold water and the egg yolks and whisk immediately until the yolks thicken and the mixture gets like cream. Turn off the heat, whip in the butter, which has been softened until it is creamy, adding this gradually but continuing to beat without pause. Now beat in the lemon juice and finally the stiffly whipped cream *and serve immediately*.

ONION SAUCE
(Sauce Soubise)

Mince 2lb peeled, Spanish onions finely. Place in a pan or bowl, cover with boiling water, leave for 3 minutes, strain, press into a clean cloth and turn into a pan in which you have dissolved 2oz butter with 2fl oz oil or 4oz of goose, duck or chicken fat. Allow to simmer gently until the onions are completely tender. Add ½ pint Sauce Béchamel (pp.176-7). Work in until thoroughly blended, taste, correct seasoning with salt and black pepper, then add 1 teaspoon of sifted icing sugar, cook gently for a further 5 minutes, rub through a sieve and work in 2oz butter rubbed through the fingers in small flakes.

Note: The final distinction to this sauce is the addition of 2–4 tablespoons thick double cream.

OXFORD SAUCE

This is an excellent long-keeping sauce for cold meats or for brushing onto items to be roasted or grilled.

Ingredients: 1lb soft brown (pieces) sugar; 4oz made English mustard: 17fl oz olive oil; 2oz salt; 1oz freshly milled black peppercorns; 8½fl oz wine vinegar.

Method: Mix sugar, mustard, salt and pepper with sufficient oil to make a thick, well-beaten paste. Add a few drops of vinegar and continue adding oil and vinegar with vigorous beating between each addition until all ingredients are absorbed. Store in screw-topped jars.

Note: Make the mustard with ordinary tap water to the consistency that will enable it to flop very slowly from a lifted spoon. Runny mustard will ruin the sauce.

PAN SAUCE

Our worst enemies could not possibly accuse us of having a grain of affection for meat cubes or 'gravy substitutes'. As the Eskimos said when they saw the Sahara Desert, 'Alas! this is not for us!' The fact remains that a very pleasant sauce can be made from the pan sediments after roasting a bird or a joint. With the item itself in a warm place, pour off all but a thin surface of fat from the baking tin. Place the pan over a thread of heat. Then with a wooden spoon add small quantities of flour and work up with the back of the spoon until a smooth paste is achieved. Thin this down to a shade thicker than the desired consistency with additions of stock or the liquor made by simmering the neck and giblets of a bird while this is roasting. Add 1 tablespoon to every pint in the pan of any of the following cooking-quality wines: dry sherry, dry Madeira, claret or burgundy types or dry white wines. Your choice will be governed solely by the item for which the sauce is intended. Work this in, taste, correct seasoning with salt and pepper and strain either over the item or into a separate sauceboat.

PROVENCE SAUCE
(Sauce Provençale)

We can do no better than quote the 'Master' on this sauce. Escoffier says:

'Peel, remove the seeds, press and concass* twelve medium tomatoes. Heat in a sauté-pan one-fifth pint of oil, until it begins to smoke a little; insert the tomatoes seasoned with pepper and salt; add a crushed garlic clove, a pinch of powdered sugar; one teaspoonful of chopped parsley and allow to melt gently for half an hour. In reality, true Provençale is nothing but a fine fondue of tomatoes with garlic.'

WINE DRESSING

Proceed exactly as instructed for French Dressing with Grapes (p.181), omitting the grapes and replacing the grape juice with 1½fl oz red wine to every 5fl oz olive oil.

*To concass – to chop roughly.

VEGETABLES

We grow the finest vegetables in the world; but due, we suspect, to the combined influences of Victorian refinement and Cromwellian austerity, they, like many other foodstuffs, sometimes suffer from too cavalier a treatment (forgive the pun) *after passing through British kitchen doors.*

As we said anent fish and vegetables in our *Cook's Book* (published Fontana, 6s.) the majority of vegetables should be steamed instead of boiled and 'Fine Fish Are Never Boiled'! So please, with all you have to do at Christmas time, and if you are over-harassed, skip the recipes in this chapter that need concentrated last-minute attention and stick to the ones that can be safely pre-prepared. These are: Chicory and Cauliflower in Cheese Sauce; Stuffed Tomatoes; Onions Monte Carlo; Stuffed Potatoes; Creamed Carrots and Swedes; French Potato Cakes and Baked Stuffed Sweet Potatoes. This is the easiest group as all the aforementioned can be warmed through in heat-resistant serving dishes at Gas Mark 1 or on the floor of the oven for the last 20 minutes of roasting the Christmas bird. The next easiest group, only needing final assembly and reheating or quick cooking and serving, are: Corn Fritters; Dauphine Potatoes; Sprout and Chestnut Sauté; Fried Potato Balls, Sweet Potato Croquettes; Sprout Fritters and Stuffed Cabbage Bail. All the above are basically pre-prepared ready for their final treatment but *Roesti* or Swiss Potato is a long, slow, serve-immediately job; Individual *Pommes Anna* must be taken straight through, as must Sweet Potato Pone.

BRUSSELS SPROUTS FRITTERS
(Beignets de choux de Bruxelles)

Prepare in advance the fritter batter given below. When required, heat up a pan of olive oil. Sink whole, small or halved, large steamed, cold Brussels sprouts into the batter. Drop small blobs into hot oil (375–380°F). They will swell up and turn golden brown. Pyramid on a dish that is covered with a paper d'oyley. Sprinkle with chopped parsley and serve.

Fritter Batter

Ingredients: 4oz sifted flour; 1⅛oz salt; 1 tablespoon olive oil; 1 standard egg; approximately 5fl oz water – please do not misread this and use milk!

Method: Separate the yolk from the white. Beat all the remaining ingredients together until thick and smooth. Immediately before using, fold stiffly whipped egg white into the prepared batter mixture.

BRUSSELS SPROUTS WITH CHESTNUTS
(Choux de Bruxelles aux Marrons)

You can use steamed, fresh sprouts or cooked frozen sprouts. Your chestnuts must also be cooked, peeled and diced. Do not overcook or they will crumble. This part of the work can be done 1–2 days in advance.

For Service: Dissolve 2 tablespoons olive oil and 2oz butter in a large shallow pan. When hot, toss in equal quantities of sprouts and chestnuts. Shake and fry until well browned. Drain and serve.

Remember: Really small sprouts are fried whole; medium-sized ones are halved; big ones are quartered.

Note: This dish is, in our experience, the most favourite of all for Christmas Dinner, but it is dreary beyond belief unless the sauté process is done until the sprouts – as well as the chestnuts – become well touched with brown!

CAULIFLOWER IN CHEESE SAUCE
(Chou-fleur Mornay)

Cut out the surplus coarse base stem and all coarser outside leaves. Steam the cauliflower until cooked but still firm. Divide into neat portions, set in a buttered, heat-resistant dish and cover complete with Cheese Sauce (pp.177-8). Remember, this can be done a day in advance, the top of the sauce flaked with butter and the whole reheated (under foil) at Gas Mark 2.

CHICORY IN CHEESE SAUCE
(Les Endives Mornay)

For those of us who find the slightly bitter taste unattractive, this is an admirable way of cooking this first-rate winter vegetable. Place the heads in a pan of cold water with 3 lumps of sugar to every pound. Bring to the boil and simmer for 15 minutes. Drain, cover with fresh water and cook again until tender. Cover with Cheese Sauce (pp.177-8) as instructed for Cauliflower (above).

CORN FRITTERS
(Beignets de Maïs)

Beat 1 egg yolk, 1 whole egg, 2 tablespoons olive oil and 4 heaped tablespoons flour together in a basin with 6½fl oz milk to form a smooth, very thick batter.

Add the strained contents of an 8oz tin of whole-kernel sweetcorn. Rub a heated griddle with a piece of unsalted pork fat. Drop spoonsful of the mixture wide apart on the hot, slightly smoking griddle (over a low heat). Cook until the underside is golden brown. Turn over and repeat.

CREAMED CARROTS

Emergency recipe. Heat the contents of any sized tin of carrots. Strain when hot. Mash finely with a fork. Add 1 rounded dessertspoon stiffly whipped cream to a medium-sized tin. Season liberally with freshly milled black peppercorns and finally add 1 flat dessertspoon milled parsley heads. This tastes remarkably good considering it is an expediency method.

CREAMED SWEDES

Peel enough swedes to yield 2lb peeled weight. Cut up roughly, steam until really tender and then treat exactly as for Creamed Carrots.

DAUPHINE POTATOES
(Pommes de terre Dauphine)

Ingredients: 6oz Choux Pastry (pp.239-40); 1lb Duchess Potato mixture (below); raw beaten egg; flour; fine bread-crumbs; oil for frying.

Method: Beat the choux pastry and cold potato purée together. Shape 1oz pieces into small balls or corks. Turn in sifted flour, pass through raw beaten egg, coat thickly with fine soft breadcrumbs and fry exactly as for Fried Potato Balls (p.192).

Note: 2oz minutely diced cooked lean ham and/or 1 rounded dessertspoon freshly milled parsley may be added to the above mixture if desired.

DUCHESS POTATO 'PEARS'
(Pommes de Terre Duchesse en 'poires')

Ingredients: 1lb stiff potato purée (see Fried Potato Balls, p.192); 1oz butter; 1 large egg yolk; salt and pepper to season; flour, raw beaten egg and fine breadcrumbs; a few fine 'stems' cut from blanched almonds; deep fryer of heated oil.

Method: Beat the egg and butter and seasonings into very stiff, well-dried-out potato purée. Scale off into 2oz pieces. Roll in sifted flour and shape into 'pears'. If you find any difficulty in this moulding, chill the mixture in the refrigerator before handling it to make it extra firm. Turn the pear shapes in raw beaten egg, then coat thickly with fine soft crumbs and drive a thin sliver of almond into the pointed end. If desired, refrigerate for up to 24 hours on a baking sheet base covered with the same fine breadcrumbs. Prior to serving, place one or two gently on a slice and lower into slightly smoking hot oil (390–400°F) until richly browned. Drain and arrange slantwise around your chosen Christmas bird on a heated dish.

FRENCH POTATO CAKES
(Crêpes Parmentier)

Ingredients: 4 generously heaped tablespoons flour; 1 standard egg yolk; 2 tablespoons olive oil; 6½fl oz milk; 1lb dried, sieved potato purée (p.195).

Method: Place the flour, egg yolk and oil in a bowl and beat in the milk gradually until the batter is completely smooth. Beat in the sieved potato mixture. *Only add seasoning of salt and pepper when serving with a savoury item.* Rub a griddle or deep iron pan that has been heated dry over a very low heat with a small piece of raw, unsalted pork or mutton fat. Drop small dessertspoonsful onto the greased griddle, being careful to space them widely apart. Pat out into thin circles. When browned on the underside, flip over and cook the reverse side. Serve either sprinkled with grated cheese as an accompaniment to the Christmas main course or serve as a family pudding dusted thickly with sifted icing sugar.

FRIED POTATO BALLS
(Pommes de Terre Amandines)

Mix together equal quantities of Choux Pastry (pp.239–40) and Duchess Potato (p.191). Season with salt and pepper and pipe through a plain 1in writing pipe, lopping off 1in pieces with a knife dipped in cold water or just roll into small balls – pass through flour and egg, and roll in flaked almonds. Fry in hot oil (390–400°F) until swollen and golden brown. For a more economical version use very firm Duchess potato only instead of the above with choux pastry, otherwise follow the given recipe completely.

INDIVIDUAL POTATO MOULDS
(Pommes Anna d'Escoffier)

This is a method and not a recipe. If care is taken, it will always prove successful. For it, you must have small individual moulds called dariole or madeleine moulds and you must cut and dry in a cloth transparently thin slices of peeled, raw old potatoes using either a knife (the hard way), a small cucumber cutter (the quick and easy way) or a mandoline (the classic way). You must also have a tin or bun loaf tin a minimum 2½in in depth.

You must heat some frying oil in a saucepan from your deep-fry stock – this is the one exception to the rule in that the oil can be as old and dirty as you like because it never comes in contact with the food, but it *is absolutely essential*! To try to obtain the same results with water instead of oil will pre-determine total failure.

Having got so far, burnish the interiors of the dariole moulds vigorously and thoroughly with oil or melted butter. Season the potato slices with salt and pepper and pack them in the prepared darioles, ramming them down tightly until the containers are filled to the brim. Dot the tops with flakes of butter, place in your chosen tin and pour hot oil in until it comes two thirds of the way up the dariole moulds. Place on the highest possible oven shelf at preheated Gas Mark 8 and allow to bake for 35 minutes, when the tops will be crisp and brown. Lift out each mould carefully. Hold firmly in several folds of tea towel, run a sharp knife round the inside to loosen each, give each a smart tap and out will fall richly browned sandcastle shapes, which are soft and gooey in the middle.

Warning Always remember when working with hot oil to take the pan or whatever *to the hot oil* and not the hot oil to the whatever. Otherwise, as the authors have done in moments of idiocy, you may very well burn yourself severely!

POTATO RISSOLES
(Pommes de Terre Croquettes)

Turn 2oz portions of Duchess potato (p.191) in flour and shape into small, neat sausages. Proceed exactly as instructed for Duchess Potato 'Pears'.

ROAST POTATOES
(Pommes de Terre Anglaise)

Parboil peeled, evenly divided old potatoes for 10 minutes in slightly salted water. Drain thoroughly and place in butter or oil (or, if you must, in dripping) around the roasting meat, game or poultry for the last 45 minutes of roasting time. Remember to 'turn' the potatoes at half-time.

SAUERKRAUT Mme. JEANNE
(Choucroute Mme. Jeanne)

Place 2lb sauerkraut (tinned or fresh) in a basin. Work in ½oz caraway seeds. Moisten with ½ pint beer, still white wine or non-vintage champagne. Reheat as required over hot water (*au bain marie*).

Note: The addition of caraway seeds must remain optional as people are so sharply divided between loving and loathing their existence in any food.

SAUTÉ OF PARSNIP
(Panais Sauté)

Peel and divide the requisite number of parsnip and steam until tender. Drain and chill. When required for service, sauté in equal quantities of olive oil and butter until the outsides are a rich golden brown. Sprinkle with salt and pepper and serve with cut lemon.

SIEVED POTATO PURÉE

When steamed and rubbed through a sieve, the potatoes *must* be returned to a clean, dry pan and stirred with a wooden spoon over a low heat until the surplus moisture has dried out in a gentle steam. If you do not do this, the mixture will be too flabby to pipe properly.

STUFFED CABBAGE BALL
(Sou-Fassum)

An ideal vegetable dish, which the housewife can pre-prepare for Christmas dinner.

Use a round-headed or Savoy cabbage. Plunge into boiling water and leave on a table for 5 minutes. Allow to cool before peeling off the outer leaves. Ease back the inner leaves until the centre or core can be withdrawn completely. Replace this with any suitable forcemeat, cover with the outer leaves, set in a sieve lined out with several layers of muslin or a linen cloth. Place the sieve over a basin and steam for 2 hours.

If the sieve is lined with an outer layer of aluminium foil, pudding and cabbage can be steamed alongside or above each other, as the foil will ensure the flavours are not transmitted.

THE FORCEMEAT
(an example)

Chop up the centre core of cabbage (which you have removed!). Add 2oz finely sliced, blanched white of leek; ½lb pork sausage meat; 1½oz lean bacon, diced and fried; 1 very small onion, chopped fine and fried until soft and uncoloured in butter; 1 skinned tomato; ½ small crushed garlic clove (this can be omitted); 1oz half-cooked rice and 1oz frozen uncooked peas or half-cooked fresh peas. Season with salt and pepper.

STUFFED POTATOES
(Pomme Farcies)

Scrub and bake at Gas Mark 4/5 for 1 hour (unless giants, in which case 1¼ hours) the requisite number of large Dutch potatoes. Split lengthwise and scoop the pulp into a dish. Mash well, season with salt and pepper, add a little butter, a little very finely chopped ham, a little parsley and chives. Fill the mixture into the potato cases. Smooth off the top, brush with beaten egg and brown under the grill before serving.

STUFFED TOMATOES
(Les Tomates farcies)

Slice small 'lids' from a dozen firm, medium-sized tomatoes, scoop out the pips and flesh and cut away the cores with a small pair of scissors. Press the pulp through a sieve, and scrape the sieved pulp into a bowl. Now mix together with the following ingredients:

2oz soft breadcrumbs; 1 teaspoonful Worcestershire sauce; 1 teaspoonful freshly milled parsley or chives; 1 teaspoon raw grated onion pulp; 1 tablespoon sherry (add more crumbs if the mixture is too runny – it should be a pap). Spoon this mixture back into the hollowed-out tomatoes. Replace the lids, pack closely together – a Victoria sponge tin does very well – and bake on the middle shelf for about 20 minutes at Gas Mark 4 when desired.

SWEET POTATO CROQUETTES

Ingredients: 4 medium sweet potatoes; 1½oz butter; salt and pepper to season; 2 rounded tablespoons soft brown sugar; fine soft white breadcrumbs; 1 strained raw beaten egg.

Method: Peel, steam and sieve the potatoes into a roomy bowl. Add the butter, salt, pepper and sugar. Beat thoroughly. Refrigerate until firm enough to handle easily. Shape up like round scones ¾in thick. Pass through the egg and coat thickly with the crumbs. Refrigerate up to 24 hours. Fry in slightly smoking hot oil (390–400°F) until a good golden brown immediately prior to service.

SWEET POTATO PONE

Ingredients: 3 large peeled sweet potatoes; 14fl oz boiling water; 1 flat teaspoon salt; ¼ teaspoon black pepper; 2 flat teaspoons allspice; 2oz butter; 4 gently rounded tablespoons soft brown sugar.

Method: Grate the potatoes medium fine. Place in a bowl, cover with boiling water and leave for 5 minutes. Add all remaining ingredients, beat thoroughly, turn into a shallow buttered baking tin and bake on the centre shelf at Gas Mark 4 for 1 hour or until crusty and brown.

SWISS POTATO
(Roesti)

Ingredients: 2lb peeled, steamed potatoes; rendered-down unsalted pork fat; 1 small teacup each of grated Parmesan, soft-fried onions and thick cream; salt and pepper to season.

Method: Grate the potatoes coarsely. Melt sufficient pork fat to cover the base of a frying pan. Mix the remaining ingredients together, and level the mixture into the pan over a brisk medium heat. Use a metal spatula or slice to scrape and turn as a fine crust forms on the base. Finally press into a flattish gâteau shape.

VICTORIAN RED CABBAGE

Ingredients: 1 medium red cabbage; 1 large, thinly sliced onion; 1 tablespoon butter; 8oz cold Brown Sauce (p.176); ½ saltspoon pepper; 2 flat teaspoons salt; 4 tablespoons wine vinegar; 1 heaped tablespoon soft brown sugar.

Method: Separate the cabbage leaves. Cut away the hard stems. Slice thinly. Place the onion, butter, Brown Sauce, pepper and salt in a thick pan over a low heat. Simmer until the mixture bubbles and then pay in the cabbage, turning it over as you do so. Add the vinegar, cover and cook very gently for 1 hour. Add the sugar, stir again and continue cooking until the cabbage is very tender and the moisture is almost completely absorbed. Serve piping hot.

Note: 4 tablespoons single cream may be added a moment or two before serving and/or the strained juice of ½ lemon may be poured over.

SALADS

Before you align salads with any chosen dishes on your Christmas dinner menu and if you are serving wine, it must be remembered that the given incidence of wine vinegar in any of the following dressings is not very kind to wine and really should be replaced by grape juice. Remember that although the French regard a tossed green salad as a vital part of any meal, they love it as a separate course after the main one before the cheese and then pudding, and carefully abstain from drinking wine while demolishing the salads. The word vinegar derives from the French '*vin aigre*' or sour wine; therefore it is obvious that you cannot produce sour wine from malt and that we always mean wine vinegar because there is no other! Even so, sour wine is no partner for sound wine, as you probably know very well already. If, however, you happen to have a more humble Burgundy than the one you may be serving for Christmas Dinner, you can also use this in your dressing instead of the wine vinegar, or a modest claret when serving claret with the main course, or if serving a dry white wine with a fish course and desiring a salad, use a little modest dry white wine in the dressing. It is equally implicit that the Orange Salad is primarily intended for service with duck; that the French Potato Salad is intended for the buffet like the salads made with beans, lentils, cabbage, tomato and beetroot and endive mixed. Even so the Celeriac and Beetroot Salad constitutes an excellent way of cutting the richness of a goose, and a classic

Green Salad suitably dressed can be served either way with or after any main course.

A BASKET OF RAW VEGETABLES
(Les Crudités)

This most popular and healthy fashion in French homes and restaurants has still not sufficiently penetrated English ones – *Les Crudités* are nothing more than decorative assemblies (on trolley, sideboard or buffet) of raw vegetables from which guests make their own selection, grating, shredding or separating according to the requirements of the chosen vegetable or salading. A bowl of Mayonnaise (pp.182-3) and a bowl of French Dressing (pp.180-81) are set beside the salads and again guests help themselves. All green salad items should be cleaned, trimmed and torn – but never cut!

For grating coarsely: Carrots, parsnips, turnips, onions, swedes, flower of cauliflower, cabbages (white and red), beetroot and Jerusalem artichokes.

For slicing: Raw unskinned mushrooms, cucumber and pimentos (red, yellow and green).

For eating whole: Radishes, separate bowls of shelled pecans, walnuts, beech nuts, brazils and almonds (plain and salted).

Preparation: Any large salad bowl will do, but the effect is far greater if the whole raw items are arranged carefully in a large-handled wicker basket.

P.S. Do not forget a sharp knife, a grater or mandoline and a chopping board.

BUTTER BEAN SALAD
(Salade aux Flageolets)

For this salad 1lb of beans must be soaked overnight, cooked and, if large and coarse, also divested of their overcoats. To a pint of ordinary French Dressing (pp.180-81) add 1 teaspoon each of tarragon, chervil, chives and parsley (dried herbs can always be used if you pre-soak them in a few drops of absolutely boiling water first and then squeeze out in a clean, dry cloth). Also add half a dozen finely chopped anchovy fillets and a heaped teaspoon of powdered paprika. Toss the beans in this mixture and serve liberally sprinkled with milled parsley leaves.

Note: The above yields a buffet quantity but is easily divisible by 2 or 4!

CELERIAC AND BEETROOT SALAD
(Salade d'Hiver)

Toss shredded celeriac and shredded beetroot in French Dressing (pp.180-81), turn into a salad bowl and smooth off to a neat dome. Overlap circles of sliced cooked beetroot (stamped with a small, fluted pastry cutter) around the outer edge. Place an inner circle of half-walnuts, another circle of beetroot and so on to the centre where a stem of celeriac must be driven down to finish.

CELERY SALAD
(Salade aux Céleris)

Shred the inner hearts of celery heads either into matchsticks with a knife or with a mandoline for the easy way. Mix together equal parts of cream and Mayonnaise (pp.182-3). Stir in 1 level teaspoon lemon juice to every ¼ pint. Toss the celery shreds in this mixture. Turn into a salad bowl, sprinkle with finely chopped walnuts and garnish with a tuft of celery heart driven in centrally and a band of walnuts around the rim.

CORN SALAD
(Salade Lorette)

Escoffier salad admirably suited to winter limitations.

Ingredients: 6 'heads' carefully picked corn salad (*romaine*); 1 teacupful celery heart cut into matchsticks (*en julienne*); French Dressing (pp.180-81); 1 medium, cooked, skinned beet-root cut into matchsticks (against the grain), i.e. *en julienne*.

Method: Mix all salad ingredients together at the moment of service and turn in French dressing. If you try to do this in advance, the salad will be a mess, discoloured by the beetroot, which stains on contact with any other substance.

GREEN SALAD
(Salade Verte)

The hardy perennial is made with cos or cabbage lettuce dressed with plain French Dressing (pp.180-81) made with wine, grape juice or wine vinegar, but all or any of the following may also be served as a green salad, either separately or mixed together: watercress, corn (*romaine*), cress, young spinach leaves, young nasturtium leaves, blanched dandelion leaves, endive (*chicorée*), very young green radish or turnip centre leaves from the tops. First, pick the chosen salad over carefully, discard any blemished areas, wash in icily cold water, shake in a salad basket (*saladier*) and only toss with your chosen dressing immediately before serving. Ideal service is of course in a wooden salad bowl. Just one final thing to remember: these items inevitably weep out their flavour if cut up with a knife or scissors. The leaves, when too large, must be torn into convenient sizes. At will any of the green items may be served separately or together with top sprinklings, after dressing, of milled parsley heads or very, very finely scissored chives.

LENTIL SALAD
(Salade aux Lentilles)

Soak 1lb lentils in cold water overnight. Simmer in plenty of strained meat or game stock until tender. Drain the stock back into the stock pot and turn the lentils in the French dressing mixture given for Butter Bean Salad (pp.200-201), adding to it a teaspoon of real curry paste, i.e. Masala Paste.

Note: The quality of these when purchased in England is extraordinarily variable. We abstained from giving you the cooking time as two separate lots purchased recently took (a) 45 minutes and (b) 1½ hours to reach the stage just past *al dente* and this side of collapsing.

MERCEDES SALAD
(Salade Mercédes)

Assemble equal quantities of cooked beetroot cut in matchsticks (*en julienne*), celery heart cut in matchsticks (*en julienne*) and finely torn heart of endive. Make a dressing as follows:

2 finely chopped hard boiled eggs; sufficient olive oil to bind to a light paste; 1 rounded teaspoon of French mustard; strained juice of 2 lemons. At the moment of service, arrange in decorative heaps on a glass dish, pour on the dressing and serve immediately. If kept waiting, the beetroot will 'bleed' and render all unsightly.

MUSHROOM SALAD
(Salade aux Champignons)

One of the best of the simplest. Just slice unskinned mushrooms very thinly, stalks and all. Swill them with lemon juice, spoon a ladle full of olive oil over them, add a grating of pepper, turn once or twice and serve immediately.

Do not skin mushrooms. Place in a colander, clean by pouring hot water over them, dry and use.

ORANGE SALAD
(Salade aux Oranges)

It is all in the cutting of the orange. Sharpen a small, 'comfortable' knife and with it slice both pith and peel away from each sweet orange, so that the flesh is completely exposed. Then drive the knife between skin and flesh against the skin and turn it so that the segment flicks out whole and skinless. Do this all round the orange so that you are ultimately left with a core and a circle of the segments' skins and can squeeze this like a sponge to expend the remaining juices. When sufficient segments have been assembled (we allow 1 orange per 2 persons), present in one of the two following ways:

Presentation 1: Orange segments heaped into pulled chicory leaves, which when filled are lightly dusted with paprika and lightly sprinkled (a) with salt and (b) with orange juice.

Presentation 2: Arranged in a 'flower' on individual salad plates with a centre of thinly sliced chicory, and a moistening of sherry instead of orange juice.

RUSSIAN SALAD
(Salade Russe)

This is composed of 1 level teacupful of each of the following: cooked, diced potatoes, French beans, carrots and turnips; raw, unskinned cucumber (cucumber is only indigestible when the skin is removed); strained, tinned sweetcorn, whole cooked *petits pois* and half-quantity of soaked, cooked, small white beans (*flageolets*). Mix all well together and mix thoroughly in mayonnaise. We prefer to serve this in a panel. If you would like to copy us dissolve 1oz gelatine in 4 tablespoons of water over a low heat and stir into 1 pint real Mayonnaise (pp.182-3) and blend thoroughly into the mixed vegetables. Turn the mixture into an oiled mould and leave until set. Unmould, garnish with decorative squiggles of mayonnaise, sliced hard-boiled eggs and petals of peeled black and green olives.

SALAMAGUNDY

A moderate version of a very old English dish.

Ingredients: 2 finely torn lettuces; the skinless, neatly trimmed segments of 2 lemons; about 2 dozen slices of cold game or poultry; 2 sliced hard-boiled eggs; 2 rounded table-spoons chopped or milled parsley; 1 dozen very small, cooked shallots; ½lb peeled grapes; 1 dozen boned, washed, dried anchovy fillets; French Dressing (pp.180-81).

Method: Lay down a bed of the torn lettuce, which may well be mixed with torn spinach leaves if liked. Cover with the meat slices. Scatter the diced anchovy evenly and continue sprinkling over the chopped lemon segments, the grapes and the parsley. Arrange hard-boiled egg slices and shallots around the edge and at the moment of service dress liberally with French dressing.

Note: There are many versions of this dish, beloved by our ancestors and sometimes known as Solomon-Grundy.

TOMATO SALAD
(Salade de Tomates)

Slice firm, unskinned or skinned tomatoes as cleanly and thinly as possible; this can only be done with a very sharp knife. Range the slices in overlapping lines down a shallow dish. Swill them lightly with oil, sprinkle with parsley, lay an overlapping line of the thinnest possible raw onion rings over the top surface and serve.

TRUE FRENCH POTATO SALAD
(Salade de Pommes de Terre)

Dice 2lb peeled old or new potatoes neatly and steam. Refresh in cold water and drain very thoroughly. Spread 1 whole thin crust from a sandwich loaf with 1 crushed garlic clove. Cut into narrow strips and then halve the strips. Place in salad bowl and swill with 1 generous ladleful of hot, strained stock or consommé. Turn carefully and gently and at the moment of service add French dressing with herbs.

Note 1. Fine small sprigs of endive, finely sliced chicory, dice of *charcuterie* sausage, diced anchovies, peeled French green olives or black olives may be added '*à choix*'. The subtle delight of flavouring depends upon the addition of that stock or consommé.

Note 2. A whole garlic is called a head. The name 'clove' is given to a section of the head.

WINDSOR SALAD
(Salade Windsor)

Hollow out a large, tight white cabbage very thoroughly. Grate up one small teacupful of the removed cabbage and mix with equal quantities of raw grated carrot and Jerusalem artichokes, finely chopped raw mushrooms and raw grated beetroot. Stir in sour cream and mayonnaise in equal proportions. Fill into the hollow cabbage, decorate centrally with a stuffed hard-boiled egg and encircle with stuffed hard-boiled eggs for service.

PUDDINGS

'The things we eat by various juice control
The narrowness or largeness of our soul'.
Dr King

Although we rarely eat puddings we revel in making, garnishing and presenting them. Even the most wine-wise men adore
them and most women will forsake their diets for the ones that
look really tempting.

Puddings, in fact, can be monstrous deceivers or the one
item which above all makes eyes sparkle, whether the eyes
belong to what Fanny's papa called 'octogeraniums' or to what
the late Sir Archibald McIndoe always referred to as 'squeakers'.

They can be an outrage when, as in many catering trade
buffets of our bitter experience, they *appear* excellent . . . cream-
laced and painstakingly decorated . . . yet taste rather like bath
sponge garnished with shaving cream. If anyone is aiming for
this brand of flavour, they will most readily achieve it with
synthetic sponge, bought custard powder, ersatz cream and
meringues made from a fluid which we understand to be a
by-product of nylon.

A party pudding is of necessity a *luxe* item; only the best is
good enough for it and there must be no scrimping; better a
bowl of fruit macedoine with just a touch of liqueur from
a miniature bottle than a trifle with too little cream, a tipsy

cake with insufficient alcohol or a *Charlotte Russe* flavoured with vanilla essence and not a vanilla pod. The policy should be lash out or leave severely alone. Moreover at Christmas-time the garnish or decoration can be much more elaborate than at any other time in the year and indeed needs to be when it has to hold its own in a room garlanded and swagged, beribboned and sparkling with candlelight and glitter balls.

LET YOURSELVES GO

Tie up your *Charlotte Russe* with narrow scarlet ribbon; bejewel the top with angelica and glacé cherries, which, remember, are not only sold in red but also in green and golden colour; encircle the base with lavish rosettes of whipped cream and surround these with a garland of almond-paste holly leaves.

Give the Italian cake/pudding so oddly named *Zuppa Inglese* (Italian Trifle), which is encased in biscuit-coloured meringue mixture, little sprigs of angelica leaves and jewel cherries at the corners and in the centre.

Set a bowl of syllabub on a silver tray and mass the rim with sprigs of holly, real or fake berries.

Pipe brandy butter into a pyramid on a pedestal dish, tie up the stem with an enormous shiny emerald or crimson bow and bejewel the pyramid with scraps of crystallised or glacé fruits. Do the same with mistletoe sprigs around the family fruit salad but keep ivy off the table – the dust is poisonous.

If you have need of paper d'oyleys, let them be gold or silver, not just plain white.

THE PRESENTATION OF CHRISTMAS PUDDINGS

Pray do not boil them in dreary old pudding basins. If you burnish the insides of any jelly moulds, no matter how decorative, sufficiently thoroughly with *liquid paraffin* soaked into a piece of lint or cotton waste, the puddings will turn out perfectly and look a deal more attractive than those pudding-basin humps.

If you wish to be very different, then press your raw Christmas Pudding mixture into a large, oiled metal border mould and steam it in this. It has the added advantage of taking less time to cook. When you turn it out, have ready a garland of holly sprigs, which will fit around the outside of the border mould – thus enabling you to put the brandy in the middle and light it without the fear that the holly will also catch fire. (Which ours has done before now!)

If you prefer to be really classical in the manner of the great Escoffier, then use our favourite, the *Pouding des Rois Mages* recipe (pp.216-17). For it, you may wish to obtain a log-shaped mould into which you pack your pudding mixture, first lining the tin carefully and thoroughly with aluminium foil, which you then oil liberally. We did it this way at the Royal Albert Hall before nearly 7,000 people so you can be quite confident that it works! It also looks superb when blazing with brandy from end to end and it is remarkably neat to serve, in slices as you would a Swiss roll. Naturally the flavour is unimpaired when cooked in a plain pudding basin!

Some years ago the eminent and very correct General Manager of a famous television company shared a lift with

Fanny. As the lift stopped and he moved towards the doors, he demanded abruptly, 'What's happened to the round Christmas Pudding, Fanny? Please revive it,' and so saying, disappeared. It must be remembered that when the copper clothes-boiler went out of fashion, so did the round Christmas Pudding, which had hitherto been shaped into a ball, tied up in a cloth and dropped into a great deal of boiling water, where it simmered and bounced away merrily without constriction.

We solved the problem with a sieve, some aluminium foil and a basin. Shape up the raw pudding mixture in a large sieve lined with aluminium foil and well-buttered papers. When the mixture is well pressed down and you have achieved a fairly good dome on top, cover with more butter papers, draw over the foil and turn upside down so that the un-shaped half is now in the sieve. Stand the sieve over a basin, stand the basin on a piece of wood and set both inside a large, covered pan, not so full of water that it reaches the pudding. Steam for about 10 hours (turning the pudding reverse side up at half-time).

BOILED PLUM PUDDING (1777)

'Take a pound of Beef-fuet fhred very fine, then ftone three quarters of a Pound of Raifins, then take fome grated Nutmeg, a large Spoonful of Sugar, a little Salt, fome Sach, four eggs, three spoonfuls of Cream, and five Spoonfuls of Flour; mix thefe together, tie it up in a cloth, and let it boil three Hours. Melt butter and pour over it.'

ANGELICA TART

Ingredients: 10oz bought or home-made puff pastry; 1¼lb peeled, cored, fairly thinly sliced cooking apples; ¾lb diced angelica; 1 generous leaf of lemon rind, cut thinly; sugar syrup (pp.274-5); a little raw egg white; castor sugar.

Method: Place the prepared apples and angelica in a thick pan with the lemon peel and sufficient sugar syrup to come halfway up the depth of the pan filled by fruit and herb. Simmer very gently until the apples become transparent. Chill. Roll out the puff pastry fairly thinly. Line into a standard glass ovenware flan dish 8in diameter. Remove the lemon peel from the cooled fruit mixture. Turn into raw pastry or proceed as described using a medium pie dish. Then cover with trimmings of pastry rolled into lid. Brush the surface with raw egg white and sprinkle thickly with castor sugar. Bake one shelf above centre, Gas Mark 6, until the pastry is a good golden brown.

THE BRANDIED FRUIT POT

Ingredients: 1 bottle humble brandy; 1lb preserving sugar; fruit as instructed.

Method: Take a very large stone jar with a well-fitting cork lid. Place the brandy and sugar in the base. When a pound of dessert gooseberries are available, wash, top, tail, dry, sink into the jar and ram on the lid. When any or all of the following fruit are ripe but not bruised add 1lb of each, resealing and storing after each addition: raspberries, loganberries, strawberries, cherries, plums, greengages, peaches, nectarines, black grapes.

Note: After the final sealing leave for 3 months. Always re-seal after taking any desired quantity.

THE BRANDY MIXTURE WHICH ALWAYS BURNS FOR A LONG TIME

For this you employ a trick. Use equal quantities of inexpensive, young brandy (not a good one, please) and tasteless, odourless vodka, which has a very high alcoholic content indeed – this is what facilitates the burning, provided you put both in a small, thick pan and warm through until the heat nips a very clean finger, over a low heat first. We did this at the Royal Albert Hall and we kept the mixture burning for 9 minutes.

CHARLOTTE RUSSE

This was an integral part of so many Christmas-party tables in our youth that we feel it essential to include it.

Ingredients: Savoy finger biscuits; 4 tablespoons redcurrant jelly; 2 tablespoons port; 5fl oz water; ½oz powdered gelatine.

Method: Wet the base and sides of a 7½in-diameter sliding-based cake tin with cold water. Cut one tip off each biscuit (so that they stand well) and arrange them all round the inside of the tin. Warm the water, soften the gelatine in it, add the jelly, stir until clear, add the port and strain into a bowl. Pour sufficient into the wetted, biscuit-edged tin to cover the base. Set over ice. Decorate with cut petals of glacé cherry and curved stems of angelica. Set this decoration with a carefully spooned covering of the jelly. Allow this to set. Now use more of the jelly with the crumbled biscuit tips to make a pap and fill in any interstices with this pap. When set, make the filling (see below), pour in and leave in refrigeration overnight. Unmould and immediately tie round just below the top and just above the base with very narrow red or green satin ribbon. Fork up the remaining jelly and arrange in a narrow encircling band around the Charlotte. Decorate with sprays of maidenhair fern.

The Filling:

Ingredients: 15fl oz double cream; 5fl oz milk; 2½fl oz water; ½oz powdered gelatine; 2 stiffly beaten egg whites; 1 vanilla pod; 6 level dessertspoons castor sugar.

Method: Whip the cream until it holds a peak. Boil the milk with the sugar and vanilla pod very slowly and leave to infuse till cold. Remove the pod, stir into the cream, dissolve the gelatine with water, stir into the cream/milk mixture, beat in the egg whites and continue beating until the mixture starts to thicken. Turn into a prepared tin.

Notes: Vanilla pod may be deleted and in its place 1 tablespoon of strongly reduced coffee syrup added. In this case also delete 1 tablespoon of water and replace it with the coffee syrup. Alternatively, a tablespoon of rum, kirsch or brandy may be added to the mixture, in each case deleting the equivalent amount of water.

To make coffee syrup, collect the lees for long enough to give you a pint. Then simmer down to about 3fl oz maximum of strongly reduced coffee syrup. Do not add any sugar. Store in a screw-topped bottle.

CHESTNUT PUDDING
(Mont Blanc aux Marrons)

Ingredients: 2lb peeled, cooked, sieved dry chestnuts; 6oz loaf sugar; 1 small wineglass Madeira; 1 vanilla pod; 1½ pints Chantilly Cream (p.232).

Method: Melt the sugar with the Madeira and vanilla pod in a thick pan over a very low heat. Bring to the boil, simmer for 2 minutes, add the chestnut purée gradually and work up to a smooth, very thick, workable paste. Pipe this through a fairly thick, plain writing pipe to form a border in a shallow dish. Fill the centre with a pyramid of ornamentally piped Chantilly Cream, chill and serve.

CHRISTMAS PARCELS
(Petits Pacquets en Surprise)

Ingredients: 2 very fine and delicate pre-made pancakes per head; 1 small, fat rectangle cut from a Frozen Christmas Pudding (pp.218-19) per 'parcel'; a shallow container of ground almonds, another of raw beaten egg, and a pan of oil (slightly smoking hot) for frying the 'parcels'.

Method: Place a rectangle of frozen pudding in the centre of each pancake. Fold up into a small, neat parcel. Slip the parcels swiftly through the beaten egg, coat thickly with the ground almonds and slip into the hot oil to brown rapidly. Serve at once with sifted icing sugar or Champagne Sauce (p.231).

CHRISTMAS PUDDING LEFTOVERS

1. Slice, lay on a buttered heat-resistant dish, moisten with brandy, cover with foil and heat at Gas Mark 1. Sprinkle with sifted icing sugar and serve with Brandy Butter (pp.230-31) or Punch Sauce (p.233).

2. Slice, dip slices into raw beaten (strained) eggs and turn in ground almonds until thickly coated. Deep fry in olive oil until golden brown and serve with the following sauce:

   Sauce: Heat 3 tablespoons golden syrup in ½ pint water with 1oz butter and the strained juice and grated rind of 1½ lemons. Flavour strongly with rum, stir in a further nut of butter to 'finish' and thicken with a little potato flour (*Fécule de pommes*) mixed with cold water.

3. Re-steam in a basin under foil, shape into small balls, set on a heat-resistant dish, cover with piped meringue

(pp.247-8) and bake at Gas Mark 2 until golden brown. Hand Brandy Butter separately.

4. Cut into leaf-thin slices. Clap together in pairs over a liberal spread of Brandy Butter. Cut into triangular 'sandwiches' and arrange on a d'oyley-covered, oval flat dish. Sprinkle thickly with sifted icing sugar and decorate with pipings of Brandy Butter, coloured pale green with harmless vegetable colouring.

CHRISTMAS PUDDING SNOWBALLS
(Beignets de Noël)

Cold Christmas Pudding, re-steamed until pliable, forms the basis for one of the most simple and effective winter party puddings.

Ingredients: Shallow containers levelled off with (a) ground almonds (sieve these if they are at all lumpy); (b) sifted icing sugar; (c) beaten, strained raw egg; olive oil to fry; little sprigs of almond-paste holly or mistletoe, or little gold leaves and halved glacé cherries used together; warm Christmas Pudding remains.

Method: Shape small portions of the re-steamed Christmas Pudding (with well-scrubbed hands!) into balls, which are roughly the size of small tangerines. Roll these in the beaten egg. Drain thoroughly and roll in the ground almonds until well covered. Lift with a slice and slide into the heated olive oil. Fry to a good, rich golden brown. Lift out, drain and bury in the icing sugar. Arrange on a heated dish and keep hot in the oven until required. At the moment of service decorate each one with a tiny sprig of either almond-paste holly, or a gold leaf and a piece of glacé cherry. Hand Brandy Butter separately (pp.230-31) or serve with soft brown (pieces) sugar and cream.

ECONOMICAL CHRISTMAS PUDDING

Ingredients: 10oz flour; 5oz soft breadcrumbs; 6oz suet; 4oz mixed golden syrup and black treacle; ¼ nutmeg, grated; 1 level tablespoon mixed spices; 1 raw, finely grated carrot; 2oz minced, raw beef; 4 eggs; ½lb sultanas; ¼lb currants; ¼lb dates; ¼lb figs; old ale to mix.

Method: Mix all the dry ingredients in a large bowl. Add warmed syrups and beaten eggs. Stir in sufficient ale gradually to achieve cake-mixture consistency. Turn into buttered basins, fill three-quarters full, cover with butter papers, cover with kitchen foil and steam for 8–10 hours.

ESCOFFIER'S PLUM PUDDING
(Le Pouding des Rois Mages)

Here is our favourite Christmas Pudding recipe. It is very much lighter in texture than the traditional recipe. It was created by the greatest chef of all – Georges Auguste Escoffier. We consider it the best in the world.

Ingredients: 1lb fine breadcrumbs; ½lb suet; ½lb flour; 4oz chopped cooking apples; ½lb sultanas; ½lb seedless raisins; ½lb currants; 2oz mixed chopped peel; 4oz soft brown sugar; strained juice of ½ orange; strained juice of 1 lemon; 1oz finely chopped ginger; ½oz allspice; 1oz flaked almonds; 2 small eggs; 2½fl oz brandy; sufficient old ale to bind this mixture to a loose batter paste.

Method: Mix the breadcrumbs, suet, flour, sugar, all fruits, almonds, spices, peel and apples together in a large bowl. Whip the eggs and add the brandy, lemon and orange juices. Work up into a dry mixture, adding ale until it makes a very loose batter. Cover with a cloth and leave overnight before filling into buttered containers. The bread swells during the waiting time and by morning the mixture is thick and firm. Press into moulds or bowls and cover with (a) buttered paper, (b) foil. Steam for 10 hours. Re-steam for 4 hours on Christmas Day.

FAMILY FRUIT SALAD
(Salade de Fruits familiale)

Fanny's Mother said English Fruit Salad was like pond water with bits floating about in it. She never allowed anyone to use any liquids at all in a fruit salad . . . only the fruit, icing sugar, liqueur and lemon juice. Like this:

Take a large wide-necked jar and lay into it (in winter) a layer of peeled, stoned grapes. Cover with sifted icing sugar. Cover with a layer of thinly sliced eating apple (with the skin removed – remember to use a silver knife), dredge with lemon juice to prevent discolouration, dust thickly with sifted icing sugar and cover with a layer of thinly peeled pear. Dust again with sifted icing sugar. Cover with a layer of rough-cut fresh pineapple, more icing sugar, then a layer of sliced bananas and finally a layer of absolutely skinless tangerine or orange segments. Make one final thick layer of sifted icing sugar. Pour on 2½fl oz rum; 2½fl oz brandy and a tablespoonful of maraschino. Cover and leave for at least 24 hours. Serve without cream.

FRENCH PLUM PUDDING
(Le Pouding de Noël)

Light but very pleasant and highly suited to those unable to stomach our traditional 'indigestible'.

Ingredients: ½ pint milk; 2oz butter; 4oz sifted flour; 3oz castor sugar; 6 egg yolks; 4 egg whites; 3 medium cooking apples; 1 liqueur glass kirsch; 2oz finely chopped walnuts; ¼lb sultanas; ½lb chopped stoned raisins; 1 heaped teaspoon powdered cinnamon.

Method: Bring the milk and butter to the boil together in a thick pan. Stir in the flour and continue stirring with a wooden spoon until a smooth paste is obtained. Cool to blood heat. Add the sugar and the egg yolks (lightly beaten). Beat well. Add the stiffly beaten egg whites. The peeled, cored, finely chopped cooking apples are then stirred in, together with the kirsch. Add the remaining ingredients. Stir slowly and lightly. Turn into a large, buttered mould and steam for 2½ hours. Serve with Vanilla Sauce (p.233).

FROZEN CHRISTMAS PUDDING
(Le pouding de Noel glacé)

This is very much our own. Make ½ pint of Confectioners' Custard (p.232), fold into it ½ pint of stiffly beaten cream and add a heaped tablespoon each of chopped glacé cherries, chopped angelica, chopped glacé ginger, chopped crystallised pineapple and 1 tablespoon each of sultanas and currants, all of which have been soaked previously for 1 hour in sufficient dry white wine to cover them and strained thereafter.

Tip into a soufflé mould or solid (not sliding-based) cake tin and freeze, to serve whole, garnished with whipped cream. Alternatively, cut into small balls with a small ice cream server. Set with at least 2in spaces between each one on a flat dish. Pipe all over with Chantilly Cream (p.232), using a nylon icing bag and a small ornamental pipe. Decorate each ball with two 'leaves' of angelica and a glacé cherry. Replace in the freezing compartment until required for serving. Take out 10–15 minutes before eating. Please note that you cannot cut a number of these and pipe them all in one go or the ice cream will begin to melt. Do two or three at a time, put them back in the freezer and then take out and do two or three more.

OUR MINCEMEAT

Ingredients: 1lb currants; 1lb rough-chopped seeded raisins; 1lb sultanas; 1½lb beef suet; 1lb darkest possible soft brown (pieces) sugar; 1oz mixed spices; 1lb peeled, cored, minced apples with their juices; grated rind of 2 lemons and 3 oranges; 1 teacupful each of rum and brandy.

Method: Mix all together thoroughly.

MINCEMEAT PANCAKES

This is a treatment, not a recipe. Make very thin pancakes. Bake mincemeat at Gas Mark 6 for 10 minutes or until bubbling, spread on pancakes, roll up, arrange on a heated dish and sprinkle thickly with sifted icing sugar. Pour on warmed rum and send flaming to the table.

HOW TO MAKE A BIG MINCE PIE

> *'The while the meat is a-shredding*
> *For the rare mince-pie,*
> *And the plums stand by*
> *To fill the paste that's a-kneading…'*
> *Hesperides*, Herrick

Authors would ask you to note particularly that Herrick refers to mince pie in the *singular*, for which we campaign today!

Use a steep-sided, shallow fireproof dish (round) or a plain, steep-sided Victoria sponge tin, or a flan ring. Roll out the pastry, roll it up over a handleless rolling pin and unroll it over the chosen container. Press in the sides. Press the surplus pastry lightly over the rim and run the rolling pin round the edge so that the pastry surplus falls away cleanly without leaving a clumsy, thick border. Roll out the pieces to form sufficient for a lid.

Fill the mincemeat into the pastry-lined container. Roll up and unroll the pastry as before to form the lid. It is quite unnecessary to wet the edges. Roll the rolling pin round again to lock top and bottom together securely and leave a neatly finished rim. Bake at Gas Mark 5, one shelf above centre, without brushing the top surface of the pastry with *anything*.

Bake until pale golden brown (allow for reheating if you intend serving your big mince pie hot), take out and dust thickly with sifted icing sugar.

NESSELRODE PUDDING
(Pouding Nesselrode)

This is a monster of extravagance, but every cook ought to make at least *one* for a special party at some time in her cooking life.

Ingredients: 1½ pints Confectioners' Custard (p.232); 8½oz chestnut purée; 5oz finely chopped, mixed, glacé cherries; 4oz diced angelica soaked for 30 minutes in Bual or Malmsey; 5oz Malaga raisins brought to the boil in water, wiped, seeded and soaked in Bual or Malmsey; 2¼ pints double cream, flavoured to taste strongly of maraschino (it will be twice reduced by the bulk of the confectioners' custard and by its own frozen state, which always diminishes flavour).

Method: Mix the custard with the soaked fruits and chestnut purée, add the fairly stiffly whipped cream and turn into a well-oiled, really decorative mould. Freeze until required.

Unmould about 10–15 minutes before service. Garnish with asparagus fern and crystallised mimosa.

NURSERY CHRISTMAS PUDDING

When very small tummies are incapable of coping with richly endowed dried-fruit Christmas Puddings, give them the following substitute.

Ingredients: 2oz butter; 2oz castor sugar; 1 egg; 4oz flour; 3oz cooking chocolate (or chocolate chips); 1 tin peach and apricot baby food, an equal amount in cream.

Method: Cream the butter, add the sugar and cream again. Add the egg, flour and 2oz softened chocolate (or softened chocolate chips). Then fold in the remaining ounce of chocolate (not softened). Fill into a small, liberally buttered basin, cover with butter papers, cover with foil and steam for 1¾ hours. Mix the peach and apricot baby food and cream to make a sauce, heat and serve.

If feeling 'fancy', place the raw prepared mixture into a liberally buttered rabbit mould. When the pudding has been turned out onto a dish, remember to affix two small glacé cherry 'eyes', 'ears' of softened angelica, and touch up the apricot and cream sauce with harmless green colouring. Pour around rather than over the rabbit and he or she will appear to be sitting upon the greensward.

OLD-FASHIONED BAKED PLUM PUDDING

Ingredients: 1 small milk loaf; milk; 4 eggs; ½lb suet; ¾lb chopped, seeded raisins; ¾lb currants; 2oz chopped glacé cherries; 3oz soft brown (pieces) sugar; 1 eggspoon powdered ginger; ½ eggspoon grated nutmeg; 1 port-glass brandy.

Method: Cut the crusts from the loaf, break up the crumb roughly, stand in a bowl, moisten with milk and leave for two hours. Drain away all the surplus milk, beat in the eggs, add all the remaining ingredients, press into a buttered heat-resistant dish and bake at Gas Mark 4 until springy to the touch.

ORANGE FOOL
(Crème aux Oranges)

Definitely extravagant.

Ingredients: Strained juice of three oranges; 3 well-whipped eggs; ½ pint cream; 2½oz sifted icing sugar; generous pinch of nutmeg and cinnamon; 1 small nut of butter.

Method: Mix all the ingredients except the butter in the top of a double saucepan. When completely blended, place over the outer pan, half filled with boiling water. Stir the mixture over a very low heat until it becomes very thick and smooth. Remove from the heat and plunge the top pan at once into a bowl of crushed ice. Toss in the butter in very small flakes and continue stirring until the temperature has dropped to blood heat. Pile into glasses or coupes and serve with *gâteau* or *petits fours* biscuits.

PLUM PUDDING

Ingredients: ¾lb fine white breadcrumbs; ¾lb sifted flour; ¾lb currants; ¾lb seeded raisins; 1½lb suet; 6 eggs; 1½fl oz old ale; ½ pint brandy; ¼lb finely chopped cooking apples; ¼lb diced mixed peel; ½oz mixed spices; 1 rounded teaspoon powdered nutmeg; 1 eggspoon salt.

Method: Mix the crumbs, flour, suet, spices, salt and dried fruits together. Whip up the eggs, add the beer and brandy and pour onto the dry ingredients. Mix very thoroughly.

Three-quarters fill into well-buttered basins or moulds and steam rather than boil. The longer you steam them, the better they will be.

PUNCH CAKE
(Ponche Gâteau)

This is a French version of the Italian *Zuppa Inglese* (pp.228-9) and both are members of the trifle family.

Ingredients: 3 rounds of stale sponge baked in Victoria sponge tins; 1 pint strong sugar syrup flavoured to taste with rum; 8oz apricot jam, preferably rubbed through a sieve.

The Meringue Mixture: 1½fl oz rum; 4oz sifted icing sugar; 4oz sieved apricot jam; 6 stiffly beaten egg whites.

Method: Moisten the three sponge layers with the rum mixture, spreading each liberally with apricot jam and mounting each above the other on a heat-resistant flat dish. Now blend the 1½fl oz rum with the 4oz apricot jam, add the icing sugar and fold gently into the very stiff egg whites. Spread over the assembled *gâteau* and decorate as desired using an icing bag with a large ornamental pipe. Cook one shelf below centre at Gas Mark 1 until a pale biscuit colour. Garnish with sprigs composed of cut glacé cherries and 'leaves' cut from angelica.

Note: Remember to soften the angelica in a little hot water before cutting. Be sure to use stale sponge.

ROUND CHRISTMAS PUDDING

For the finest results please use Escoffier's Christmas Pudding (pp.216-17). Steam a made Christmas Pudding until malleable. Line a common sieve with a big square of turkey-width kitchen foil. Line this liberally with buttered papers and shape the

Christmas Pudding into a ball inside. Fold the corners of the paper over, then bring up the foil sides. Press the handle of the sieve gently upwards to fit into a steamer. Stand in a basin in a steamer and re-steam for 2 hours. Then turn over the pudding, press well into the sieve again and steam for a further 2 hours. The pudding will now be well rounded. Stab the top with a sprig of holly. Additional steaming time will depend on your pudding and judgement.

Note: If wishing to make a Round Christmas Pudding with raw mixture, see pp.221-22, 222-23.

RUM SORBET
(Sorbet au Rhum)

Ingredients: ¾ pint boiling water; 8 lemons; 7oz loaf sugar; ¼ pint rum.

Method: Peel the lemons thinly. Place the rind in a roomy bowl. Pour on boiling water. Stir in the loaf sugar; allow to descend in temperature to blood heat. Add the strained juice of 6 lemons only. Stir in the rum. Pour into a plastic, seal-lidded container and freeze. Scrape into the roomy bowl, whisk vigorously (preferably with an electric mixer), return to the freezing container and re-freeze until required. Serve in glasses which have been rim-dipped into (a) cold water and (b) castor sugar. Place in refrigeration until the moment of service.

SYLLABUB 1
(Victorian)

Ingredients: Thinly peeled rind of 1 lemon; 1 pint sweet sherry or Madeira; castor sugar to taste; 1½ pints double cream; 1 egg white; strained juice of 1 lemon; 3 tablespoons brandy.

Method: Place the peel, 2 tablespoons castor sugar and the chosen fortified wine in a bowl. Cover with foil or a plate and leave overnight. Taste and, if desired, add more sugar until the mixture tastes very sweet, because the bulk of the cream will considerably reduce the sweetness. Stir in the brandy, tip in the cream and egg white and start whipping. Whip relentlessly. If your whipping is done thoroughly, a froth will rise upon the top. Skim it off into a well-chilled glass dish. Continue whipping and skimming until there is too little left to whip. Place in refrigeration and leave overnight. This kind of syllabub should always be made the day before it is eaten. Aim to pile the froth or foam as high as possible in the dish. Serve with dry *petits fours*.

SYLLABUB 2

Keeps for a week.

Ingredients: ½lb sifted icing sugar; strained juice of 2 lemons; grated rind of 1 lemon; 1 claret glassful Madeira; 1 claret glassful sweet white wine; 1 teaspoon ratafia; 1 quart cream; 6–8 macaroons; 1 generous pinch cinnamon.

Method: Break up the macaroons roughly and line into the base of a glass bowl. Dissolve the sugar in the lemon juice. Add the rind, wines and ratafia. Stir until the sugar is completely dissolved. Add the cream and whip relentlessly until the froth begins to rise. Skim off and place over the macaroons and so continue, whipping and skimming off the froth until there is too little left to whip. Pile the froth high in the dish and keep in mild refrigeration until required.

TANSY

We have rephrased this 1856 recipe.

Ingredients: 1 pint double cream; 8 egg yolks; 2 stiffly beaten egg whites; ½ pint Bual or Malmsey (Madeiras); icing or castor sugar and grated nutmeg to taste.

Method: Fold the egg yolks into the cream in a large bowl. Add the egg whites and beat them in, adding the chosen Madeira slowly and steadily. When this is done, season to taste with the nutmeg and chosen sugar.

Turn into a liberally buttered soufflé mould and stand the mould in a meat baking tin quarter filled with hot water. Bake one shelf below centre at Gas Mark 4 for 30–40 minutes or until set. Sift thickly with icing sugar when cold and immediately before serving.

TIPSY CAKE

This was also an indispensable adjunct to the Christmas Party, if only for the teetotallers! You can still buy moulded sponges in the form of pyramids, hedgehogs, ovals, etc. from pastrycooks in Soho and orders may be placed in advance. These sponges can be very stale when used, so we make ours considerably in advance of Christmas and store them in a tin or kitchen foil.

Ingredients: A 'moulded' sponge; 1 pint sweet white wine with 1 port glassful of brandy; 20oz sweet, blanched almonds; 1 pint Confectioners' Custard (p.232); harmless vegetable colouring; ½ pint double cream; 2 tablespoons brandy.

Method: Split the almonds lengthwise into slender spikes and drive them in all over the sponge cake in a shallow dish. Mix the wine and the brandy together and spoon slowly and carefully over the cake. Go on ladling and scooping up the liquid as it seeps into the dish, until all is absorbed. Whip the cream, whip into the confectioners' custard, add the brandy, colour palely with any desired colour, pour round the base of the sponge and chill well before serving.

Note: If using an animal mould, do not forget a squiggly tail in a strand of angelica or lemon peel, glacé-cherry eyes and leaf-thin angelica whiskers.

OUR TRIFLE

The trifle mixture is as follows:

1st layer: Crumbled macaroons – either almond or coconut – well soaked beforehand in strained orange juice and sherry. Alternative is rum – but use more sparingly and increase the orange juice.

2nd layer: Apricot jam.

3rd layer: Confectioners' Custard (p.232).

4th layer: Chantilly Cream (p.232).

Garnish: Chocolate leaves in a central cluster and all around the edges (pp.278-9).

TRIFLE (VICTORIAN)

Ingredients: 1 pack sponge cakes or 8 home-made; 1oz blanched almonds; 7½fl oz sweet white wine; 12 ratafia biscuits; 1 liqueur glass Noyau; 1 dozen leaf-thin slices lemon and orange candied peel; 1 tablespoon apricot jam; 1 table-spoon redcurrant jelly; 1 tablespoon raspberry jam; ¾ pint Confectioners' Custard (p.232); grated rind of 1 lemon; pinch of nutmeg; pinch of cinnamon; 6 lumps of sugar, crushed finely; ½ pint whipped double cream; 1oz hundreds and thousands.

Method: Split the sponge cakes, stab with splinters of almond and pack into the base of a crystal dish. Moisten with the wine. Soak the ratafias in the Noyau and lay on top.

Cover with the peel, dot the jams and jelly over the surface, cover with the confectioners' custard, sprinkle on the spices, cover with the whipped cream – preferably piped in decorative rosettes – and scatter with hundreds and thousands. Serve well chilled.

THE 'FAMILY' CHRISTMAS TRIFLE

Ingredients: 1 dozen sponge cakes or 2 dozen sponge fingers or 1, 10–12in long Swiss Roll filled with apricot jam (pp.237-8); 15fl oz sweet white wine; 5fl oz cooking brandy; ½lb cooking chocolate chips; 1½ pint Confectioners' Custard (p.232); ½ pint Chantilly Cream (p.232); green and red glacé cherries for garnish and chocolate leaves (pp.278-9).

Method: Slice the Swiss roll into a wide bowl, or split the sponge cakes or fingers, spread with apricot jam and clap together again and lay down in the bowl. Press well to form a solid base. Mix the brandy with the wine. Moisten the chosen sponge with this mixture. Cover with half the custard and leave until cold and set. Soften the chosen chocolate in a small pan over a low heat and spoon gently and swiftly over the cold custard, spreading carefully to form a complete coverage. When set, coat with the remaining custard. Decorate with pipings of Chantilly Cream, border with chocolate leaves, make a central cluster of chocolate leaves and finish with glacé cherries and angelica sprigs.

ZUPPA INGLESE
(Italian Trifle)

This curiously named dish is extremely good, provided the chef is not an Italian peasant who believes that all other flavours should be superseded by Strega!

Ingredients: 4 rectangles of sponge (pp.237-8) – use two Swiss rolls cut in halves; 1 pint Confectioners' Custard (p.232); ¼ pint cream; apricot jam; 1 batch meringue mixture (pp.247-8); Strega; white wine; sugar syrup (p.274).

Method: Spread the first sponge rectangle with jam, cover with confectioners' custard, lay on the second, repeat and thus assemble all four. Mix about 1 pint sugar syrup with Strega to taste – do not make it any stronger than tastes agreeable in this state. Add white wine (sweet rather than dry) and heat without boiling. Pour gently over the assembled sponge until it is thoroughly moistened. Chill and, when cold, mask completely with the meringue mixture, either spreading some of it on and then decorating the top and sides with meringue pushed through an icing bag with an ornamental pipe, or roughing up peaks all over the meringue with a fork. Bake at Gas Mark 1, one shelf below centre, until the meringue is a pale biscuit colour. When cold, decorate with angelica leaves and glacé cherries. Hand the cream separately.

Notes: If authenticity is not necessary, then forget the Strega and use sugar syrup well laced with white wine and fortified by 2 tablespoons per pint of peach or apricot brandy, mirabelle, kirsch, maraschino or cherry brandy. If using mirabelle, use plum jam; if cherry brandy, cherry jam.

A more elaborate *Zuppa* can be made by layering fruits between sponge, jam and custard.

Crystallised fruits can be used instead of more glacé cherries if desired.

SWEET SAUCES

This is a small, lean chapter – almost inexcusably so for the sweet section of the greatest culinary art – but not, we suggest, completely so. It could of course be considerably extended but the modem housewife, we feel, could not as she has more than enough to contend with already . . . going flat out! She will, we believe, be sufficiently hard-pressed to find it difficult to devote her full and complete attention (as is necessary for all sauce-making) to these few!

BRANDY, RUM OR GRAND MARNIER BUTTER
(Crème au beurre parfumée)

This is not to be confused with brandy sauce. Real brandy butter is seldom correctly given in English publications but this one came by a roundabout route from a royal household that really knew what it was eating and drinking.

Ingredients: 8oz pure, best-quality unsalted butter; 1lb finely sifted icing sugar; 1 teaspoon orange flower water; 1 teaspoon rose water; as much brandy, rum or Grand Marnier as the mixture will take; green vegetable colouring (optional).

Method: Cream the butter very thoroughly indeed. Add about a quarter of the sugar and cream again. Add another quarter of the sugar, the rose and orange flower waters and cream again. If you cream thoroughly, the mixture will now take and hold the remaining 8oz of sugar. Cream it in and then add as much chosen alcohol as the mixture will absorb and still hold a gentle peak. Now colour it pale green with harmless vegetable colouring. Place in a nylon icing bag with an ornamental pipe and pipe onto a pedestal dish in a pyramid. Stud the pyramid with bits of glacé cherry, angelica, and other crystallised or glacé fruits. Chill in the refrigerator until really hard, mask with crimson cellophane, tie in at the waist of the pedestal with an emerald satin bow and get the whole thing out of the way at least a week before Christmas. The dust cannot reach it, the brandy preserves it, and you can get on with other things.

Serve sifted icing sugar in a separate bowl; the above is not sweet enough for some palates.

Note: You can get orange flower water and rose water from the *chemist*, not the grocer!

CHAMPAGNE SAUCE
(Sauce Champagne)

Ingredients: 2oz castor sugar; 2 dessertspoons cold water; 4 separated egg yolks; 4fl oz champagne; ½ pint lightly whipped double cream.

Method: Place all the ingredients except the cream into a thick, roomy pan (ideally copper). Hold a hand loop whisk or hand electric whisk ready. Turn up the heat to fullest and start whisking as you put the pan over it. Whisk continuously until the mixture rises up the pan sides, turns to pale yellow foam and on still till this foam thickens sufficiently to hold a soft peak when the pan is taken from the heat and a spoonful of mixture pulled up. Plunge immediately into a bowl half filled with ice. Resume whipping until the mixture is down to blood heat. Whip in the cream spoonful by spoonful and refrigerate in a bowl until required.

CHANTILLY CREAM
(Crème Chantilly)

Ingredients: ¼ pint double cream; 1 egg white (stiffly whipped); sifted icing sugar to taste; apricot or peach brandy (optional).

Method: Whip cream until it hangs loosely from the whisk. Add icing sugar, teaspoon by teaspoon, stirring in gently until the required sweetness is achieved. Add the chosen liqueur drop by drop. Finally whip in the egg white until smoothly blended.

CONFECTIONERS' CUSTARD

Ingredients: 4oz castor sugar; 1oz flour; 3 egg yolks; 1 vanilla pod; ½ pint milk.

Method: Bring the milk to the boil slowly with the vanilla pod. Whip the egg yolks, flour and sugar together until pale in colour, creamy and absolutely free from streaks. Pour the hot milk onto this batter. Whisk well, turn into the top of a double saucepan over hot water over heat and stir until the mixture coats the back of a wooden spoon. Remove the vanilla pod. Store in mild refrigeration until required under a fitting circle of wetted greaseproof paper. (This stops the mixture from forming a crust and should be used for the storage of all basic sauces made with flour or potato flour.)

Note: If keeping for 3–4 weeks, add 1 tablespoon brandy to the given quantity. Beat in after making and before storing.

Freezing: We have also frozen this mixture. Always in small containers; once thawed, it cannot be returned to the freezer.

PUNCH SAUCE
(Sauce Ponche)

For plum or Christmas puddings.

Ingredients: ½ pint dry white wine; strained juice of 2 lemons; grated zest of 1 lemon; 2oz unsalted butter; rum to taste; 1in stick of cinnamon; sugar to taste; 1 heaped dessert-spoon potato flour (*fécule de pommes*).

Method: Mix the potato flour with the lemon juice. Warm the wine, with the lemon zest, cinnamon stick and butter. When hot, stir in the potato flour mixture and stir steadily until all becomes thick and clear. Add the sugar and rum to taste. 'Finish', if not perfectly clear, with a few additional stirred-in flakes of butter.

VANILLA SAUCE
(Sauce Vanille)

Ingredients: 1 pint Confectioners' Custard, i.e. double given quantity (p.232); ¼ pint double cream; 1 tablespoon brandy.

Method: Mix together and serve hot, cold or just reheated in the top of a double saucepan over hot water.

CAKES, PASTRIES AND ICINGS

Certain items in this chapter have been chosen specifically for very busy women who want to make a show at Christmas. They can use sweet short pastry for large mince pies, put these up in ovenproof glass flan dishes and deep freeze them for at least one month to thaw overnight on Christmas Eve and bake on Christmas Day. The basic recipe and the chocolate version of the Swiss Roll on p.239 can also be frozen for the same period. It will emerge just as spongey and featherweight as when it went in.

Let us suppose that you want to freeze several for over the Christmas period using one for trifle, another for a plain Swiss roll, a third for a chocolate log cake and two or three for local bazaars. Lay the uncut cold baked panel on its floured greaseproof paper on a piece of board, cover with a second layer of floured greaseproof, then freeze immediately while you make the next. When this is cold, take the board from the deep freeze, lay No. 2 on top and continue in this way until you have assembled your chosen quantity. Wrap the whole lot in kitchen foil and that's that!

You may not know that Sand Cake, Seed Cake, Wendy's Gingerbread and Madeira Sponge cake can all have the one-month freezing treatment too, as indeed can your puff pastry – this raw, of course, not cooked! Sweet short pastry may be frozen too, but not if you intend thawing it out and then refreezing it. Nothing should be frozen twice.

The most extravagant recipe in this section is Chocolate Log Cake No. 2. We gave one to a friend in 1963, the year we created it, and after she had eaten some over Christmas in our house. She and we made it together subsequently and she told us three months later she still had one foil-wrapped piece left, which she was saving for the next time she went to bed alone with a book!

Gâteau Religieux (Choux Pastry Cake) is both typically French and tiresome to anyone who is fraught because the choux pastry should be made in the evening before service, baked and assembled a maximum three hours before it is served; so do not embark upon it unless you have made these due allowances in your overall plan!

The shortbread will keep for a long time in a tin; Lemon Jumballs for a week or more, hard Ginger Nuts for a long time in tins and any form of meringues for a week if stored in an earthenware container or a glass jar, always provided that both have very well-fitting lids.

CHEESECAKE

Line a standard heat-resistant glass flan dish with thinly rolled raw puff pastry. Spread the filling evenly over this surface and bake for 15 minutes, centre shelf, at Gas Mark 5. Pull sufficiently from the oven to strew leaf-thin slices of citron peel on top. Continue baking until the mixture and pastry edges are a good light brown.

The Filling: ½lb cottage cheese; 6oz castor sugar; 2oz butter; 6 egg yolks; generous grate of nutmeg; pinch of salt; grated zest of 2 small lemons; 3oz sultanas.

Traditional Method: Place all the ingredients except the sultanas in a mortar and pound with a pestle until blended. Stir in the sultanas.

Modern Method: Place all the ingredients except the sultanas in the mixing bowl of an electric mixer and beat at slow until blended. Stir in the sultanas.

CHOCOLATE GINGERBREAD
(Pain d'Epice au chocolat)

Ingredients: 12oz self-raising flour; 7oz soft brown (pieces) sugar; 11½oz black treacle; 6fl oz milk; 6fl oz olive oil; 1 rounded teaspoon baking powder; 1 dessertspoon lukewarm water; 1 rounded teaspoon soda bicarbonate; 1 level teaspoon powdered ginger; 1 level teaspoon powdered cinnamon; 1 level teaspoon mixed spices; 5oz chocolate chips.

Method: Line three Victoria sponge tins with greaseproof paper, which you must brush thoroughly with olive oil. Dissolve the sugar in warmed milk and treacle. Sift the baking powder, spices and flour together into roomy bowl. Add the chocolate chips and stir in the warmed liquids. Add oil, stirring well, and finally add the soda bicarbonate dissolved in the lukewarm water. Divide evenly between the three tins and bake one shelf below centre at Gas Mark 4 for 25–30 minutes. Spread the cooled layers with butter cream flavoured with ginger syrup (p.257). Dust the top with sifted icing sugar or coat with softened cooking chocolate or chocolate chips mixed with 1 tablespoon sugar syrup (p.274) to every 3oz.

CHOCOLATE MERINGUES

Fold 5oz chocolate chips into a batch of standard meringue mixture (pp.247-8). Drop in peaked ovals with a spatula onto carefully oiled, greaseproof-paper-lined baking sheets. Bake at Gas Mark ¾ for approximately 1 hour, depending on size.

CHOCOLATE LOG CAKE NO. 1
(Buche de Noël)

'Gâteau symbolique que l'on prepare chez tous les pâtissiers de France, à l'occasion de la fête de Noël.'

Prosper Montaigne

This log is made singly or by joining two Swiss rolls together with a little butter cream and then coating both completely with softened cooking chocolate. If a soft icing is preferred, cover the whole cake with Chocolate Butter Cream (p.257) roughed up with a fork and liberally sprinkled with finely chopped pistachio nuts. Tie up centrally with a ribbon – we suggest scarlet wrapping ribbon with a gold spangled edge – and set on a panel of wood cut to size and wrapped in aluminium foil. Our Swiss roll will not crack when rolled up cold after being spread with butter cream, *if the instructions are followed exactly*.

Ingredients: 2½oz sifted flour; 4oz castor sugar; 3 standard eggs.

Method: Line the base of a Swiss roll tin (14in × 10in × ¾in) with a piece of oiled greaseproof paper. Light the oven at Gas Mark 7. Cover a small fireproof plate with a piece of aluminium foil, place the sugar on the foil and pull up the comers to protect the sides. Bake this one shelf above centre for 6 minutes. Meanwhile break the eggs into a basin. Tip the baked sugar onto the raw eggs and whisk continuously until the mixture is thick, creamy and free from streaks. Fold in the sifted flour lightly with a spatula. Spread this mixture evenly over the paper-lined tin. Bake one shelf above centre at Gas Mark 7 for 9–10 minutes. Remove from the oven and run a knife down all four sides to loosen the sponge. Leave in the tin on the table for 1 minute.

Then turn it upside down on the prepared paper base. When cold, cut away the lengthwise edges. Spread evenly with chocolate butter cream. Pick up the greaseproof at the end nearest to you. Make a ¼–½in maximum crease in the sponge edge by lifting the paper and pressing the edge down onto the filling, then tow the greaseproof steadily away from you, thus rolling up the sponge. Brush off any surplus flour.

Prepared Paper Base. Cut two sheets of newspaper and one sheet of greaseproof paper about 2in wider all round than the Swiss roll tin. Lay the greaseproof over the newspapers and dust the surface with sifted flour.

Note: If you want a chocolate-flavoured Swiss roll, remove 1 rounded tablespoon from the given quantity of flour and replace with 1 heaped tablespoon sweetened drinking chocolate. See below for presentation suggestions.

CHOCOLATE LOG CAKE NO. 2
(Buche de Noël)

Very rich indeed. One of our specials.

Ingredients: 2oz sifted icing sugar; 1lb cooked, sieved chestnuts (skinned, cooked weight); ¼lb Butter Cream (pp.256-7); 2 tablespoons brandy; 1 tablespoon rum; 8oz cooking chocolate or chocolate chips.

Method: Work the butter cream and chestnut purée together to a very stiff paste. Soften the chosen chocolate in a cool oven, beat well and beat into the prepared mixture. Continue beating, adding the rum, brandy and icing sugar. Turn onto a sheet of carefully oiled greaseproof paper or waxed paper and gradually work up into a roll. Wrap tightly in paper, then in brown paper and refrigerate for 24 hours. Unwrap, set on a board and mask completely with Royal Icing (p.261). Pull this into 'peaks' and leave to set. Tie with a scarlet or emerald-green ribbon.

Note: It will keep for several weeks in a tin.

CHOCOLATE SWISS ROLL
(Buche au chocolat)

Ingredients: 4 egg yolks; 4 stiffly beaten egg whites; 1 heaped tablespoon powdered drinking chocolate; 1 heaped teaspoon powdered coffee; 6oz castor sugar.

Method: Whip the egg yolks with the sugar until white and creamy. Whip in the chocolate and coffee powder, fold in the egg whites and spread the mixture into a Swiss roll tin. Cook for exactly the same time and temperature as for the Bon Viveur Swiss Roll (pp.237-8), 9–10 minutes at Gas Mark 7. When turned out and cold, spread with ¼ pint whipped cream into which you have folded 2 tablespoons of softened cooking chocolate or chocolate chips.

Note: This is made without any flour – we have not omitted anything.

CHOUX PASTRY

Ingredients: 5fl oz cold water; 2 eggs; 2oz butter; 2½oz sifted flour.

Method: Place the water and butter together in a small, thick pan. Bring to the boil sufficiently slowly to allow the butter to melt. Toss in the flour and allow the liquid to foam and begin to rise. Remove from the heat and beat vigorously until smooth and thick. Beat in the eggs singly, beating well between each addition. Cover with a plate or saucer. Leave in the pan until cold but do not refrigerate. Baking temperature of Gas Mark 7½ remains constant for all shapes and sizes using this mixture. Choux pastry must always be baked to a rich golden brown.

CHOUX PASTRY CAKE
(Gâteau Réligieux)

This is a French classic served on feast days, notably Christmas Day. The base of the cake is an 8in-diameter, ½in-deep sweet short pastry flan case. The 'uprights' are 4 cream or confectioners' custard filled eclairs, top-iced with chocolate glacé icing (p.260) and 4 identical eclairs top-iced with coffee glacé icing (p.260), plus 1 large, round choux bun top-iced with chocolate glacé icing and filled with either cream or confectioners' custard. One end of each eclair, working alternately chocolate/coffee, is stood on the base of the flan case and stuck to its neighbour almost upright but so that it slopes in at the top to the dimensions of the solitary choux bun, which sits on top. Having so disposed of the 8 eclairs, pipe large enough rosettes of cream around the flan-case rim to mask the base of the eclairs standing inside it. Then pipe another circlet of smaller cream rosettes around where the tops of the eclairs meet the base of the bun. This locks all into place. Pipe tiny rosettes of cream between each eclair from top to bottom. Decorate the top of the bun with a further spiral of whipped cream and remember this cake must be eaten on the day of making and assembled as late as possible before service. Choux pastry deteriorates by the hour and is inedible the following morning!

How to Make Eclairs: Pipe cold choux pastry (pp.239-40) through a nylon icing bag with a ½in writing pipe affixed onto baking sheets brushed with pure oil. Have a tumbler of cold water with a knife in it beside you. Pipe each eclair 3in long and lop off the end with the knife dipped in cold water, which gives you a clean finish.

How to Make the Choux Bun: Use a 1in writing pipe in a nylon icing bag. Hold the bag vertically above the baking sheet, squeeze a large blob onto the sheet and smooth the top with a wet knife.

Note: The very lushest versions in France have Chantilly Cream filled into the central hollow after the eclairs have been placed in position and before affixing the bun on top.

FRENCH TWELFTH NIGHT CAKE
(Gâteau de Rois)

Ingredients: 7oz butter; 7oz sifted icing sugar; 8 eggs; ⅜oz very fine salt; grated rind of lemon; 1oz baking powder; 9oz flour; 12 lumps of sugar.

Method: Sift the flour, baking powder and salt together into a roomy bowl. Soften the butter until creamy but in no circumstances allow it to oil. Turn the flour mixture onto a cold surface, push out into a ring, place the eggs, butter, lemon rind and icing sugar in the centre and work up into a pastry (see Sweet Short Pastry, p.252). Cover with a cloth and rest overnight out of refrigeration. In the morning use the pastry to make one large or several smaller rings. To do this take the chosen amount, work into a long sausage, brush the ends with melted butter, form the ring and work with your fingertips until the join is concealed. Place on thickly buttered baking sheets, and tent trays with kitchen foil. Place over a saucepan or meat baking tin of slightly bubbling water. Allow to rise until half as fat again. Brush with raw beaten egg, sprinkle thickly with crushed lump sugar. Bake one shelf above centre, Gas Mark 5/6, to a rich golden brown.

Note: To crush sugar place between thick folds of brown paper, bat with a rolling pin wrapped with a tea cloth and then roll down with the pin.

GINGER NUTS

Ingredients: 4oz butter; 4oz soft brown (pieces) sugar; 1 teaspoon powdered cloves; 1 tablespoon powdered ginger; 7½oz black treacle; grated rind of ½ lemon; 4oz sifted plain flour.

Method: Cream the butter, add the sugar and cream again until loose and light. Add the flour, spices, lemon rind and treacle. Work up into smooth balls. Press down slightly on the buttered and floured baking sheets, leaving plenty of space between each ball. Bake on the centre shelf at Gas Mark 3/4 for approximately 20 minutes or until set. Remember, biscuits tend to harden after cooling so do not overbake.

GINGERBREAD HOUSE

Study Diagram 21. Begin by preparing your cardboard patterns to the sizes marked in A, B, C, D and G. Roll out the gingerbread dough (p.245) to just under ½in thickness and lay on the patterns. Cut round very evenly and carefully. Use two slices to lift from the table onto one or two lightly floured baking sheets. Bake on the centre shelf at Gas Mark 4 for 25–30 minutes. Take out of the oven and leave on the baking sheets until cold. Now slide a spatula slowly and gently underneath and make sure you have completely loosened the parts of your cooked gingerbread house before you try lifting them off. Lift them with two slices once again. Take off A first and set on a silver, gold, scarlet or green paper-covered board. Mark off

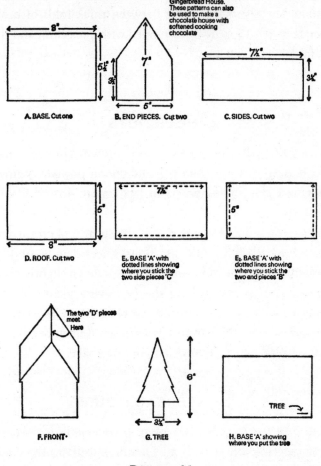

Diagram 21

on your base A, the two lines shown on E1. Follow the measurements exactly.

Put 16 lumps of sugar in a small saucepan with 4 tablespoons of cold water. Bring to the boil without stirring and boil until a tiny bit of mixture sets to a nice firm but soft ball when dropped into a cup of cold water.

Dip the base of both C pieces in the sugar syrup and stand them quickly over the marked lines (see E1). Hold them a moment to grip firmly. Wait 5 minutes. Then dip the base of both B pieces in the sugar syrup and stick them on the dotted lines shown in E2. Dip the base of both D pieces in the sugar syrup. Put them at the angles as shown so that they meet in the middle. Dip a spoon handle into the sugar syrup and smear enough on where they meet to hold them firmly in position.

Mark the place for your tree as shown in H. Take your G piece of gingerbread – the tree – and dip in the sugar syrup and stand over the line G that you have made. Leave it all for 5 minutes.

Make some Royal Icing (p.261) and put it in a nylon icing bag with a fairly fine icing pipe inserted in it first. Copy all the trimmings drawn in H.

Lastly, take some finger chocolate biscuits. Cut them in halves. Dab the cut ends in a tiny scrap of royal icing and stand them all around the rim of the base piece of gingerbread to make a little fence. Finish by adding a dab of royal icing through the pipe to the tip of each little chocolate biscuit fencing. Your house is complete!

You can add a tiny Father Christmas, or a snowman, or a reindeer or anything else you fancy. You can put the house on a much bigger board than it really needs and make a fence going right down a path, with sifted icing sugar for a snow pathway, sifted icing sugar lawns and a little cluster of gingerbread Christmas trees standing at the end of your snowbound garden if you want to take even more time and trouble. In Sweden, where we first saw this kind of little house, every child has a gingerbread house at Christmas-time.

P.S. No chimney? Stick 4 pieces of chocolate-finger biscuits together ½in long, dab a bit of cotton wool on top and stick on the roof.

GINGERBREAD MIXTURE
(made over two days)

You can use this mixture for both a Gingerbread House and for Gingerbread Men.

Ingredients: 5fl oz double cream; 10oz (pieces) soft brown sugar; 5fl oz black treacle; 1 level dessertspoon powdered ginger; 1 level dessertspoon grated lemon rind; 1 level tablespoon soda bicarbonate; 20oz flour.

Method: Whip the cream until it hangs loosely from the whisk. Pour on the sugar, ginger, treacle, grated lemon rind and soda bicarbonate. Stir and stir, taking 10 minutes over the job. Now stir in the flour and work on it, stirring and pressing carefully until the mixture is absolutely smooth. Put a cloth over the bowl and leave in a cool place until the next day.

Then put the dough onto a floured slab or other cold table surface. Roll out to just under ½in thick for the Gingerbread House. Roll out thinly ¼in for all animals and men stamped out with fancy cutters.

GINGERBREAD MEN

Trace the drawing in Diagram 22 by laying a piece of greaseproof paper over it and when you have made the outline, cut it out and trace round it onto a piece of cardboard. Cut that out neatly and you have a gingerbread man pattern, which will last a long time. Lay the pattern on the rolled-out mixture and use the point of a small, sharp knife to cut round it very neatly indeed. Lay the men on a lightly floured baking tray. Do not put them too closely together. Bake on the centre shelf at Gas Mark 4 for 15 minutes. Leave on the baking trays until cold. Then decorate them, copying the lines in the diagram, with Royal Icing (p.261), using a plain writing pipe in a nylon icing bag.

Diagram 22

LEMON JUMBALLS

Ingredients: 4oz castor sugar; 4oz butter; 4 eggs; 1 teaspoon rose water; 8oz sifted flour; grated rind of ½ lemon; strained, raw beaten egg.

Method: Cream the butter until very light and creamy. Beat in the sugar. Add a little flour, rind and rose water. Beat in the eggs singly alternated with additions of the remaining flour until the mixture becomes a good, thick dough. Roll out in strips about ¼in thick and 4–5in long. Shape half into the letter S. Form the remaining half into circles. Lay the S shapes on the circles, joining together with a little raw beaten egg. Lay on a well-buttered, floured baking sheet and bake one shelf above centre at Gas Mark 6 for 10–14 minutes.

MACAROONS
(Macarons)

Ingredients: 3oz castor sugar; 4oz ground almonds; 2 egg whites; rice paper.

Method: Whip the egg whites stiffly. Whip in the almonds and sugar previously mixed together. Drop small spoonsful onto a rice-paper-covered baking sheet and bake one shelf above centre at Gas Mark 3½/4 until really well coloured (approximately 20 minutes). *Then* these macaroons will be crisp on the outside and gooey in the middle.

MADEIRA SPONGE CAKE
(Gâteau Madère)

Mildred Blandy's recipe.

Ingredients: 7 eggs; 10½oz castor sugar; 7oz self-raising flour; sifted icing sugar.

Method: Separate the eggs. Whip the yolks till light and creamy. Add sugar and whip again very thoroughly indeed. Fold in the flour gradually. Whip again with equal vigour. Draw in the stiffly whipped whites gently and fold in without beating until smoothly blended. Tip into standard *small* rectangular bread tins, which have been liberally buttered.

Cook on the centre shelf of a preheated oven at Gas Mark 4 for 16 minutes. Slide a little hood of aluminium foil over each to prevent over-browning and continue baking until the sponge is set and springy. Overall time about 1 hour. Invert over racks for cooling. Remove the tins when these are down to blood heat. Invert the cakes and sift thickly with sifted icing sugar.

MERINGUES

These are the meringues which never weep. Meringue is extremely porous. It is vulnerable to moisture in the air. Thus you may succeed by beating sugar into egg whites in the English manner if the day is a dry one. On another (damp) day, the same meringues will flop or weep. OUR way, they are impervious.

Ingredients: 5 egg whites (not too fresh); 2oz *and* 6oz castor sugar.

Method: Whip the egg whites until stiff, stir in the 2oz castor sugar and continue beating for exactly 5 minutes by hand or 3 minutes at fastest speed on an electric mixer. Stop beating and fold in the remaining castor sugar carefully and lightly. Now spoon onto trays, pipe onto flans – use how you like, and the mixture will hold a perfect peak.

MINCEMEAT ROLL

This is only a treatment and not a recipe. Make a Swiss Roll (pp.237-8). Bake about 1lb mincemeat for 10 minutes at Gas Mark 6. Spread on the Swiss roll, roll up and dust thickly with sifted icing sugar. Makes either a cake or a pudding when served with a real custard (p.232).

OUR RICH BLACK PLUM CAKE
(Gâteau de Noël Maison)

Ingredients: ½lb flour; 1 flat coffeespoon ground nutmeg; 1 flat coffeespoon powdered ginger; 1 flat coffeespoon powdered cloves; 1 flat coffeespoon powdered cinnamon; 2oz ground almonds; 1oz chopped walnuts; 4oz chopped glacé cherries; 4oz mixed diced peel; 12oz sultanas; 12oz currants; 4oz chopped seeded raisins; 8oz butter; 8oz soft brown (pieces) sugar; grated rind and strained juice of 1 small orange and 1 small lemon; 3 eggs; 2½fl oz brandy; 2½fl oz Madeira or Marsala; 2½fl oz port; 1oz golden syrup; 1oz black treacle; 1 coffeespoon orange flower water; 1 coffeespoon rose water; 1 coffeespoon Noyaux (if possible).

Method: Assemble all the dry ingredients (except the sugar) in one bowl. Beat the butter until creamy and add the sugar gradually, beating very thoroughly. Mix all the wet ingredients together in another bowl. Place the butter cream in large bowl and add, alternately and gradually, all dry and liquid ingredients, beating thoroughly between each addition. Turn into an oiled, paper-lined 12in diameter cake tin (preferably with sliding base), level off the top and bake one shelf below centre at Gas Mark 3 for 1 hour, reduce to Gas Mark 2 and cook (minimum 3 hours) until the mixture ceases to sing when you bend closely over it. When cold, store the cakes wrapped tightly in aluminium foil.

PUFF PASTRY

1st Stage: Sift 1lb finest self-raising flour and a generous pinch of salt. Turn onto marble or another surface. Hollow out the centre and, working with the fingers, draw in and work up with sufficient icily cold water to bind to a light, dryish pastry. Use the smallest amount of kneading possible. This causes elasticity in the pastry.

2nd Stage: Dust the working surface with flour. Place the pastry in the centre. Cover with a clean cloth. Rest for 30 minutes.

3rd Stage: Squeeze 14oz butter through clean linen to expel all possible moisture. Work the butter in the cloth until very pliable.

4th Stage: Roll out the pastry into a neat, narrow rectangle, using minimum pressure and rolling in little jerks to assist aeration. Place the prepared butter in the centre of the rectangle and fold up the nearest end to the centre, the farthest end to the centre. Fold together. Poke a finger into the nearest end of the pastry. Lay on a floured cloth. Refrigerate for 30 minutes and place the pastry so that the finger indent is now right as you work.

5th Stage: Roll it out *from you* into an even strip, 18in in length. Fold as before. Press the pin upon the edges to join the superimposed layers. Turn the pastry to the right so that it is crossways onto its previous rolling position. Repeat the rolling and folding. Mark the top again with a finger indent. Set the pastry in the coldest place possible for 1 hour. Give two more rolls and turns as previously described. Rest for 1 hour. Repeat the rolls and turns twice more with the same intervals between. Keep the pastry during 'resting periods' in moderate refrigeration or the coldest possible corner, but never set it directly on ice.

Baking: Preheated Gas Mark 7½.

Oven Position: One shelf above centre.

Method of Baking: Rinse baking sheets under a cold tap. Shake off surplus drips and place the puff pastry in position.

Covering During Baking: Here there are two schools of thought. Some like to place a lightly oiled sheet of greaseproof paper over vol-au-vents and similar large or small cases for the first 10 minutes of baking time, as this is said to assist even rising. Some do not. You must choose.

Golden Rules: Always use first-quality flour and sift before using. Always protect flour in storage from any danger through damp. Never wash the rolling pin. Scrape lightly if you have naughtily accumulated scraps upon it. Wipe it with a clean cloth and keep in a dry place.

SAND CAKE

This Victorian cake was regarded as quite essential at Christmas-time. It is considered difficult to make. If this recipe is followed meticulously, it will not be difficult any longer.

Ingredients: 8oz butter; 5oz sifted icing sugar; 3oz sifted flour; 3oz potato flour (*fécule de pommes*); 6 egg yolks; 3 egg whites; additional sifted icing sugar; finely grated zest of 1 medium lemon (optional).

Method: Cream the butter and optional lemon zest very thoroughly and then beat in the sifted icing sugar. Sift the flour and potato flour together, add a third of this mixture to the butter cream, then add 2 egg yolks, and repeat this procedure twice more with the remaining flour mixture and egg yolks. Fold in the stiffly whipped egg whites and turn into a buttered and floured 9in × 5¼in × 2½in rectangular tin. Bake on the middle shelf at Gas Mark 4 for 55 minutes. Invert on a cooling rack and dust very thickly with sifted icing sugar.

SEED CAKE

This is as inseparable from Christmas fare in our household as punch and Prunes in Port Wine (p.272).

Ingredients: 10oz castor sugar; 7 eggs; 7oz sifted self-raising flour; 2–2½oz caraway seeds.

Method: Separate the eggs and whip the yolks until creamy and free from streaks. Slide in the sugar and beat very thoroughly until the mixture is light and airy. Work in the flour – it will make a very stiff mixture indeed. Whip up the egg whites stiffly. Beat these in gradually, working the first addition until the mixture becomes malleable. Stir in the caraway seeds, turn into a well-buttered and floured, slightly slope-sided bun tin (base 7½in × 3½in, top 8in × 5in) and bake on the centre shelf at Gas Mark 4 for 1 hour 15 minutes or until a skewer driven into the centre comes away cleanly. Invert over a rack and, when cooled, dust thickly with sifted icing sugar.

SHORTBREAD

Ingredients: ½lb sifted flour; ¼lb ground rice; ½lb butter (squeezed in a cloth to expel all moisture); 4oz castor sugar.

Method: Work the butter and sugar together by hand on a wooden board until well blended. Mix the flour and ground rice together and work gradually into the butter cream, until the dough is the consistency of short pastry. Be careful it does not become oily. The less kneading, the more short and crisp the shortbread will be. Press the mixture out with your hand into two round cakes ¾in thick. Pinch the edges neatly all round with finger and thumb. Prick all over with a fork. Bake on the middle shelf, Gas Mark 5, for the first 15 minutes, then reduce the temperature to Gas Mark 4 and continue baking until a light golden brown.

Note: When rice flour is obtainable, use this in preference to ground rice.

SWEET SHORT PASTRY
(Pâte à foncer fine)

Ingredients: 8oz sifted flour; 4oz castor sugar; 4oz butter; approximately 2½fl oz cold water; 2 egg yolks; 1 flat eggspoon of both powdered cinnamon and nutmeg.

Method: Place the flour on a cold surface and push out to form a ring. Put the butter, sugar, egg yolks, spices and a little water in the centre and work to a smooth paste. Then gradually work in the flour from inside of the ring, using two table knives and adding more water sparingly until all the flour is incorporated and the mixture forms a consistency firm enough for rolling. Sift a little more flour over the pastry, cover with a clean cloth and leave if possible in mild domestic refrigeration for 24 hours before using.

TUTTI FRUTTI

This is an elegant and suitable cake for Christmas-tide.

Ingredients: 1 batch Swiss Roll mixture (pp. 237-8), baked in 4 very thin layers in 6in-diameter tins; 2oz almond paste (p.256); 8oz of as many different varieties of crystallised and glacé fruits as possible, chosen to suit your personal taste, all soaked in 5fl oz kirsch; ½lb hot, sieved apricot jam (add a nut of butter to it); plenty of the nuts sold as 'almond nibs'; 1 ring of crystallised pineapple; 1 glacé cherry; 7 large, very thin slices of candied peel, preferably melon.

Method: Spread each layer of sponge with the kirsch-soaked mixture. When all are assembled, brush the cake sides thickly with the apricot mixture. Roll in the almond nibs until completely covered. (The professional trick for coating the sides of any cake with anything is to fill a large soup plate or Victoria sponge tin with the chosen item, hold the cake between both palms like a wheel and trundle it across the plate or tin. The coating item will adhere immediately.) Now set the cake on its board or stand. Shape the almond paste into a little cone. Set this in the top centre of the cake. Brush all the top surface and little cone with the jam mixture. Press the top of the cone down sufficiently to make a little flat top shelf. Overlap the slices of candied peel around the top like an opened deck of cards. Set the pineapple on the almond paste, the cherry over the pineapple, and that's done.

VIRGINIAN FRUIT CAKE
(Gâteau de Noël Americain)

Long keeping.

Ingredients: 4oz butter; 4oz castor sugar; 4oz flour; 3 eggs; 1lb rough-chopped seeded raisins; ½lb crystallised pineapple; ½lb crystallised cherries; 4oz finely cut citron peel; 1oz redcurrant, grape or crab apple jelly; 4oz stoned chopped dates; 2oz soft brown (pieces) sugar; 2fl oz water; ¼ pint grape juice;

½lb mixed chopped nuts (walnuts, pecans and almonds or substitute hazelnuts for pecans); 1 level teaspoon powdered cinnamon; ½ level eggspoon of grated nutmeg; ½ level eggspoon mixed spice; a generous pinch of powdered cloves; 1 dessertspoon brandy.

Method: Place half the dates and all the brown sugar with water in a small, thick pan and simmer over a low heat until the mixture becomes thick and very soft. Refrigerate overnight. Mix all the remaining fruits with the jelly and grape juice, cover and soak overnight *out of refrigeration.* The following morning cream the butter until light and very soft. Whip in the castor sugar until the mixture is again light and creamy. Sift the flour with the spices and add gradually to this cream, together with the egg yolks, added singly. Mix together the soaked fruits, cooked dates mixture and nuts. Work gently into the mixture. Turn into a paper-lined, buttered and floured sliding-based 12in-diameter cake tin. Bake at Gas Mark 2, middle shelf, for 3½–4 hours or until the mixture stops 'singing.' Listen and you will know.

WENDY'S GINGERBREAD
(Pain d'Epice Familial)

Moist and long-keeping rib-sticker!

Ingredients: 7oz plain flour; 2 rounded teaspoons ground ginger; 5oz lard; 5 tablespoons black treacle; 2½oz soft brown (pieces) sugar; 1 egg; 2 tablespoons milk; 1 saltspoon soda bicarbonate.

Method: Dissolve the lard in treacle over a low heat. Sieve the flour and ginger together. Mix the egg and sugar together. Mix the milk and bicarbonate together just before using. Pour the lard mixture onto the flour mixture in a roomy bowl. Add the egg and sugar mixture, stir well and add the milk and bicarbonate mixture. Turn into a well-oiled, greaseproof-paper-lined standard Swiss roll tin and bake one shelf below centre at Gas Mark 4 for 20–25 minutes. For long keeping just cool in the tin, cover the tin with foil and store in a dry place.

WHITE PLUMB CAKE
(Gâteau de Noël blanc)

(From an eighteenth-century family recipe book).

Ingredients: 1lb sifted flour; ½lb castor sugar; ½lb butter; ⅛oz powdered mace; ⅛oz powdered nutmeg; 8 eggs; 1¼lb currants; 4oz lemon candied peel; 4oz ground almonds; 2½fl oz sherry or brandy; 1 teaspoon orange flower water; 1 teaspoon rose water.

Method: Cream the butter thoroughly. Cream in the sugar. Separate the eggs. Whip the yolks up thoroughly and whip into the creamed mixture with gradual additions of flour. Fold in the stiffly beaten whites. Mix all the other dry ingredients together, mix the liquids together and add alternately to the mixture. Give one final very thorough beating, turn into a buttered and floured, paper-lined, sliding-based cake tin (12in diameter). Bake at Gas Mark 3 for approximately 2 hours. Invert over a cooling rack in the tin and only remove the tin when the cake has cooled.

Note: If the 'singing' test (p.254) makes you nervous, drive a thin skewer or steel knitting needle in centrally. When either comes away cleanly and not beaded with moist mixture the *cake is cooked*!

ALMOND PASTE

Ingredients: ¼lb ground almonds; ½lb sifted icing sugar; 1 egg white; a few drops orange flower water, rose water and Noyaux.

Method: Mix the sugar in a bowl with the ground almonds. Add the orange flower water, rose water, Noyaux and part of the egg white. Stir with a round-ended knife or metal spatula, pressing and working in more egg white gradually so that the mixture becomes a very firm paste. Turn it onto a marble slab and knead gently and steadily for a few minutes. Store in refrigeration, closely wrapped in aluminium foil.

BASIC BUTTER CREAM
(Crème au Beurre Anglaise)

Ingredients: 4oz butter; 8oz sifted icing sugar; 2 raw separated egg yolks; 1 small teaspoon rose water; the same of orange flower water.

Method: Cream the butter thoroughly, cream in half the sugar, add the flower waters and 1 egg yolk; then the remaining sugar and egg yolk.

Note: If a teaspoonful of brandy is added to the above mixture it will keep under a tight covering of kitchen foil for up to 4 weeks in refrigeration.

OUR BUTTER CREAM

Ingredients: 4oz sifted icing sugar; 3 egg yolks; 4oz butter.

Method: Whisk the egg yolks and sugar together over hot water until thick, creamy and absolutely free from streaks. Remove from the heat and whip down over a bowl of ice until cool. Cream the butter until very loose and soft and whip in the egg yolk and sugar mixture a spoonful at a time. Flavour, colour and use.

CHOCOLATE BUTTER CREAM

Ingredients: 3oz cooking chocolate or chocolate chips; 6oz sifted icing sugar; 1 egg yolk; 3oz softened butter.

Method: Beat the icing sugar gradually into the softened butter until the mixture is loose and creamy, adding the egg yolk when the first half of the given quantity of sugar is absorbed. Beat in the softened chocolate and use as required.

GINGER BUTTER CREAM

To spread upon slices of gingerbread.

Ingredients: 6oz butter; 2oz soft brown (pieces) sugar; syrup from a jar of preserved ginger; 1 teaspoon rum (optional).

Method: Cream the butter. Work in the sugar with sufficient ginger syrup alternated with the rum to achieve a soft, spreading consistency. Pot and refrigerate for several weeks if desired.

HOW TO APPLY ALMOND PASTE

Brush the cake all over with a brush lightly dipped in cold water. This will remove any surface crumbs and enable you to go to work on a *clean* cake, not a crumby one!

Melt redcurrant jelly in a small pan over a low heat and brush the *chosen* top of your cake with this immediately before affixing the almond paste (the bottom of the cake usually provides the better top-surface).

Roll out the almond paste (p.256) to the desired thickness, sprinkling the table with cornflour, *never* flour. Press the jelly-brushed cake top gently onto the paste. Cut round with a sharp knife and turn over. This way the paste adheres evenly and firmly to the cake top and gives a precise and very neat 'edge' all round.

Roll out a long strip of almond paste to the required thickness for covering the cake sides. Remember that the circumference is three times the diameter. Trim one side of the length with a knife and ruler. Measure the side-depth of the cake. Mark this off on the almond-paste strip and cut off any surplus – thus making a clean edge top and bottom. Brush the sides of the cake with jelly. Trundle the jellied sides carefully along the almond-paste strip on the table. Cut off any surplus so that the ends join exactly. Smooth off with a fingertip. This is the way to obtain a perfectly even surface to which you can therefore apply your royal icing with some guarantee of success! Conversely, if almond paste is slapped on and then rolled over the top and sides with a rolling pin you will almost certainly not be able to guarantee a smooth and precise finish.

HOW TO APPLY ROYAL ICING

When the almond-paste-covered cake has dried out, set the cake on a cake base on a turn table. Slap a big blob of Royal Icing (p.261) onto the top of the cake and 'work' it over with a metal spatula. This 'working' movement is best described as a press-pull turn of the wrist, which, if the icing has been properly made in the first place, ensures *no bubbles* and no dabbing about with sucked darning needles either!

The Top

When you have achieved a *thick*, rough spread of royal over the cake top, take your scraper and, angling it very slightly away from yourself as you hold it in both hands, start on the farther side of the cake, so that you will be pulling towards yourself. Now, in one steady, even pull, draw the scraper right across the surface of the cake and pull it away with any surplus icing adhering to it. Try to ease off the pressure slightly as you come to the edge nearest to you as you work. If at first you do not succeed, put on some more royal and try again. It is only a question of finding out for yourself what is the right amount of pressure to use and what is the exact angle at which to hold the scraper. The rest is merely a matter of practice. When the top is satisfactory, coat the sides thickly all round with royal icing. Then do a cross-hands exercise, which will need a moment's practice before you start.

The 'Crossed Hands' Bit

You are aiming to pull a plain scraper right around the cake in one long, steady pull, thus scraping off surplus royal and achieving a smooth surface all the way round. To do this – assuming you are right-handed: take the scraper in the right hand (mime it first) and put it against the wall or side of the cake as far over to the left as possible with the cake inside the curve of your right arm. Now hold the rim of the cake board with your left hand and as far over to the right as possible. This is rather like playing cross-hands chopsticks until you have got used to it, *but once you have, it works*! You will now perform two actions simultaneously: with your right hand you will hold the scraper edge against the side of the cake and with your left hand you will pull the cake round in the opposite direction to the hand that holds the scraper! When set, apply the chosen decorations.

PROFESSIONAL ROYAL ICING
(Glacé Royal Professionel)

Ingredients: 1½lb sifted icing sugar; 3fl oz water at blood heat; 2 rounded teaspoons albumen powder.

Method: Dissolve the albumen powder in the water. Add the icing sugar gradually, beating well between each addition until the mixture holds a floppy peak on a spatula (for icing) and an erect peak (for piping decorations). Keep covered with a damp cloth while working so that no skin forms on the top. If using an electric mixer, be sure to beat slowly, and do the majority of beating in the early stages when the mixture is very loose.

SIMPLE GLACÉ ICING
(Fondant simple)

Place sifted icing sugar in a bowl and add sufficient water at blood heat to make a very thin paste. Beat relentlessly until the paste is absolutely smooth and just flops slowly and heavily from a wooden spoon. Insufficient beating means those dreary bubbles that deface the top of beginners' cakes.

Note: Water may be flavoured, before using, with standard orange or lemon juice, coffee syrup, or any desired liqueur, *eau de vie* or brandy, Armagnac or marc. Equally, chocolate powder may be mixed with the dry icing sugar in the proportions of 1 rounded teaspoon to ¼lb icing sugar.

SOFT CHOCOLATE ICING

Ingredients: 4oz chocolate chips or cooking chocolate; 2¼–3 tablespoons unsweetened black coffee; ½oz butter; a few drops rum or *crème de cacao* (optional).

Method: Place your chosen chocolate and coffee in a small pan and soften over a very low heat. When this mixture is smooth and creamy, remove from the heat and beat in the butter in small flakes. Add rum or *crème de cacao* if using. Use immediately.

TRADITIONAL ROYAL ICING
(Glacé Royal Familial)

Ingredients: 3 egg whites; strained juice 1 medium lemon; approximately 1½lb sifted icing sugar; 2 drops blue vegetable colouring.

Method: Whip the egg whites, lemon juice and colouring for 30 seconds, if using an electric mixer or rotary whisk, or beat vigorously for 5–6 minutes with a wooden spoon. Continue whipping or beating while adding the sugar; continue until the mixture is smooth and holds a floppy peak. If at this stage you work in a teaspoon of glycerine, you should be able to achieve a classically firm royal icing, which does not crack and fly in all directions!

PRESERVES, SWEETMEATS AND ACCOMPANIMENTS

BLACKCURRANT, RASPBERRY OR STRAWBERRY PURÉES FOR SORBETS

Hull the strawberries and raspberries; string the currants. Pack the chosen fruit into a stone jar without any water at all, cover and place in the oven, Gas Mark 1, low down so as to leave cooking area for other items. When absolutely collapsed, rub through a sieve, bottle and sterilise exactly as for bottled fruit.

CANDIED CHERRIES

Remove the stones and stalks from 2lb firm ripe black cherries. Place 2lb preserving or granulated sugar in a pan with 1 pint water, bring to a slow rolling boil and maintain for 2 minutes. Pour over the prepared cherries in a heat-resistant bowl, cover and leave for 24 hours. *Strain off the syrup gently and thoroughly. Add another 1lb sugar, *bring once more to a slow rolling boil, maintain for 2 minutes* and recover the cherries. Leave this time for 48 hours. Repeat this last process* twice more. When finally strained, wash the cherries in cold water. Now prepare a fresh syrup of 2lb sugar to 1 pint cold water and bring this to a slow rolling boil. Maintain until the sugar reaches the 'crack' stage (310–315°F.). Dip the cherries in this syrup. Place on a rack in a cool oven (Gas Mark ½ with door ajar) and remove when thoroughly dried out. Store in an air-tight tin between layers of waxed paper.

CHOCOLATE BALLS

Ingredients: ½lb stoned dates; 3oz shelled walnuts; 2 large pieces preserved ginger in syrup; 1oz angelica; 1 pack chocolate chips or 4oz *couverture* (professional cooking chocolate); 1oz glacé cherries.

Method: Place the chosen chocolate in a heat-resistant bowl and allow to soften in a cool oven. When soft, beat well. Add the finely chopped dates, walnuts, ginger, glacé cherries and angelica, working in a few drops of ginger syrup to achieve a blended mixture, which can be rolled easily into small balls. These can be placed in little sweet paper cases. For more elaborate service impale each ball on a cocktail stick, dip into more softened chocolate and drive the opposite end of each cocktail stick into the top of a loaf (foil-covered) or into a very large old potato. When set, remove the chocolate balls from the cocktail sticks, place in sweet paper cases with the pierced side uppermost and drive a tiny sliver of angelica or almond into the holes. Yet another method is to dip the balls into the chocolate as instructed above, then to drop them one by one into a shallow container of almond 'nibs' – these are sold ready chopped for immediate use.

COCONUT ICE

Ingredients: 1lb granulated sugar; 2½fl oz double cream; 2½fl oz milk; ¼lb desiccated coconut; harmless vegetable colourings.

Method: Dissolve the sugar in milk and cream over a very low heat and on no account let the mixture boil until the mixture is absolutely clear and free from any little grits. Raise to boiling point, simmer, stirring occasionally, for 15 minutes. Stir in the coconut and work over a moderate heat for approximately 4 minutes or until the mixture is very thick indeed. Pour into shallow oiled tins, about 2–2½in in depth. When cold, divide and store in waxed papers with an outer protective wrapping of aluminium foil.

Note: If a large slab is desired, double the quantities, turn into an oiled bun tin and store when cold in one piece. If different colours are wanted, divide the mixture into three parts – colour one pale pink, another pale green with harmless vegetable colourings, pour either of these into the base of a bun tin, level off, pour on the white third next, complete with the remaining coloured part, and when level allow to set.

DRIED-APRICOT JAM

Ingredients: 2lb very best dried apricots; 6 pints cold water; 6lb preserving or loaf sugar; strained juice 1 lemon; the thin peel in a strand of 1 lemon.

Method: Soak the apricots in the water for 24 hours. Bring to the boil and simmer until tender. Add the sugar and peel and stir until the mixture reaches a slow rolling boil. Maintain until a small spoonful 'sets' on a saucer slipped into refrigeration. Stir in the lemon juice. Raise again to boiling point and instantly scum rises to the rim of the jam kettle; skim off and turn off the heat. Ladle some of the mixture into a strainer over a basin and pot up the resultant fruitless purée into two 12oz heated glass jars. Return the strained fruit residue to the jam, stir, remove the lemon peel and pour into heated jars. Cover when cold.

DRIED MUSHROOMS

Use only the freshest mushrooms. Remove all stalks and with a trussing needle and fine trussing string, thread the mushrooms into long strands; the length must be determined by the width from wall to wall of the airy, dry room where they will be stored. When each strand is completed, tie one end of the string to a hook on one wall and draw the other end very tightly before fastening to a hook on the opposite wall. Before securing the second end make sure that all mushrooms have a space between them. They must not touch or they will mould and collapse. Leave on the line until completely shrivelled and dry; then take down, tie into circles, and hang from a nail or hook until needed.

To use: Soak well in cold water until puffed out and swollen. Discard this dirty water. Pat with a clean cloth and use as desired.

FONDANT

Ingredients: 1lb granulated sugar; 5fl oz cold water; 2¼fl oz liquid glucose.

Method: Brush the sides of a small, thick, clean pan with cold water to stop the sugar from graining. Cover the sugar with water, add glucose and allow the sugar to dissolve before reaching boiling point. Simmer to soft-ball stage (with saccharometer 240°F). Tip into a wooden or iron confectioners' frame on a marble slab. Remember to sprinkle the slab with cold water first. Sprinkle the fondant with cold water. When cooled down sufficiently to handle, work up with a small metal spatula until creamy and set. Pack into a jar, cover with very damp cloths. By keeping the cloths moist, the fondant can be preserved indefinitely.

GARLIC BREAD (HOT)

Ingredients: Use a fat 'flute' of French bread sliced through at a slight angle; or a Hovis loaf, large or small, or individual miniature ones; Garlic Butter.

Method: Slice the chosen loaf or loaves from end to end in such a way that each slice is severed almost to the crust base. Thus the loaf remains whole but opens out like a fan. Spread *one* side of each slice with garlic butter. Press all slices closely together again to re-shape the loaf. Wrap in foil and when required heat at Gas Mark 2, middle shelf, for 10–12 minutes.

GARLIC BUTTER

Ingredients: 4oz salt butter; 2 heaped tablespoons milled fresh parsley; 3–4 small, crushed garlic cloves.

Method: To do at speed, whip the butter with an electric mixer. When it is pale and creamy add the remaining ingredients and whip again until thoroughly blended. Turn into a bowl. Cover tightly with kitchen foil (to insulate the garlic odour!) and refrigerate for 3–4 weeks.

GRANDMA'S INDIAN CHUTNEY

Ingredients: 8oz crystallised ginger; ½oz peeled garlic cloves; 10 medium-sized tart cooking apples; ½lb seeded raisins; 3oz *gros sel* or rock salt; strained juice of 3 medium lemons; thinly grated rind of 1 lemon; 8oz soft brown sugar; ¼oz cayenne pepper; 1 quart best wine vinegar.

Method: Peel, core and chop the apples coarsely. Place in a thick pan with the vinegar and simmer until tender. Add the lemon rind with the finely chopped ginger, raisins and very finely crushed garlic. Stir until thoroughly incorporated. Add all the remaining ingredients. Bring the mixture to the boil and, stirring with a wooden spoon at intervals, maintain for approximately 45 minutes or until the chutney is really thick and pungent. Pour into warmed jars. Tie down when cold.

Note: This mixture improves with keeping.

HOW TO CURE A HAM (1)

Place the ham in deep receptacle, rub all over with common salt and remember to turn each day for 3 days. Mix together 4oz saltpetre, 1lb coarse salt and 1lb soft brown sugar. Remove the ham from the brine fluid and dry. Place in a pickling container, rub in the saltpetre mixture very thoroughly indeed and keep returning the mixture to the top of the ham when it slides down the sides and for a period of 4 days. Then swill all over with 2 pints good wine vinegar, baste frequently and turn every day, keeping the ham in this curing mixture for 4 weeks. Remove, drain and smoke over *wood* for 2–3 weeks. Sew into muslin bags and hang in a dry place.

HOW TO CURE A HAM (2)

Ingredients: 1 large handful coarse salt; 1 cake prunella; 2 cloves; 1lb treacle; ½lb coarse salt; 2 pints ale; 1 small handful soft brown sugar.

Method: Pound the cloves and prunella together in a mortar with a pestle. Add the given handsful of salt and sugar and rub the ham thoroughly with the mixture. Repeat frequently for 3 days. Place the ale, treacle and ½lb salt and any liquor which has come from the first mixture in a sturdy pan and bring to the boil. Place the ham in the pickling container, pour the boiling mixture over, cover and turn every day for 1 month. Dry the ham thoroughly and sew into a bag to hang in a very dry place.

LEMON AND ORANGE CREAMS
(Fondants)

Ingredients: 8oz sifted icing sugar; a generous pinch cream of tartar; oil of lemon; yellow and orange colourings; strained lemon or orange juice; candied lemon and orange peel (optional).

Method: Place the sugar in a bowl, add the cream of tartar and work up with sufficient citrus fruit juice to form a stiff paste. Add a drop or two of oil of lemon (*not more*), your chosen colouring, and turn onto a marble slab where it must be worked up like a dough with more sifted icing sugar for a few minutes. Then roll out over a dusting of sifted icing sugar. When ¼in in thickness, stamp out with miniature fancy cutters and decorate, if desired, with scraps of candied lemon and orange peel.

MARASCHINO CHERRIES

It is advisable to use small, screw-topped jars as you are not expected to employ this preparation in large quantities and of course it does not need any cooking. If only using with sweet items, select prime White Hart cherries. If wanting some for savoury use, choose Morello cherries. Remove the stalks and wash the fruit. Fill into the jars. Cover with maraschino, screw down tightly and store in a dry place. If a few of either or both are required for very special garnish, put up one or two bottles with the cherries *left on their stalks.*

MUSCAT JELLY

Ingredients: 6lb tart gooseberries (thinnings will do very well); preserving sugar; 1 bunch (the size of a pudding plate) of elder-flowers when open; water.

Method: Just cover the fruit with water, bring to the boil and simmer until collapsed and fluffy. Pour into a jelly bag and leave to drip into a bowl overnight. Measure the syrup, place in a thick pan, bring to the boil and level off to a gentle simmer.

Add 1lb sugar to every pint of syrup and allow to simmer for 20 minutes. Tie up the elderberry flower sprigs securely and leave a loop. Hitch the loop round the pan handle and allow the flowers to trail their heads in the syrup while continuing simmering until a small amount of jelly sets on a saucer. Remove the elderberry, pot into warmed jars and, when cold, tie down and store in a dry place.

Note: We learned the above from the late, great Mrs Constance Spry, who told us that the above procedure produces a jelly which tastes like muscat grapes. She was of course perfectly correct.

PEPPERMINT CREAMS

Ingredients: ½lb sifted icing sugar; 1 very generous pinch cream of tartar; peppermint flavouring; 1 small teaspoon strained lemon juice; 1 egg white.

Method: Sift the icing sugar and cream of tartar together in a bowl, make a central well and drop in the egg white, a few drops of peppermint flavouring and lemon juice. Work up with a wooden spoon until the mixture forms a very firm lump. Roll out over a cold surface (marble is best), which has been lightly sifted with icing sugar. When ½in thick, stamp into small discs with a round sweet cutter or just cut into small, neat squares. Store in an air-tight tin between layers of waxed paper.

Note: These peppermint creams can be left for 2 hours on the open board and then dipped into softened cooking chocolate or chocolate chips.

PICKLED WALNUTS

Wear rubber gloves! Prick the young nuts all over with a darning needle. Prepare a brine composed of 3oz salt to 1 pint water and steep the pricked walnuts for 3 days. Replace with a fresh brine and leave again for 3 days. Drain the nuts, wipe them and immerse in clear, cold water. Leave for 6 hours. Now spread out on trays and dry off in the sun, turning them until they are completely blackened. Pack in jars with warm spiced vinegar. Cover and keep for 2 months before using.

Spiced Vinegar: 3oz peppercorns; 1oz root ginger (bruised in a muslin bag); 10 cloves; 2 small bay leaves; 1¾oz allspice. Bring all the ingredients to boil together. Maintain at boiling point for 12 minutes. Strain. When not too hot for a testing finger, pour over the walnuts.

POTTED CHESHIRE CHEESE

From an eighteenth-century family recipe book.

Ingredients: 1½lb Cheshire cheese; ½lb best, fresh butter; 2–2½fl oz Madeira (Bual or Malmsey); ¼oz finely powdered mace.

Method: Ancestor's way: Pound the cheese and butter in a mortar with a pestle, working in the mace and Madeira until the whole forms an absolutely creamy mass. Pot very firmly, cover with melted butter and store in a cool place. *Our Way:* Grate the cheese very coarsely or slice thinly. Whip the butter in an electric mixer, adding the cheese, mace and Madeira gradually until the mixture becomes thick and creamy. Refrigerate for 2 hours. Shape into a pat. Serve with hot toast. Alternatively, spread on buttered toast or croutons and bubble under a steady grill.

PRESERVED CHESTNUTS
(Marrons glacés)

The high cost of bought *marrons glacés* is due to the enormous wastage during the repeated poaching procedure in syrup, when the chestnuts collapse and crumble very easily, even more than to the cost of the labour involved.

We hit on the happy compromise of poaching cooked, peeled chestnuts in stock sugar syrup *once only* for 30 minutes in a wide, shallow pan. Then transfer them very carefully into wide-necked bottling jars, picking each one up gently with a pair of lifting tongs. Strain the sugar syrup in which they have been poached, fill up the jars with it, cover, affix closures and sterilise at 165°F on a bottling thermometer for 1 hour. IF YOU ALLOW THE TEMPERATURE TO RISE BEYOND THE GIVEN DEGREE, THEY WILL PROBABLY COLLAPSE! All that is left to do is to repeat the sterilising process at the given temperature and for 1 hour daily until the chestnuts look brown and semi-transparent. Store in a dry place. Lift out and wrap each whole one in a square of silver paper for dessert.

The Crumbled Bits which will inevitably accumulate can be bottled separately if you choose to sort out before storage. Otherwise just use them up when you have emptied each jar of its whole *marrons glacés*.

(1) Pour bits in syrup over vanilla ice cream.

(2) Spread some into leaf-thin pancakes, roll up and top-dress with more syrup and bits.

(3) Dab waffles with butter and serve a jug of the residue mixture for pouring over.

(4) Blend ½ pint slightly whipped double cream into ½ pint syrup and bits; dissolve ¼oz powdered gelatine in 3–4 table-spoons cold water, stir thoroughly into the mixture and pour into an oiled mould. When set, unmould and hand a jug of the syrup and bits separately.

Note: If given a light flavouring of rum, this cold pudding becomes gorgeous.

PRESERVED RASPBERRIES

Pick from bushes straight into a jar – up to the shoulder of a fairly slender bottling jar. Bang them down and pack 'em again, and repeat until, without actually pressing, you have as many in as possible. Fill to the rim of the jar with castor sugar. Press down like crazy, and fill up again with more castor sugar. Then put the lid on and seal it down and keep in a dry place.

PRUNES IN PORT WINE

This is a simple family recipe, which has been used for generations, and generations of total-abstainer maiden aunts have thawed under its influence.

Ingredients: ½ bottle tawny port; 1lb best prunes; 3 heaped tablespoons soft brown (pieces) sugar.

Method: Cover the prunes with cold water and leave overnight to soak. Drain, wipe and pack *lightly* into a large screw-topped jar or 2 smaller ones. Put the sugar on top, shake the jar vigorously, fill to above the prunes with the port, screw down and leave to swell and mature.

Note: Serve these in small bowls and among other desserts.

REDCURRANT JELLY

This is a method which may be applied to all fruit jelly. Place the available amount of unhulled redcurrants in a roomy saucepan or jam kettle. Cover with cold water, bring to the boil and simmer until purged and flaccid looking. Strain through a jelly bag and leave overnight. Measure the fluid, place this in a clean pan and bring to the boil. Stir in 1lb of preserving sugar to every measured pint of fluid, raise to boiling point, steady off at a simmer, stir until the sugar has completely dissolved and continue simmering until a small quantity jells on a saucer. Pour into warmed pots and either screw up or tie down when absolutely cold.

ROQUEFORT CREAM
(Crème de Roquefort)

Ingredients: ½lb unsalted butter; ¾lb Roquefort cheese; 2–2½fl oz tawny port; 2 packets pretzels; ground almonds (optional).

Method: Cream the butter thoroughly. Break up the cheese and add gradually in small pieces. Work in the port. Chill in refrigeration. When thoroughly cold, shape into a gâteau-like circular pat. Dust the top surface (optional) with ground almonds. Press pretzels upright all round the sides to form a wall. Ideally serve with hot French bread. Wrap this in foil and slip into the oven at Gas Mark 1, one shelf above centre, until the bread nips a (clean) finger when prodded.

SALTED ALMONDS

Skin* and dry 1lb of Jordan almonds. Place 2 tablespoons of melted butter in a shallow frying pan and heat through gently. Toss in the almonds and keep shaking and tossing until they are browned. Remove from the heat. Sprinkle on 1 level dessertspoon of salt, toss and shake until the oil, salt and browned nuts are thoroughly incorporated. Leave in the pan overnight, then shake into a dish and serve.

Note 1: Treat pecan nuts, cashew nuts and peanuts in the same fashion.

Note 2*: Place unskinned almonds in a bowl. Cover with boiling water. Leave for 6 minutes. Plunge into cold water. Leave for 1 minute. Now the skins will pop off at speed.

STOCK SUGAR SYRUP

Stock sugar syrup for storing and using as required is an essential ingredient of any serious kitchen. *Babas* and *Savarins* are soaked in it, it is used in making fondant for sweets and icings, it is employed with cooking chocolate and chocolate chips and also in ices and sorbets – to give only a few examples.

Brush the sides of a thick, clean pan with cold water to stop the sugar from graining. Cover 2lb preserving or granulated sugar with 1¼ pints cold water. Allow to dissolve without stirring. Then raise the heat and maintain until the mixture reaches boiling point. Skim carefully, simmer for 3–4 minutes longer, re-strain, chill and store in lidded glass containers in mild domestic refrigeration.

STUFFED DATES

Remove the stones from the required number of dates. Fill the cavities with sufficient almond paste to force the top sides apart and smooth off neatly. Press a lengthwise quarter of walnut down the central almond paste. At this stage these may be stored for several days. On the day of serving, mask them with sugar at the crack (310–315°F). Place 16 lumps of sugar with 4 tablespoons water in a very small pan, allow to dissolve over a low heat, bring to a slow rolling boil and maintain, testing a drop in a small bowl of iced water from time to time and until the syrup turns to crack. Then with a pair of eyebrow pluckers plunge each stuffed date fast into the syrup, shake off the surplus and put into a little paper case. If correctly done, the sugar syrup will almost instantly form a thin, hard skin like ice.

TO PRESERVE WALNUTS

Shell freshly gathered ripe walnuts carefully to ensure minimum breakages. Remove the central cores and halve. Set on trays and dry out in strong sunshine! Or in the coolest ovens. Store in air-tight jars. Check thoroughly after the first 4 weeks of storage. Walnuts, above all other nuts, are especially prone to maggots.

WORCESTERSHIRE SAUCE

Ingredients: ½oz peeled garlic cloves; 5fl oz Indian soy; 2 pints wine vinegar; ⅛oz black peppercorns.

Method: Mill the peppercorns, place in a mortar with the garlic and pound to a smooth paste. Then, like making French dressing, add a little wine vinegar, a minute quantity of soy, more wine vinegar, another minute addition of soy and so on until all are absorbed in the mixture. Place in a bottle with a tightly fitting cork or screw-topped lid. Shake, as if you were making one of those 'dreadful cocktails'. Store in a dry place and affix a label stating 'Home Made Worcestershire Sauce – Shake Well Before Using'.

CHRISTMAS FOOD DECORATION AND PRESENTATION

ALMOND PASTE HOLLY LEAVES

Colour a small ball of almond paste with harmless green vegetable colouring. Sprinkle a cold surface lightly with *cornflour*. Roll the paste out fairly thinly. Take a 2½in-diameter fluted pastry cutter. Use a bit of one edge of the cutter to stamp out a small crescent. Then think of a diamond shape. Stamp the second side to make the top half a fluted diamond shape, i.e. a pointed, fluted tip, which becomes broad (1in wide) about ¾in from the pointed end. Join a side of the cutter to the tip of the broad part and repeat in reverse, so that you end up with a simulated holly leaf with fluted edges and four little points. Pinch in one end (lengthwise) to simulate the beginning of a minute 'stem'. Brush over with raw, unbeaten egg white, press a tiny cluster of edible holly berries just above the miniature stem, sprinkle all over the leaf surface with castor sugar and, when dry, store in an air-tight tin.

Note: The 'holly' berries are sold alongside mimosa flowers, gold and silver balls, etc. in the cake decoration department of food sections in large stores or in large pastrycooks who sell ornaments for cakes.

BREAD FOR GARNISHES

The Large Bread Wedge. This is used on a buffet to support such items as a whole glazed tongue, a whole lobster or a cold leg of lamb. Cut all crusts from a day-old standard sandwich loaf. Then divide from the tip of one end to the base of the other – thus making two slanting wedges. The wedges can be used plain, deep fried in slightly smoking hot oil, and kept for days in a tight wrapping of kitchen foil. For the extra-patient, the wedges can be 'pineappled' before frying. To do this, cut 1in-deep grooves slantwise across the back or wide end. Then cut reverse grooves across those already made. This is 'pineappling'. Repeat the cutting on both the sides down to the tips of each wedge.

Small Bread Bases. These can be made from either 4in-thick crustless squares cut from a sandwich loaf, or from whole crustless sandwich loaves – whether 'pineappled' or not; or round ones can be obtained by de-crusting the base of one or more cottage loaves and trimming off thereafter into true circles. As with bread wedges, the prepared bases are deep fried to a good golden brown and foil-wrapped for storage.

Bread as a Decoration. Stamp out any number of plain 2in-, 3in- or 4in-diameter crustless circles using a *plain* round pastry cutter. Stamp out the centres of some with 1½in, 2½in or 3½in plain pastry cutters. Now cut a sliver off the edge of each circle or ring measuring about 1–1½in. Deep fry all prepared rings and circles. It will be found that the removed 'slivers' enable you to stand both rings and circles upright. They do, however, stand much more firmly when each one is pressed into position around the edge of a dish of savoury buffet food if a tiny rosette of creamed potato is first piped into position and the flattened edge of circle pressed into it. Such an encircling decoration, if interspersed with sprigs of green stuff, gives a very good appearance.

CHARLOTTE RUSSE

It helps to know exactly how to arrange the cherries and angelica on the base-layer of jelly for a *Charlotte Russe*. Put all cherries cut side *uppermost*. Place one half-cherry in the centre, and four more 1½in towards the rim – all four equally spaced and leaving room for four diamond-shaped pieces of angelica to be placed between.

CHOCOLATE LEAVES

These are one of the most absurdly simple, versatile garnishes, made in moments, happy in storage for months on end, and requiring only two items: softened cooking chocolate or chocolate chips, and leaves. Just remember – we cannot emphasise this too strongly or too often – the *chocolate must not be allowed to get hot*. The melting is best done very slowly.

Once the chocolate collapses when touched with a wooden spoon, beat the daylights out of it and all will be well. Take a rose leaf with a tiny scrap of stem attached. Tow the leaf, upper-side downwards, across the chocolate until it is completely coated. Lay the leaf chocolate-side uppermost on a cold surface. Leave until set. Then peel the leaf away gently and every single vein will have repeated itself on the leaf. This is a dazzling bit of one-upmanship to those who do not know the trick!

Use to stick in the top of whipped-cream spirals on individual party puddings; or mass in a cluster on the centre-top of a chocolate cake: just for two examples to set you thinking of many more.

CHOCOLATE SWANS

Study Diagram 23. Cut the set of patterns in scraps of plastic curtaining. Pull each pattern twice across softened chocolate and leave time in between for the chocolate to set, to make them strong. Peel off the patterns. Stand any number of bases on a piece of looking-glass. Stick on the head at one end of the base, wings on either side, and the tail at the opposite end to the head, using little dabs of butter cream (p.256) to hold them securely in position. Place a blob of ice cream in the centre of each to make a swan's body. Top with piped whipped cream.

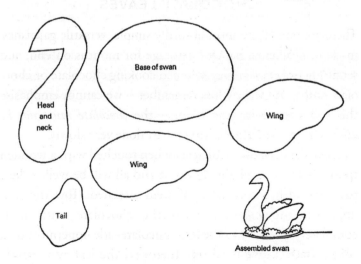

Diagram 23

Dust sifted icing sugar lightly over the swans on the look-ing-glass to look like snow.

Note: Chocolate components will keep indefinitely in an air-tight tin, provided the cooking chocolate (*couverture*) or packet of chocolate chips has not been allowed to over-heat. When this occurs, chocolate turns grey/brown and becomes speckled! The ideal means of softening is to put chocolate in a heat-resistant bowl in an oven set at low with the door open.

CHOUX PASTRY SWANS

Turn to pp.239-40 for Basic Choux Pastry. Pipe the mixture out through a nylon icing bag with a 1in plain writing pipe affixed onto oiled baking sheets. Pipe into flat, short sausages, if possible wider one end than the other. Bake one shelf above centre at Gas Mark 7½ for 30 minutes, or until thoroughly browned on top. Pale beige ones invariably collapse when cold. They also taste like flannel!

On a separate oiled baking sheet pipe a number of 'heads' and 'necks'. These are made all in one piece by piping the pastry through a ¼in plain writing pipe and in the shape of a figure 2 with a flat base. The top of these, when baked for 12–15 minutes and cooled on a rack, makes the head, and the base pushes through the whipped cream in the body. When the 'body' cases have been baked and rack-cooled, split length-wise just above half the depth. Mound the base cases with whipped cream into a reasonably high dome. Split each lid lengthwise and centrally. Push these two tilted upwards into the sides of the whipped cream to form the 'wings'. Pipe little whipped-cream tails to the narrow end of each body. Finally drive the flat base of the figure 2 into the cream at the fat end. Dust overall very thickly with sifted icing sugar.

CHRISTMAS LOG CAKE

If, after forking up chocolate or coffee butter cream over the whole length of the log and small 'branch-stumps', you wish to further decorate with minute trails of ivy, place a small amount of green-coloured plain butter cream in a small paper icing bag *without* any pipe. Nip a fractional amount from the tip and pipe fine 'trails' so that they meander over the top and sides. Pinch the tip of the icing bag and cut out a tiny 'V'. This enables you to pipe tiny 'leaves' here and there, being careful to use a press–pull movement, which ensures a good tip to what would otherwise be a small blob and not a 'leaf'. (Turn to p.51 and study the diagram of Yule Log Candle Holder.)

COCKTAIL KEBABS

Take any number of slim ring-headed skewers and tie a glitter bauble to each ring with a bow and ends of the narrowest Christmas coloured ribbon. Then thread on such items as cubed, seasoned cold ham, or turkey; cubed cheeses; trimmed, round radishes; savoury cheese balls rolled in flaked cheese; stoned stuffed black and green olives; whole small prawns; scraps of fried puff pastry cut in triangles . . . you choose. When all are prepared, cover the outsides of ordinary tumblers with shiny red, green or white paper, fill up inside with Oasis, moisten with cold water and drive the 'kebab' skewers in, fanning them out well. Just refrigerate until serving.

FORCEMEAT BABY DUCKS

This is a fine way of achieving a pretty garnish for any bird, and at the same time avoiding stuffing the bird. Choose your stuffing – any which is not full of lumps, and is bound with egg, either whole or yolk only will work! For each baby duckling, shape a forcemeat ball the size and approximate shape of a large Victoria plum. Flatten the base so that it stands steadily on the table. Make a much smaller ball for the head. The best way to give you the size for this is to provide the circumference – 2¼–2½in. Dab the base of the 'head' into raw, beaten egg, and press onto the top of one end of the body. Now pinch up the soft stuffing on the sides of the body to simulate two little tufty wings. Flatten a scrap into a tail peak and pinch this in upright at the top of the opposite end to the head. Push a sliver of blanched, skinned almond into the head to form a beak. Refrigerate. Before baking, brush all over with melted butter. Then bake for 20 minutes on a buttered baking sheet at Gas Mark 4 – lowest shelf. Arrange so that they appear to 'swim' around the bird when sending to table.

THE GARLAND CAKE

Having completed the Christmas Garland or Wreath for the door, we found ourselves with very little time left and a new design and presentation needed for a Christmas party cake. What we did have was three plain Swiss roll panels intended as a reserve for the deep freeze (see pp.237-8). By chance we also had a 20in-diameter silver cake board. This is how it was done:

Spread the three sponge panels with plain or chocolate butter cream (pp.256-7), roll them up, and very gently shape all three (they are very pliable) into a rough circle on the board. You will find as you do so that the inner edge of the ring has too much sponge, and the outer edge does not quite meet. Cut a sharp angle off one end of each Swiss roll, thick side to the middle; then smear a little more butter cream on each side of the cut sections and, reversing them, push the sections into the spaces left – so that the thick part of each section is now on the outside and the tapering tip is inwards. Press firmly until they come together and so complete your circle.

Cover the whole of the top and sides with pale green butter cream. Rough it up with a fork to simulate bark, decorate with 1in-wide shiny crimson ribbon, press single or clustered crystallised fruits or fruits modelled in almond paste around the top, and affix a bow, cluster of loops or chou of the same 1in ribbon as shown in the illustration heading this chapter.

GARNISH FOR A HAM

This is a simple and effective garnish. Cut five thin slices from an unskinned cucumber. Overlap them into the shape of a flower at the head of the saddle end of the ham (which means the top end farthest away from the bone). Dab half a stoned black olive into the centre of the 'flower'. Place a small crescent of unskinned tomato on each cucumber 'petal' where these overlap. Form a long stem down the saddle by laying on in a slight curve the thinnest-possible strips of cucumber skin, green-side uppermost. Add further very narrow strips as laterals or branches. Tip the end of each one with a snowdrop shape in bud, by first dabbing a halved black olive over the tip of the skin and then arranging a petal of hard-boiled egg white on either side of the olive, drooping downwards, and finally lock in all this by spooning more aspic gently over all. Keep in mild refrigeration until service.

HAM AND PÂTÉ CORNETS
(Cornets de Jambon)

Ingredients for six: 6 leaf-thin neatly trimmed slices of lean ham; scant ¼ pint aspic; 6oz *pâté*, or *pâté de foie gras*; 1 rounded tablespoon thickly whipped cream; 1 tablespoon cooking sherry; generous pinch pepper; 1 bread and butter plate thickly spread with freshly milled fresh parsley heads.

Method: Beat the pâté to a smooth cream with sherry and cream. Fill into a small nylon icing bag with an ornamental pipe affixed. Shape each slice of ham around a cornet mould, grip with the palm of the hand curled around it and slide off. Pipe in the *pâté* filling. Smooth off neatly at the broad end of the cornet. Dab these ends into the parsley. Chill in refrigeration. When really cold, set wide apart on a spotlessly clean cake cooling rack over a flat dish. Spoon aspic over the cornets until they are completely masked. Refrigerate until required. These make an ideal edible garnish arranged around a cold ham for a buffet, or use on top of a meat, game or poultry mousse 'set' in a solid-based round cake tin, or use them as a border for a dish of *chaudfroid* of turkey, or other game or poultry.

HARD-BOILED EGG GARNISH

If you happen to possess a box of miniature cutters for an open sandwich and cocktail canapé garnish, egg white can be used very effectively. Cut out your chosen 'leaf', 'heart', 'diamond', 'star', etc. and arrange around the rim of a mould in aspic or an aspic-glazed savoury mousse. Decorate any *chaudfroid* item, being sure that this *chaudfroid* is coloured first to throw up your tiny decorations. Always remember that if whatever-it-is is not being served immediately, another layer of syrupy aspic must be spooned on top or the garnish will look shrivelled and dejected by the time it comes to table.

Note: Rub leftover egg yolk through a sieve and use as scattered or narrow edging garnish.

HARD-BOILED EGG SWANS
FOR CHILDREN'S PARTIES
(Or as a garnish for cold savoury buffet items)

You need one egg for each swan, so hard-boil the requisite number and, when shelled and cold, cut a very thin slice of the white from the base of each egg. Do this with the egg lengthwise; do not cut off pointed or rounded ends. Place the eggs on these cut bases so that they stand steadily. For each one, shape a yellow pipe cleaner into a figure 2 with a flat base. Push this through the centre of the rounded end of each egg. Then cut two thin petals of egg white from the sides. Pipe squiggles of anchovy butter over the 'saddle' and the cut sides, and press the petals back onto the anchovy butter, tips upwards towards the pointed end to make the 'wings'. Finally affix the base petal to the top of the pointed end with a squiggle of anchovy butter to simulate the 'tail'. Sprinkle the 'saddle' with freshly milled parsley for service.

Note: Anchovy butter is simply butter creamed and flavoured to taste with bottled anchovy purée.

HOW TO COVER A HAM, SALMON OR SIMILAR
ITEM WITH CHAUDFROID SAUCE

Beat ½ pint aspic at the syrupy stage into ½ pint of warm, freshly made thick white sauce (pp.176-7). Allow to cool. Test frequently by pouring a teaspoonful over a tomato. If *chaudfroid* clings and forms a glossy covering, pour or spoon over the chosen item. If requiring edible top decoration, make sure to have a reserve supply of aspic for covering or locking in the garnish so that it cannot deteriorate by shrivelling through exposure.

LETTERED ROYAL ICING PLAQUES

A fair amount of precious last-minute time can be saved if these 'Happy Christmas' plaques are advance-made and stored. Make up a quarter of the given quantity of Professional Royal Icing (p.260). Dust a cold working surface thickly with sifted icing sugar. Turn the royal icing onto this. Dust this thickly with sifted icing sugar. Knead with more sifted icing sugar added gradually until the mixture becomes fairly dry and of the consistency of paste for pastry. Roll out to ¼in thickness. Stamp into a 4–5in-diameter circle. Lift onto a baking sheet. Re-form the remainder, re-roll and cut more, because when you do the writing, your first attempts might possibly be a little bit wobbly! Repeat until the mixture is used up. Leave uncovered in the kitchen until absolutely dried out. Pipe 'Happy Christmas', 'Merry Christmas' or 'Christmas 19-whateveritis' with a medium-fine plain writing pipe and when satisfied with your lettering, overpipe, using a very fine writing pipe, in either red or green coloured royal icing. Store in an air-tight tin to snatch up and press out onto the top of the cake after it has been iced.

ROYAL ICING PENGUINS

Using icing-sugar-stiffened royal icing (pp.260, 261), take about a ping-pong-ball-sized piece for a large penguin, or a chestnut-sized piece for a small one. Roll this into a pointed-topped, slim, unopened fir cone. Bend this point over slightly, at the same time pinching the front to make the pointed part of a penguin's 'face'. About a quarter of the way down, make a small cut with a pair of scissors each side for 'flippers'. Make two tiny 'feet' blobs of icing and stick these on at the base front, left and right. Colour the tip of the beak and the feet yellow with saffron, and add darkest caramel spots left and right of the 'face' for 'eyes'.

SMALL ASPIC SHAPES

Thoroughly rinse a standard Swiss roll tin under the cold tap. Fill to the brim with aspic. *When set, use in any of the following ways:*

1. Stamp into small circles with 1½in-wide fluted cutters. Halve and arrange cut-sides downwards as a continuous border to cold, savoury dishes.
2. Cut out 1¼in-wide strips and then cut these into little triangles. Arrange the triangles with points uppermost in a continuous border to cold, savoury dishes.
3. Stamp aspic into fluted crescents using a 2½in-wide fluted pastry cutter. Arrange these flat around the rim of any dish containing cold savoury mixtures. This looks particularly elegant if a tiny scrap of parsley head is set at the tip where each crescent tip meets the next. Crescents may also be arranged one up, one down, alternately all round. When a whole skinned fish, salmon or turbot, for example, is served on a long platter, arrange crescents around the rim, and then put a line of them all going one way down the length of the top of the fish. Put 'bands' made from very thin strips of cucumber skin across the width of the fish to divide each crescent from the next.

SLAP HAPPY 'CRISIS' SUBSTITUTES FOR SERIOUS COOKERY

EMERGENCY HORS D'OEUVRE

If you have kept a sharp eye on such an eventuality, you will be able to assemble a good selection in a few moments. Just try, if at all possible, always to have home-made mayonnaise and French dressing.

(1) *Open a small jar of black olives and another of green ones.* Stab an apple with as many fanned-out cocktail sticks as possible. Impale the olives black/green alternately.

(2) *Open a tin of new potatoes.* Slice them into rounds, pile into a dish, souse with French dressing and sprinkle with milled parsley.

(3) *Open a tin of sardines.* Arrange them tails inwards in a half-circle on a flat, round plate. Moisten with their own oil, sprinkle with pepper and heap sliced 'chips' of bottled beetroot like spillikins on the opposing half of the plate.

(4) *Open a tin of whole French Beans.* Tip them into a rectangular dish. Stir up 2 tablespoons cream with a generous squeeze of lemon juice and a teaspoonful of powdered paprika. Swill over the beans.

(5) *Open a small tin of sweetcorn.* Strain and arrange as a bed on a small dish. Spread the contents of 1–2 tins of Junior Cheese savoury on top and scatter chopped or milled nuts overall.

(6) *Open a tin of curried baked beans* into a basin. Open a tin of luncheon meat, dice this and fold into the beans. Turn into a dish and scatter with tiny pine kernels.

(7) *Open a tin of spaghetti in tomato sauce* and mix with the contents of a matching-sized tin of strained vegetable macedoine. Toss together, mound on a round flat platter and scatter with flaked almonds.

(8) *Open a tin of salted pecan nuts* and tip into a small bowl.

(9) *Open a packet of pretzels* and tip into a small bowl.

(10) *Open a jar of cocktail onions* and tip into a small bowl.

(11) *Open a packet or tin of Twiglets* and tip into a small bowl.

(12) *Serve* with Bath Oliver biscuits, Dorset Knobs, water biscuits, *Gressins* or *Gressinettes* and slap a pat of butter onto a dish.

IT ONLY COSTS MONEY!

No First Course for Christmas Dinner and No Time Left!

Mix 1 tin turtle soup (ideally) or 1 tin julienne soup or consommé with 6fl oz clear stock or stock made from a *chicken* bouillon cube and 1 small sherry glass of sherry.

Bang the Stuffing into the Trussed Bird!

Do not waste time trussing and re-trussing. Fill stuffing into a large nylon icing bag without any pipe affixed. Push the stuffing down to the tip, shove this into the vent end and SQUEEZE LIKE CRAZY. Does the job in seconds and leaves no mess to clear from the table.

The Ham – Wot No Fine Breadcrumbs!

Then emulsify half a dozen rusks or two generous handsful of plain cornflakes at speed. Scatter them thickly over the freshly skinned surface of a hot ham.

Distinguished Party Pudding Wanted at Speed?

Make *Désir de Reine* (quite untranslatable). Beat 1 tablespoon brandy, 1 dessertspoon kirsch and 1 dessertspoon orange Curaçao into 1 pint cold, standard Confectioners' Custard (p.232). Turn into individual custard glasses (or small claret 'tulips'). Whip ¼ pint double cream till it hangs from the whisk loosely. Place in a nylon icing bag with a large ornamental icing pipe and hold vertically above the centre top surface of each glass in turn. Push down as you press the cream out so that each squirl is like an iceberg, seven-tenths submerged into the liqueur custard. Ideally sprinkle with milled pistachio nuts. Stab a teaspoon into each. When eating, stir with a spoon first to blend the cream into the mixture.

Note: This specially made bit of culinary one-upmanship was created by M. Dubois of Hostellerie de l'Air Pur at La Roche-en-Ardennes.

Ice Cream Pudding (Fudged)

Cut up two vanilla ice cream bricks and whip until creamy. Whip in 3fl oz stiff cream and 1 dessertspoon brandy. Fold in 2oz each of chopped glacé cherries, angelica, walnuts and dates. Fill into a *well-oiled* ornamental mould, re-freeze and, when required, unmould fast. To do this, plunge the mould to just below the rim in very hot water and if still stubborn, repeat.

A Cheat Nursery Pudding

Soften one packet of strawberry or other jelly with ¼ pint water. Cool to blood heat when the jelly is completely dissolved. Whip in (fast) the contents of a tin of unsweetened milk. Pour into custard cups and top with a cone of piped, whipped cream. At the moment of service stick a fan-shaped pompadour wafer into each whipped-cream cone.

Failed to Make Your Mincemeat?

Place 4lb bought mincemeat into a roomy bowl. Add the strained juice of 1 orange, the grated rind of 2, one generous handful extra suet and 3oz extra each of sultanas, currants and chopped seeded raisins. Moisten with 3–4fl oz rum. Mix all together very thoroughly.

The Christmas Cake

Coat the base and sides very thickly with modern Professional Royal Icing (p.260). Hold the end 2in of a metal spatula parallel with the cake top and make a tap-down, pull-up series of peaks over all, which produces instant peaks of a far better appearance than those done with a fork. Repeat the spatula-peaks over the sides and rush for the stored box of Almond Paste Holly Leaves (pp.276-7). Encircle the base with these and dab pre-made Royal Icing Penguins (pp.286-7) haphazardly over the top, *or* if riddled with forethought, whip out of store a pre-made royal icing 'Happy Christmas' plaque (p.286) and press it down firmly onto the top centre, or wrap round (un-iced) sides with decorative Christmas paper.

No Time to Make Almond Paste for Cake or Sweetmeats

Buy bought almond paste, which we can fairly recommend as a substitute.

Getting Desperately Low on Bread? Make Gran's Quick Bread

Sift 1lb self-raising flour into a roomy bowl with 2 rounded dessertspoons of baking powder and a generous pinch of salt. Then, as fast as possible, using a knife and not a spoon, bind to a rough paste with very cold water. Cut into pieces like rock cake, place on a floured baking sheet, bake Gas Mark 5, one shelf above centre, for 15–20 minutes, or until the peaks are very *slightly* brown.

Note: These are delicious while hot – quite horrible when cold, and they do not reheat successfully.

CHRISTMAS DRINKS

WINES FOR CHRISTMAS

Five Reasons for Drinking
'If all be true that I do think,
There are five reasons we should drink:
Good wine – a friend – or being dry –
Or lest we should be by and by –
Or any other reason why!'

Henry Aldrich

The choosing of Christmas wines is always something of a problem. Considerable thought must be given not only to their selection but to the doomed stomachs which will receive them. These stomachs are due for a monumental pasting anyway, not only during the feast that celebrates the birth of Christ but thereafter for days and days of parties and dishes made up from the leftovers.

There is of course a simple solution – at least simple for anyone remaining on this island who is entirely bereft of financial worries – to serve champagne throughout Christmas dinner if you can afford it with a little dill water on the side for Auntie who puts hand to upper stomach when she hears what is in store and murmurs reproachfully, 'Champagne, dear . . . how nice . . . it is such a pity it repeats so!'

There is also a 'Christmas wine' but it would not do at all. It is bottled in a cream porcelain container, all dimpled and bestrewn with pretty little rose buds, which so far as we know have absolutely nothing to do with Christmas. However, if you think the whole idea is charming; if, in fact, you can obtain it at all in this country, which we doubt, and if you are prepared to send down rather thin, sweet Italian wine, have a go! After all, Johnnie does say to all his young students when he starts teaching them something about wine, 'The wine you like is the wine for you regardless of what the so-called experts say. As you mature and as your palate develops you do in general lose your initial predilections for sweet wines and develop a liking for the drier, finer ones.'

Well, we are prepared to assert that the majority of adults in Britain are long past the stage of 'Christmas wine'. Wine drinking, despite the iniquitous and totally unselective wine taxes of today, is on the increase and the graph rises steadily year by year; so, in an effort to meet the requirements of what we believe to be the majority – and at the same time to cater for as many differing tastes as possible – we have worked out a wine chart listing some of the wines that can be drunk harmoniously with our suggested Christmas menus. Our selection has been governed by the overall determination to achieve so far as is possible a harmonious partnership with the given dishes, which is after all what is meant by a 'happy marriage' at the table.

Before you start buying wines for Christmas the odds are you will check on your stock of glasses and start wailing: 'Half of them are broken – what's happened to our port . . . champagne . . . sherry . . . hock glasses?' Relax. There is not a wine in the world that cannot be served with classic correctness in an ordinary 6fl oz tulip glass costing as little as 2*s*. 9*d*.

Before you resign yourself to doing without traditional port and nuts ('We haven't got a decanter and what would rich Uncle George say!'), tell yourself firmly that *if* Uncle George is like the great port experts, he will know it loses nothing by being served from the bottle. The decanter tradition is charming and elegant but necessary only for vintage and crusted wines. Just pass that bottle, which need not be vintage. Go for a tawny port; no connoisseur will disdain it, and it costs considerably less than any vintage one.

If you wisely decide on a red Beaujolais to drink with the Christmas bird, buy a young one. Do not go hunting for veterans. Beaujolais should always be drunk when between two and five years old, after which its descent in quality is inevitable. Then always choose cheap wines for brew-ups. Mulling is even more lethal to fine wines than popping them into hot water. We recommend Spanish claret-types from the Rioja for hot red wine mixtures and the Spanish Chablis types for white wine cups.

Lay in gallon and half-gallon jars of red, white or rosé for teenage parties and general thirst-quenching.

Soups. Any gourmet will tell you that two floating items are best kept apart, so keep sherries and Madeiras as aperitifs, or with pudding and dessert. All sherry is naturally dry; *finos* and *manzanillas* are generally sold in their natural state. Nearly all *amontillados* in the English market have been sweetened in the blending. Sercials are dry Madeiras and Verdelhos are medium ones.

Fish. A dryish white wine is called for here – a Graves, a white Burgundy, a Loire wine, a fresh young Alsatian wine or a dryish Moselle. Do not over-chill them and do not be afraid of putting them in mild refrigeration for an hour or two. But just abstain from drawing the cork before doing so.

The Bird. Make your choice between red Bordeaux, preferably from the lusty ones, either St Emilion or Pomerol, or, ideally, a red Burgundy, the lustiest of all. For those who do not like red wines the Rhines and Moselles provide highly satisfactory alternatives. Try a Rhenish Niersteiner Domthal, a Schloss Hockheimer or a Bernkasteler (the Moselle wine which is becoming very popular) and go for either the '59s or the '64s.

The Pudding and Mince Pies. These can be accompanied by the sweet wines of Sauternes (which includes Barsac), although we do prefer the sweet, fortified wines of Madeira, but to maintain equilibrium against the onslaughts of Christmas Pudding and brandy butter you will need to buy either a Bual or Malmsey Madeira or a rich brown sherry.

For a bit of Christmas Wineupmanship. Make your aperitif a Sercial dry Madeira, or a dry white port, which always beat sherry in popularity when we serve them here – say, either a Porto Fino or a Dry Tang. Remember to serve them well chilled.

Show off with a dry Alsatian Tokay, which seems like a contradiction in terms but is not. It marries beautifully with fish or chicken and also goes well with a cold buffet.

Be clever with a *white* Beaujolais Villages. Most people think of Beaujolais as red. Very few know, either, that there is both white and red Châteauneuf-du-Pape, which makes an excellent Christmas wine.

'Fan the sinking flame of hilarity with the wing of friendship; and pass the rosy wine.'

Charles Dickens

THESE WINES WILL MARRY WITH YOUR CHRISTMAS MENUS

DISH	MODEST WINE PARTNER	MEDIUM WINE PARTNER	FINE WINE PARTNER
Menu 1			
Melon Boats	Château la Dame Blanche (Graves)	Duke of Sussex, Sercial Madeira	Madeira, Gran Cama de Lobos, Solera 1864
Roast Turkey Burgundy Sauce Brussels Sprouts and Chestnuts Roast Potatoes	Fleurie '64	Chambolle-Musigny '59	Charmes Chambertin '53
Escoffier's Plum Pudding Brandy Butter	St Croix du Mont '64	Erbacher Pellet Riesling '64	Geisenheimer Mäverchen Riesling Beerenauslese '59
Menu 2			
Bortsch			
Roast Goose with Chestnuts Red Cabbage Stuffed Jacket Roast Potatoes	Côtes-du-Rhône	Clos Fourtet '59	Château Cheval Blanc '53
Escoffier's Plum Pudding Brandy Butter	Malaga Golden Muscatel	Château Rieussec '61	Madeira Terrantez 1870
Menu 3			
Potted Shrimps	Macon Blanc	Châteauneuf du Pape Blanc '64	Château Chalon '53

DISH	MODEST WINE PARTNER	MEDIUM WINE PARTNER	FINE WINE PARTNER
Stuffed Roast Turkey Monte Carlo Onions Fried Potato Balls	Côtes de Beaune	Châteauneuf du Pape Tête '59	Bonnes Mares '52
Escoffier's Plum Pudding Brandy Butter	St Macaire	Deinhard's Cabinet Sparkling Hock	Maximin Grumhauser Herrenserg Beerenauslese '59

Menu 4

Brussels Sprouts and Chestnut Soup			
Roast Turkey Creole Ham Potato Croquettes Chicory in Cheese Sauce	Gigondas Rouge	Château Loudenne	Château Leoville-Lascases '59
Christmas Pudding Ring Rum Butter	Tiger Milk, Ranina Radgona	Château d'Arche-Lafaurir '62	Château Rayne-Vigneau '59

Menu 5

Leek and Potato Soup			
Pekin Duck Brussels Sprouts with Chestnuts Yorkshire Sauce	St Nicholas de Bourgueil '61	Volnay '59	Hermitage Rouge, La Chapelle '53
Christmas Parcels Champagne Sauce	Old Trinity House Bual Madeira	Chateau Filhot '55	Niersteiner Rohr-Rehbach Riesling and Sylvaner Trockenbeere-nauslese '53

DISH	MODEST WINE PARTNER	MEDIUM WINE PARTNER	FINE WINE PARTNER
Menu 6			
Hot Baked Grapefruit			
Foil Roasted Turkey Gammon in Pastry Crust Potato Cake	Beaujolais	Château Bel-Air '61	Clos de Vougeot '59
Christmas Pudding Roll Grand Marnier Butter	Rioja Sauternes	Madeira, Old Malmsey	Madeira, Bual 1864
Menu 7			
Snails in Puff Pastry	Aligote '64	Liebfraumilch Klosterbruder '64	Le Montrachet '59
Pheasant in Foie Gras Potato Cakes Green Salad French Dressing with Grapes	St Amour '61	Vosne Romanée '59	Richebourg du Domaine de la Romanée-Conti '55
Nesselrode Pudding	Lutimer Riesling	Tokay aszu 4 puttonyas '53	Nallgartener Schonell Riesling Auslese, Hellmer '61
Menu 8			
Individual Mussel Moulds	Muscadet	Crozes-Hermitage Blanc '62	Deidesheimer Hofstück '59
Boiled Turkey Onion Sauce Creamed Carrots Swiss Potatoes	St Emilion	Château Montrose '59	Château Latour '53
Frozen Christmas Pudding Punch Sauce	Barsac	Château Coutet '61	Malmsey 1886

DISH	MODEST WINE PARTNER	MEDIUM WINE PARTNER	FINE WINE PARTNER
Menu 9			
Whitebait	Rioja Chablis	Chante-Alouette Blanc '62	Le Musigny Blanc '61
Sucking Pig Sou-Fassum Provence Sauce	Château Chinon	Clos du Moulin-à-Vent '62	Grands Echezeaux '52
Christmas Fritters Champagne Sauce	Marsala	Sauternes, La Flora Blanche '62	Veuve Clicquot Riche '59
Menu 10			
Avocado with French Dressing			
Roast Leg of Pork Apple Sauce Forcemeat Ducks Artichokes in Cheese Sauce	Château de Terrefort '60	Château Laujac '59	Château Pichon-Longueville '59 Baron
Plum Pudding Brandy Butter	Mont Bazillac	Madeira, Barbeito Crown Malmsey	Château d'Yquem '59
Menu 11			
Avocado with Madeira			
Roast Capon with Mushroom Stuffing Brussels Sprouts with Chestnuts Dauphine Potatoes	St Julien	Château Bataillery '62	Château Duhart-Milon '52
French Plum Pudding Vanilla Sauce	Gumpoldskirch-ner Spatlese	Alsatian Tokay	Hochheimer Stein Riesling Frine Spatlese '59

DISH	MODEST WINE PARTNER	MEDIUM WINE PARTNER	FINE WINE PARTNER
Menu 12			
Prawn or Shrimp Cocktail	Soave di Verona	Piesporter Michelsberg '64	Corton Charlemagne '63
South American Turkey Sweet Potatoes Cranberry Sauce Corn Fritters	Valpolicella	Aloxe-Corton '62	Hospices de Beaune '57
French Plum Pudding Vanilla Sauce	Malaga	Bristol Milk	Bristol Cream

HOT DRINKS

ALE POSSET

Ingredients: 1 pint double cream; 1 pint ale; 4 eggs; castor sugar to taste; 1 heaped teaspoon of mixed allspice, cinnamon, nutmeg and ginger.

Method: Whisk the eggs with the sugar and cream. Be careful not to whip too violently. Add the ale, spices and sugar to taste. Turn into the top of a double saucepan over hot water (eggs granule, or curdle, when boiled) and stir continuously until the mixture thickens. Serve in cups.

BISHOP

Stuff a lemon liberally with cloves. Roast as instructed for Churchwarden (pp.303-4). Pound together ½lb loaf sugar; ½ teaspoonful each nutmeg, ginger, cinnamon and mixed spice, with the finely pared rind of 1 lemon. Place in a thick pan over a low heat. Add ½ pint water, ½ pint port and 1 bottle of Tuscan (Italian) red wine, French red Bordeaux or a Spanish claret type. Add the lemon and press down with a wooden spoon. Add a miniature bottle of Cherry Brandy and heat but do not boil.

BRANDY AND RUM PUNCH

Ingredients: ½ pint rum; ¼ pint brandy; ½lb loaf sugar; 1 lemon; 1½ pints boiling water; ½ teaspoon ground nutmeg.

Method: Rub the sugar on the lemon thoroughly. Then put the sugar into a punch bowl. Add the rum, brandy and nutmeg and pour on the boiling water. Serve in warmed glasses.

BUTTERED RUM

Place 1½in of rum in a tumbler. Add 1½ teaspoons of soft brown (pieces) sugar and a walnut of preferably unsalted butter. Fill to the brim with boiling water, stir and sip – especially in bed when a cold is threatening.

CAFÉ BRULOT

This is a showy brew of considerable potency.

Ingredients: 12 coffeecups freshly made black coffee; 12 scant level teaspoons castor sugar; 1 vanilla pod; peeled rind of 1 orange or tangerine; 4 coffee cups brandy (not a good one, please) and 1 coffee cup apricot or peach brandy (*or* 5 coffee cups brandy).

Method: Place the sugar, vanilla pod and fruit rind in a punch bowl and bruise with a silver ladle, while heating the coffee to just below boiling point. In a separate pan warm the brandy or brandies. Turn out the lights, get someone to pour on the warmed spirit and set alight to it immediately. Keep working it with the ladle, lifting up the burning stream in the darkness. The flames will continue for a minute or two. Put out the flames with the hot coffee and serve, as you would ordinary coffee, in warmed cups. When serving this at the end of a dinner, do not serve any additional liqueur.

CHURCHWARDEN

Ingredients: 1 lemon; cloves; 1 bottle Tuscan red wine, red Bordeaux or Spanish claret type wine; 1 pint weak scalding-hot tea (preferably China); ¼lb loaf sugar.

Method: Stuff the lemon with cloves, place on a heat-resistant plate in the oven at Gas Mark ¼ and leave until the lemon begins to turn light brown. Heat the wine but do not allow it to boil. Immerse the roasted lemon and add the hot tea and sugar.

Note: Ideally the tea for any of this kind of brew should be green tea from Mr Laity's shop in St Ives, Cornwall.

GAELIC COFFEE

For each person: Place a silver spoon in a tumbler. Pour in a ½in–1½in depth of Irish whiskey. Pour in piping-hot coffee to within 1in of the rim of the glass. Stir in sugar to taste. Remove the spoon. Now pour on thick cream, slowly and carefully from the side of the glass so that the cream forms a half-inch 'lid' on top of the coffee mixture. On no account stir again. Drink the coffee *mixture through the cream.*

GLÖGG

The traditional recipe uses sherry, but burgundy or claret type wines may be used equally well. It is interesting to note, in view of the fact that this recipe is rather more costly than some, that leftovers can be bottled, tightly corked and kept until required. The mixture is reheated to the temperature just below boiling point before serving.

Ingredients: 1 pint inexpensive brandy; 1 pint Italian red wine, French red Bordeaux or Spanish claret type; 5oz loaf preserving or granulated sugar; 6 cloves; 2in stick cinnamon; 2½oz blanched, unsalted almonds; 2½oz seeded raisins.

Method: Put all the ingredients, except the wine, into a thick pan and warm until just about too hot to touch comfortably. Tip immediately into a fireproof bowl, set light to the mixture and stir until the sugar is dissolved and the flames die down. Pour on the heated but not boiling wine, stir well and serve.

LEMON BRANDIES

These are not only extremely grateful on the palate but amusing as well. For each person, slice the top from a lemon, remove the bulk of the flesh (with a grapefruit cutter) and press out a firm hollow with the handle of a silver spoon. Fill this cavity with slightly warmed brandy, marc or Armagnac. Set alight to it and place in the top of a very small wineglass and, balancing a large lump of sugar on a fork on the surface, stir the sugar gently in the flames until it has completely dissolved. Drive a skewer through the base of the lemon. Let the liquor run through until the lemon is dry. Drink the result – gratefully.

MULLED ALE

"Twas Christmas broach'd the mightiest ale;
'Twas Christmas told the merriest tale;
A Christmas gambol oft could cheer
The poor man's heart through half the year.'

Walter Scott

Ingredients: 2 pints old ale; 1 level teaspoon powdered cinnamon; 1 level tablespoon soft brown (pieces) sugar; 2 bay leaves; ¼ teaspoon ground ginger; slice of lemon.

Method: Place all the ingredients in a large pan and heat slowly, not allowing the mixture to boil. Meanwhile heat a poker until it is red. Plunge into the heated mixture and hold steady while it seethes crossly. When its temper has abated, pour into heated glasses, which contain a silver spoon.

MULLED WINE WITH BRANDY

This is an ideal brew to set alight with brandy in the firelight.

Ingredients: 1 bottle inexpensive red wine; 16 lumps sugar; 1 bay leaf; strained juice of 1 orange; 1 orange sliced very thinly; strained juice of 1 lemon; ½ teaspoon powdered cinnamon; 1 teaspoon powdered cloves; pinch grated nutmeg; 6½fl oz inexpensive brandy.

Method: Place all the ingredients except the brandy in a pan and bring almost to boiling point. Heat the brandy in a small pan. Pour the mulled wine mixture into a heat-resistant bowl. Pour on the heated brandy, set alight to it with a match and stir immediately because this keeps the flames alight. When you have had enough 'fireworks', stop stirring . . . the flames will die. Ladle into warmed glasses.

NEGUS

This sweetened, spiced wine mixture is frequently made with port and hot water; but other red wines such as Tuscan (Italian) red wine, French red Bordeaux or Spanish claret type can be used more economically.

Ingredients: 1 bottle port or red wine; sugar and nutmeg to taste; grated rind of 1 lemon; strained juice of 2 lemons; 1 pint boiling water.

Method: Warm the wine without boiling and pour into a heated jug, into which you have already put the sugar, lemon and spice. Stand the mixture in its container near to a fire, add the boiling water, stir thoroughly and pour into warmed glasses.

OLD ENGLISH WASSAIL

Very grand and special.

Ingredients: ½ pint water; 1 level tablespoon powdered nutmeg; 1 level dessertspoon powdered ginger; 6 cloves; ½ teaspoon mace; 1 teaspoon allspice; 3in stick of cinnamon; 2lb preserving sugar; 1 bottle brown sherry and 1 bottle Malmsey or Bual Madeira – *Or* 2 bottles of either; 3½ pints old ale; 12 eating apples; 12 eggs.

Method: Core and bake the apples at Gas Mark 4 (do not allow them to burst). Place the water, spices, sugar sherry or Madeira (or both) with the ale into a thick pan and allow to become piping hot over a moderate heat. Meanwhile separate the eggs, whip the whites stiffly and whip the yolks lightly with a fork. Fold the yolks into the whites and scoop this foam into a punch bowl. Pour the heated brew on slowly with one hand, while whisking briskly with the other (if you use a professional loop whisk, you will find this very easy). Slide in the apples and serve.

VIENNA CHOCOLATE

Scald 1 pint fresh milk. Stir in 3oz plain chocolate or chocolate chips. Whip 2 separated egg yolks in a bowl with 2oz castor sugar. Pour on the scalded milk, whip until thoroughly blended, return to the pan and stir over a very low heat until *just* below boiling point. Have ready 2 stiffly whipped egg whites. Remove the pan from the heat, whip the contents into the egg whites until completely blended. Pour into heated cups and top each cupful with a spiral of stiffly whipped cream, either plain or with 1 teaspoon *crème de cacao* from a miniature bottle or 1 dessertspoon of brandy. Sprinkle coarsely grated plain chocolate over all.

THE WASSAIL BOWL

'Wassaile the trees, that they may beare
You many a plum and many a peare;
For more or lesse fruits they will bring,
As you doe give them wassailing.'

Robert Herrick

Ingredients: 3 quarts beer; 1lb preserving sugar; 1 nutmeg; 1 rounded teaspoon powdered ginger; 1½ pints brown sherry; 1 lemon; 3 slices toast.

Method: Warm the beer. Add the sugar and half the nutmeg, grated. As the mixture heats throw in the ginger, sherry and the whole unskinned lemon sliced very thinly. Float the slices of toast upon this mixture. As it approaches boiling point, take from an open fire (or a strong gas flame) a heated poker, which has turned red. Plunge into the pan, turn out the gas under the pan, allow the mixture to seethe until it subsides and then ladle it into warm, napkin-wrapped glasses. Sprinkle with the remaining grated nutmeg.

WINE POSSET

Ingredients: 1 pint sweet, new milk; ¼ pint dry white wine; generous pinch cinnamon, bay and lavender; grated rind of ½ lemon; castor sugar to taste.

Method: Place the milk, lemon rind and wine in a pan together. Heat until the milk curdles. Strain off the whey. Liquefy the sugar in this. Add spices. Sieve the curdled milk. Beat fairly vigorously into the sweetened whey. Serve immediately.

SNAPDRAGON

This is one of those awkward recipes that does not fit into any standard category; but as it depends solely upon alcohol, we have tucked it in at the end of this mixed drinks section. Snapdragon is a famous Christmas game, which in some of the older reference books is also called Flapdragon. The game merely consists of snatching raisins with the fingers and in a darkened room from a bowl of flaming spirit. Classically, the spirit should be brandy but we long ago discovered that the flavour of the brandy is unimpaired by the addition of 1 part vodka to every 2 parts brandy. The vodka has an extremely high alcoholic content and ensures that once the spirit is warm and lighted, it will burn for a very long time. The classic container is a silver punch bowl, but in times of stress we have used a plain heat-resistant glass mixing bowl concealed by a wrapping of stiffly starched table napkins. Always use seeded raisins. The flavour of the raisins is considerably enhanced if you make up your brandy/vodka mixture a couple of hours before service, place in a screw-top jar, add the raisins and let them steep and soften. Just make sure that the jar is absolutely air-tight.

COLD DRINKS

ALEXANDERS

Revive the frail with Alexanders; 5–6fl oz ruby port whipped with 1 egg and a powdering of cinnamon sprinkled on the top.

BLACK VELVET

Strictly speaking this is a restorative (pick-me-up is such a crude and unattractive omnibus word).

One-third fill a tumbler per person with stout. Fill up very slowly indeed with champagne. Swizzle cautiously and drink slowly. Once, when almost unconscious with 48-hour flu at the moment of a public appearance, we crawled in through a side door, mixed this brew, drank it and survived until the end of the formal luncheon and subsequent lecture.

BRANDY PUNCH

Proportions: 1 part raspberry syrup; 2 parts lemon juice; 3 parts brandy; 1 part rum; 2 or 3 dashes Curaçao for each drink.

Method: Make and serve exactly as for Planter's Punch (p.315). If you have difficulty in obtaining raspberry syrup, you may use Benedictine instead, but in that case omit the Curaçao.

BREAKFAST WINE

Serve glasses of Breakfast Wine at noon aperitif parties. Place a curl of lemon peel in a tall glass. Cover with 1½in of crushed ice and bruise well with a long spoon. Add a wineglass of dry white port.

BULL'S MILK

This has quite remarkable restorative qualities. Place 3 tumblers of fresh milk in a large jug. Add 1 claret glass of rum and 1 claret glass of brandy, sugar to taste, a generous pinch of both nutmeg and cinnamon and whisk in 3 fresh eggs. Chill thoroughly; add 8 ice cubes at the moment of service. Serve in small wine glasses.

CHABLIS CUP

Ingredients: 1 pint boiling water; 6 lumps sugar; 1 thin strand of lemon peel; 1 bottle Chablis; 1 sherry glass sherry; 1 tumbler soda water; any chosen small fruits; 8 ice cubes.

Method: Dissolve the sugar in water and stand with the peel for half an hour. Strain, add the Chablis and sherry. Chill thoroughly for 30 minutes. Add the soda water and ice cubes and serve.

CHAMPAGNE CUP

Chill a bottle of champagne. Pour into a large crystal-clear jug. Add a small tumbler of brandy, 1 ribband from a dark-skinned young cucumber, 2 thin slices of orange (with the peel on), a small ribband of thinly pared lemon rind and sifted icing sugar to taste if you must! Stand in a refrigerator or the coldest possible place for ½ hour. Add a tumbler of crushed ice, stir gently until dissolved and serve.

CIDER CUP

Ingredients: 1 slice of toast; ½ nutmeg, grated; 1 eggspoon ground ginger; very thinly peeled rind of ½ lemon; 8 lumps sugar; 2 sherry glasses sherry; 3 pints cider; 1 sherry glass brandy (can be omitted); 10 ice cubes; 1 tumbler or 1 small bottle of soda water; 1–2 sprigs borage.

Method: Cover the toast with the ginger and nutmeg. Place in the bottom of a wide-necked jug. Cover with the remaining ingredients, except the ice, soda water and borage. Prepare ½ hour in advance and chill thoroughly. Remove the toast and discard, after squeezing the liquor back into the container. Add the soda and ice at the moment of service and, when possible, a sprig or two or borage.

CITRONNADE

Rub 6 lumps of sugar over the rind of 3 large lemons until the sugar takes up the oil in the lemon rind, turns yellow and crumbles. Place this in a jar or basin with 8oz lump sugar, 5 tablespoons boiled cold water and the strained juice of 4 lemons. Let it stand until the sugar is completely dissolved, stir, strain through muslin into a bottle and keep in a refrigerator. Use to taste with water, soda water or tonic water and crushed ice.

CLARET CUP

For special occasions.

Ingredients: 1 bottle inexpensive claret; 1 sherry glass brandy; 1 liqueur glass maraschino, Curaçao and yellow Chartreuse; sifted icing sugar to taste; 2 small bottles soda water or 2 tumblers from a siphon; 1 thinly sliced (small) lemon; 8 ice cubes; sprig of borage (optional).

Method: Mix all the ingredients except the ice and soda water together an hour before the cup is required. Chill thoroughly. Pour in the soda water, add the ice and, if liked, a sprig of borage (never mint).

CLARET CUP

A simpler version.

Ingredients: 1 bottle inexpensive claret; 1 sherry glass sherry; thinly peeled rind of 1 lemon; sifted icing sugar to taste; a generous grate of nutmeg; 8 ice cubes; 1 tumbler soda water or 1 small bottle; sprig of verbena or borage (when available).

Method: Bruise the sugar and peel together in a bowl. Add the wine, sherry and nutmeg. Chill thoroughly for ½ hour. Add the soda water and ice at the moment of service with a sprig of verbena or borage.

ECONOMICAL LEMONADE

Ingredients: 1 lemon; ¾lb lump or granulated sugar; 1½ pints boiling water; 1 dessertspoon citric acid.

Method: Peel the lemon thinly, squeeze out the juice and put both into a jug. Add the sugar and citric acid, pour on boiling water and stir well. Leave for about 12 hours, strain and use about 1 tablespoon to a tumbler of water. Keep in refrigeration.

ICED COFFEE

Flavour 1 pint milk very strongly with coffee syrup (p.213). Place the mixture in a thick pan with a vanilla pod and add soft brown sugar to taste. Stir until the sugar is completely dissolved. Remove from heat, pour over 6 crushed ice cubes in a large bowl or tureen and stir until the ice is dissolved. Add 2 or more tablespoons rum (taste and decide yourselves) and then add 2 small vanilla ice cream bars cut into minute pieces. Refrigerate overnight. Stir in ¼ pint single cream just before serving.

ICED VIENNA COFFEE

This is an old family recipe. Make 1 pint strong coffee and strain through muslin into a bowl containing 1 vanilla pod. When absolutely cold, add 1 tablespoon rum and 2 of brandy. Cover the base of claret glasses with crushed ice. Pour on the prepared coffee. Top each glass with a spiral of thickly whipped cream, surmounting each spiral with a sprinkling of crushed coffee beans.

KING'S PEG

This beverage is especially recommended to nervous and unsteady bridegrooms after successful wedding-eve bachelor celebrations or after Christmas indulgences. The procedure is simplicity itself. Have a bottle of dry champagne in a cooler packed with ice. When chilled, pour into goblets containing approximately 2 tablespoons of brandy.

MILK PUNCH

Ingredients: 1 tablespoon castor sugar; 2 tablespoons strained, cold China tea; 4fl oz brandy; 2fl oz rum; 3oz crushed ice; grated nutmeg.

Method: Stir the ingredients well together, pour into tumblers, and sprinkle a little nutmeg on top of each.

MISSISSIPPI PUNCH

(not for wine connoisseurs!)

Proportions: 1 part sugar syrup (p.274); 2 parts lemon juice; 1 part brandy; 3 parts whisky.

Method: Prepare and serve the same as Planter's Punch (below), but float 1 tablespoon rum on top of each drink.

ORANGEADE

Use the Citronnade recipe (p.312), substituting 3 small oranges for 3 large lemons and adding 1 lemon with the first part and 5 oranges in the second part.

PLANTER'S PUNCH

Put 1 bottle Barbados rum into a lidded glass or earthenware crock with ¼ bottle falernum; ½ breakfastcup strained, fresh orange juice; ¼ breakfastcup strained lime or lemon juice; ½ sliced, unskinned cucumber; 1 whole skinned mango or 2 small peeled peaches (sliced with a silver knife); 1 whole peeled and segmented orange (flesh segments only); ½ small, peeled, sliced, cored pineapple; a few drops Angostura bitters and a scant quarter of grated nutmeg. Cover the top tightly with foil, then with a lid, and strain before using.

Note: Do not fuss about the rarity of falernum. This colourful name conceals sugar syrup; 1lb sugar to 1 pint water, boiled, strained and sparked up with the strained juice of 1 lemon or lime.

RELAX

Put 2 ice cubes in a tall glass, add 2 fingers of white rum, 1 finger of pineapple juice and fill up with tonic water.

RUM COLLINS

Use two tumblers. Place in a tumbler 1¼fl oz rum, 1 ice cube, fill up with soda water and set aside to chill. Place the strained juice of 1 lemon and 2 teaspoons castor sugar in a second tumbler. Stir until completely dissolved, stir into the first tumbler and serve immediately.

SANGRIA

Place 1 bottle of inexpensive claret in a large jug with sifted icing sugar to taste, 2 fairly thick slices of orange, 2 fairly thick slices of lemon and the remaining strained juice of each fruit. Add a pinch of both cinnamon and nutmeg and 1 liqueur glass of brandy. Chill thoroughly. At the moment of service add one-third of a siphon of soda water and 6 ice cubes. Serve in tall glasses.

WHITE ANGEL PUNCH

Ingredients: ½ pint strained lemon juice; ¼ pint sugar syrup; 2 pints orange juice; 1 pint strong China tea; 2 pints soda water.

Method: Mix all the ingredients together except the soda water, which is added at the time of service.

FOR FREEZER AND/OR REFRIGERATOR

In addition to seasonal items which we have listed in the appropriate months of the Through the Year Christmas Calendar (pp.3–18), there are a great many cooked ones that can be advance-made and then plunged into the freezer when space and availability allow.

The great thing to remember at all times is that a relatively short period in the freezer invariably results in a more flavoursome dish than can be hoped for after a very long period. So, in the little *aide-memoire*, which we now submit, we have given what we regard as maximum periods for each item suitable for this method of storage. Overall, we have listed everything in this book that you could have made and stored in some way throughout the preceding months, either specifically for the Christmas period or for general winter use. *We would like to stress that we take off all our hats to anyone who has achieved the entire list despite the manifold obstacles which would have had to have been overcome in terms of time, labour and expenditure!*

Whatever you have managed to do to suit your plans and patterns, it is a very good idea to check them all in early December. Such a check will enable you to revise and settle final drafts of all Christmas to New Year menus and ensure that you will not overlook some 'treasure' you put up many months ago.

Nothing must ever be returned to the deep freeze after thawing, nothing must ever come out of the deep freeze for over three hours and then be returned and nothing of any sort whatsoever should be fast-thawed by putting in a cool oven or under a running hot tap. The time required for items to thaw must be related to their bulk and texture. For instance, an ice cream pudding (unless a huge one) needs only 15 minutes in refrigeration and, say, five minutes on the table before it is ready to serve; a *Charlotte Russe* can spend the night in refrigeration and very probably then be ready to serve. Soups take a very long time to thaw; frozen liquids (2, 3 or more pints) require 24 hours in refrigeration and then must be left at room temperature until all crystallisation has disappeared. A large turkey would want 24 hours in refrigeration and maybe up to 12 hours at room temperature, whereas a chicken would only want overnight refrigeration and about two hours at room temperature.

HORS D'OEUVRE

Pork *pâté* (freeze 1 month or less); Grapefruit and Orange Cocktail (freeze the skinless segments of both fruits separately in their own juices in lidded plastic containers for 6 months or less).

SOUPS

Vichyssoise (Leek and Potato Soup – freeze the cooked purée before adding any cream 2 months or less); Onion Soup (freeze 3 months or less).

FISH

Vol-au-vent cases for Lobster Patties (stamp out and freeze raw 1 month or less).

MEAT, GAME AND POULTRY

Alabama Gammon (cooked and ready for finishing, freeze 3 months or less); Raised Pies (cooked, freeze 3 months or less): Oxtail in Aspic (cooked and ready for aspic, freeze 3 months or less); Baked Gammon (freeze 3 months or less); Beefsteak and Kidney Pie (cooked with raw pastry lid ready for baking, freeze 3 months or less).

PUDDINGS

Frozen Christmas Pudding (freeze 3 months or less); *Charlotte Russe* (freeze 1 month or less); Nesselrode Pudding (freeze 3 months or less); Rum and Blackcurrant Sorbets (freeze 6 months or less); Frozen Soft Fruits (9 months or less).

CAKES AND PASTRY

Sweet Short Pastry for Mince Pie (freeze 3 months or less); Mince Pie (completed ready for baking, freeze 3 months or less); Chocolate Log Cake (sponge rolled up with filling ready to finish, freeze 2 months or less); Seed Cake (freeze 1 month or less); Chocolate Swiss Roll (freeze 1 month or less); Puff

Pastry (freeze 6 months or less); Gingerbread Men (freeze 1 month or less).

SAUCES AND ICINGS

Brandy, Rum or Grand Marnier Butter (refrigerate 4 weeks or less); Confectioners' Custard (freeze 2 months or less, refrigerate 3 weeks without brandy, 4 weeks with 1 tablespoon to ½ pint); Stock Sugar Syrup (refrigerate 3 months or less); Basic Butter Cream (freeze 2 months or less, refrigerate 4 weeks or less).

PRESERVED SWEETMEATS
AND SIDE DISHES

Purées for Sorbets; Mint/Parsley Cubes (frozen from midsummer onwards); Garlic Bread (do 14 days before heating and serving and sling in the deep freeze wrapped tightly in foil, thaw out still in foil 8 hours before using, then heat up as instructed); Garlic Butter (4 weeks in refrigeration under tight foil wrapping to insulate securely); Potted Cheshire Cheese and Roquefort Cream with Port (maximum 7 days in refrigeration before serving).

EMERGENCY SUPPLIES

Spare a glance for the following lists in case there is any item you may possibly have overlooked, which belongs in your pattern:

Biscuits and books for spare bedrooms; spare bedding, bed linen, pillows and towels; toothbrushes for absent-minded guests; stamps, writing paper and envelopes for bread and butter letters; cake candles; children's stocking gifts like a sugar mouse from Woolworth's, chocolate money, giant lollies, jelly babies, liquorice allsorts, candyfloss, barley sugar, bags of fruit and nuts, puzzle games and some of those joke things like sausages which make rude noises; jigsaws to keep kids quiet after meals; comics; 'Silent Night' gramophone record to play when the tree is lit; face pack for Mum; extra orders for milk, cream and bread; coffee and instant coffee; chocolate and cocoa; breakfast cereals; tinned fruit juices; face tissues; laxatives; loo paper; soap (household and personal); extra cards, stamps and envelopes for the ones you have forgotten on your list; Alka Seltzer; kitchen foil, greaseproof paper, paper d'oyleys and kitchen paper rolls; plenty of flour in case you run out of bread and need to make Gran's Quick Bread (p.292); salt; pepper; mustard; oil; wine vinegar; cornflour; potato flour; sugars including crystals for after-dinner coffee; vanilla pods; harmless vegetable colourings; soft drinks for children and teetotallers; beer for late-night thirsties; mulled wine and punch ingredients; cigarettes, cigars, pipe cleaners and

matches; chocolate cigarettes and cigars; Father Christmas or
tree for the cake; fuse wire; pet foods; orders for coal, coke and
wood; spare electric light bulbs, including ones for fairy lights;
wine glass and tumbler replacements; corkscrew (?); theatre
tickets (?); container and wrapping for tree base; plenty of ice
in refrigerator cube trays – order a block for buffet parties;
small money for carol singers; not-so-small-money for trades-
men's Christmas boxes.

If you are a country dweller, you may find something that
you need which is additional to the preceding town dwellers'
list:

Check fuel stocks; order solid fuel for AGAs, coal and make
sure a good stack of logs and kindling are as much under shelter
as possible and immediately adjacent to the house; paraffin; oil
for central heating; dried milk; petrol and check tyres: tooth-
paste; playing cards, indoor games and parlour games for
marooned kids; torch and radio batteries and have TV and
long player checked if either or both are showing signs of incip-
ient temperament; overhaul first-aid box and replace missing
items.

If you live in some desperately remote area, you may find
something that you need which is additional to the preceding
lists:

Rock salt to put on paths and drives in the event of snow
and ice; jars of long-keeping Double Devon cream; tinned and
packaged foodstuffs and cleaning items in the event of antici-
pating being marooned; eggs if hens show signs of rebelling
against inclement weather; cheeses like Stilton, which keep
properly; blow lamps in case the pipes freeze up (try not to
blow right through the pipe, dears, like we did once!); reserve
supplies of plain and fancy biscuits; bring in supplies of
clamped vegetables; and get some instant potato if potatoes
have already got frostbite.

CHRISTMAS DECORATION MATERIALS

EVERLASTINGS

Buy in the autumn ready-dried or plant, harvest and dry your-selves a selection of the following 'everlastings'. In any event arrangements of these make very welcome small presents and if any colours are deemed unsuitable, a squirt of glitter dust over spray-on gold or silver paint soon transforms them.

Ammobium: Silvery white flower heads.

Anaphalis: Everlasting with numerous pearly white flower heads and soft woolly foliage.

Catananche: Sometimes called Cupid's Dart. Four vars. Important to harvest just before blooms are fully matured.

Gomphrena: Pick just before reaching maturity if wishing crop to retain colour over long period. Seven varieties.

Helichrysum: Ten to choose from including *H. monstrosum*, mixed colours, large double flowers.

Helipterum: Four vars. Another straw daisy sometimes listed as *Acroclinium*.

Statice: There are 17 different varieties excluding the special *S. tataricum*, which has small white flowers and is the best for dying or spraying. The members of this family are often called *Limonium*.

Xeranthemum: Not unlike *Catananche*, white or purple.

SUITABLE ITEMS FOR DRYING

These are excellent subjects:

Achillea: These tall members of the yarrow family must be cut before colour fades. Can either be dried and hung or arranged in permanent containers immediately after harvesting.

Amaranthus caudatus viridis: Vulgarly christened in this family Green Bloody Love. Strip off leaves, retain and dry long, fat, greeny-grey tassels.

Buddleia: Pick twice – one bunch in full bloom if desiring colour retention, one bunch when dried out if intending to paint and/or spray.

Ceiosia: Or Cock's Comb. Strip off leaves, bunch and hang head downwards until needed. Very popular except with us.

Echinops: Lovely globe thistles. Can be arranged immediately or dried. Be certain to cut as long as possible.

Eryngium or Sea Holly: Treat as *Echinops*.

Hydrangea Heads: Hold cutting until tiny central flowers – like eyes – to petals of single 'blooms' (which are nothing of the sort but bracts) have finished flowering. Then leave in water for at least a month.

Lavender: Spray as Pussy Willow.

Pussy Willow: After gathering, bunch head downwards and spray with a little hair lacquer to stop the silver pads from moulting.

Onion Heads: Bunch seeded heads, hang head downwards and spray with hair lacquer. Then they will not moult.

Solidago (or Golden Rod): Bunch and dry before flower heads are fully developed.

Verbascum (or Mullein): Let the spikes dry out, harvest, spray with hair lacquer or bunch and hang dry if intending to paint and glitter. In the interests of economy we must remember that a famous London store was selling the plain dried spikes last Christmas at 7/6d. a piece!

SEEDHEADS

Delphinium; poppy; *Hemerocallis* (day lily); globe artichokes (spray with lacquer); thistle; fir cones; wild iris; *Iris foetidissima* filled with shining scarlet berries; *Moluccella laevis* or Bells of Ireland, fabulously pretty when dried, look like clustered stems of straw-coloured baby shells; honesty, one of the most valuable of all (when completely dry on plant, uproot – these are biennials – rub each coin-like seed head between thumb and first finger and grubby outer coins will fall away leaving silvery sprays; retain and replant seeds as required for rotation);

teasels; lilies of the valley; *Physalis* or Chinese Lanterns (these are gorgeous sprayed gold or silver for Christmas).

ORNAMENTAL GRASSES – TO DRY

Agrostis pulchella: bouquet grass.

Briza maxima: large spikes of bouquet grass.

Cortaderia argentea (or Pampas grass); tall and splendid.

Hordeum jubatum (or squirrel tail grass): bearded and very ornamental.

Miscanthus sinensis zebrinus: cross-barred, zebra-leaved.

Panicum violaceum: long purple and silky.

Phalaris arundinacea (or Gardener's Garters): bold striped leaves.

Tricholaena rosea: 8in-long silky spikes, wine to purple.

Zea mays gracillima variegata: fine striped foliage, ornamental corn heads.

FERN AND FOLIAGE

Beech: Ignore all exhortations to 'start in early autumn' because by this time other forms of life will have started first and a great many leaves will be picked, pocked and otherwise blemished. By midsummer the giant copper beech in our garden has always developed several surplus sun-stealing sprays. At this stage they are perfect. Remove them, select the ones which curve gracefully, trim off the lower leaves for at least 6in. Stand in a large tin in 2 parts water to 1 part glycerine, using sufficient of this mixture to achieve a container depth of 6in.

Bracken: Lay green unblemished fronds between sheets of newspaper and stuff under carpets and walk on them for weeks.

Ferns, General: Select and treat as for bracken but if wishing to cherish any special subjects in this category lift up the carpets in the car and slip them underneath. There is less Hoover activity and therefore less chance of damage!

Magnolia Leaves: Wait until they fall and turn brown. Then gather, wipe carefully and allow to finish drying out in a cool place. Then pack away in small boxes. When painted with quick-drying paint and scattered with gold or silver glitter dust they are incomparable as an encircling base to individual Christmas arrangements made with plasticine and thin silver or gold cake boards.

Ornamental Cherries: Bunch a few spring thinnings, strip for shape, peel and varnish immediately or leave untouched if intending to paint and glitter.

EVERGREENS FOR THE TRADITIONAL

Grow or beg, borrow but do not steal sprays of *Laurus nobilis*, the ideal laurel for swags; *Picea Smithiana*, the weeping spruce, and the *P. pungens glauca* or blue spruce; *Rosmarinus* and our old friend the holly, *Ilex pyramidalis* grown in pyramid form;

the silver- and gold-leaved *Ilex argentea* and *aurea* and the
wonderful *Ilex melanotricha*, beloved by that great artist, the
late Mrs Constance Spry; smokey grey *Abies Fabri* and an *A.
sutchuenensis* and of course mistletoe; the Western hemlock
Tsuga heterophylla, which is studded with small cones; the very
clear, bright green of *Thujopsis dolabrata*: the palm-like formation, which makes the umbrella pine *Sciadopitys verticillata*
invaluable for evergreen arrangements; the seemingly
windswept spikes of the Weymouth pine *Pinus Strobus*:
Chamaecyparis nootkatentsis pendula, which grows naturally in
swag formation; *Cedrus Deodora*, the Deodar – we have a small
one on the terrace, which has the grace of green plumed ostrich
feathers; the *Hederas* or ivies variegated, silvered, white marked
and yellowed and the common ivy, which ramps about the
garden; box, aspidistra leaves where exhausted and brown.

SKELETONISING LEAVES

For skeletonising leaves we cannot do better than recommend
you the method quoted by Miss Violet Stevenson from an
1884 issue of *Amateur Gardening*.

Dissolve 3oz washing soda in 2 pints boiling water. Then
add 1½oz slaked quick lime. Boil for 10 minutes (in a
condemned-for-cooking saucepan). Strain carefully, clean the
pan, re-boil. Now add the leaves, boil briskly – Miss Stevenson
suggests an hour – occasionally adding hot water to replace
that lost by evaporation. Test one leaf: put into a container of
cold water and gently rub the leaf between fingers under water.
If the skin does not separate easily maintain boiling for a
further period until it does. For bleaching these skeletons put
approximately 1 drachm of chloride of lime with 1 pint water,
adding sufficient acetic acid to liberate the chlorine. Steep
leaves in this mixture until whitened (about 10 minutes),

taking care not to leave them too long or they may become brittle. Put into clean water, float them out on pieces of paper, remove them from papers before quite dry and press them.

SUNDRIES

The odd oak apple on a short stem, the green balls that hang down on slender stems from plane trees. These we steal annually in French villages and treasure.

The huge seed clusters from *Cercis Siliquastrum* or Judas Tree. The hard-dried fruits of *Passiflora* or Passion Flower.

Seed heads of *Isatis glauca* or Woad.

Odd bits of tree bark.

Branches from the contorted Japanese-like *Corylus avellana contorta*.

Tassels of *Garrya elliptica*.

Sprays of dead wood encrusted with lichen.

Paddy pieces of ground-matted lichen and moss.

ARTIFICIAL ITEMS

Bunches of artificial holly berries – the ones which are short ends of wire with a berry at each end for twisting into position easily.

Candles, green, red, white – cake and table.

Chicken wire.

Flat white paint and turpentine substitute.

Florists' wire, stem, fine reel and medium-fine strands in bunches.

Glitter balls.

Gold glitter dust, silver glitter dust.

Gold spray, silver spray.

Kitchen foil.

Oasis.

Ribbons, narrow and wide, green, red, white.

Shiny scarlet, emerald and white paper.

Staple rings.

The long-stemmed red roses that look as though made in velvet (not shiny red plastic ones).

Thin cake bases (gold and silver coloured).

Tissue paper, scarlet, emerald and white.

UHU, plasticine, Sellotape.

White net